The Birth of a Celestial Light

The Birth of a Celestial Light

*A Feminist Evaluation
of an Iranian Spiritual
Movement Inter-universal
Mysticism*

By

Tina Eftekhar

**Cambridge
Scholars**
Publishing

The Birth of a Celestial Light: A Feminist Evaluation of an Iranian
Spiritual Movement Inter-universal Mysticism

By Tina Eftekhar

This book first published 2015

Cambridge Scholars Publishing

Lady Stephenson Library, Newcastle upon Tyne, NE6 2PA, UK

British Library Cataloguing in Publication Data
A catalogue record for this book is available from the British Library

ISBN (10): 1-4438-7048-X
ISBN (13): 978-1-4438-7048-1

به نام بی‌نام او بیا تا شروع کنیم

در امتداد شب نشینیم و طلوع کنیم

مهم نیست چگونه، چطور و چند

به یک تلنگر ساده بیا تا رجوع کنیم

ببین که خاک چگونه به سجده افتاده

چرا غرور و تفاخر بیا تا رکوع کنیم

(محمد علی طاهری)

Let's start in the name of nameless

Sit along the night and rise like a sun

No matter how

Let's go back with a simple fillip

See how the land lay prostrate

Why having vanity, let's bow

(Mohammad Ali Taheri)

TABLE OF CONTENTS

LIST OF TABLES AND FIGURES

FOREWORD

SHIRIN EBADI,
NOBEL PEACE LAUREATE

TRANSLATED BY HADI KHOJINIAN

Patriarchy in the Middle East has ancient roots. By patriarchy, I am not referring to culture of masculinity, but a culture that does not believe in equality and the slogan of "ALL FOR ONE AND ONE FOR ALL" is engraved at the heart of this culture. This is why patriarchy is at odds with democracy.

Many of the present day crises in the Middle East have their roots in patriarchy. The culture of patriarchy justifies itself by finding any excuses such as religion. This is why in a country like Iran, where over 60% of its university students are female, and where it is over 50 years since women were given the right to vote and become members of parliament, still the testimony of two women is needed to equal that of one man in a court of law; a man can be married to four wives at the same time and divorce their wives at will, but it is very difficult, and at times impossible, for wives to divorce their husbands.

It is quite natural that such rules will work towards strengthening and supporting the patriarchal culture. Iranian women have tried in every possible way to empower themselves to counter patriarchy and its discriminations. Whenever women object to these discriminatory rules, authorities, by pointing to Islamic Sharia law and its various interpretations, call them blasphemous.

Women are therefore looking for a way to continue to fight these discriminations, without being accused of blasphemy. One way has been for women to follow individuals or movements that have moderate and more modern interpretations of Islamic laws to empower themselves. In this way they can withstand the unjust accusations of blasphemy and prove that with correct interpretations of Islam they can put an end to discrimination against women in both the society and the law of the country.

This book is an in-depth research and documentation of such women's activism. Through reading this book the reader will have a better understanding of why mystical/spiritual movements receive much more attention in the Middles East.

مقدمه

خانم شیرین عبادی برنده جایزه صلح نوبل

فرهنگ پدر سالار در مشرق زمین، ریشه ای دیرینه دارد. منظور من از فرهنگ پدر سالار، جنس مذکر نیست، منظور فرهنگ نادرستی است که برابری انسان ها را قبول ندارد و شعار "همه برای یکی و یکی برای همه" در دل این فرهنگ نهفته است و بهمین دلیل است که فرهنگ پدر سالار با دموکراسی سازگار نیست.

ریشه بسیاری از تنش های موجود در خاورمیانه را می توان در فرهنگ پدر سالار جستجو کرد. فرهنگ پدر سالار برای توجیه خود از هر موضوعی از جمله مذهب استفاده می کند و بدین گونه است که فرضا در کشور ایران، ارزش شهادت دو زن در دادگاه معادل با شهادت یک مرد است، مرد می تواند چهار زن بگیرد و هر وقت بخواهد بدون عذر موجه زنش را طلاق دهد اما طلاق گرفتن برای زن بسیار دشوار و گاه غیر ممکن است. این قوانین تبعیض آمیز در کشوری اجرا می شود که بیش از ۶۰٪ دانشجویان آن دختر هستند و زنان ایرانی بیش از ۵۰ سال است که حق رای به دست آورده و به پارلمان رفته اند.

طبیعی است که چنین قوانینی باعث اشاعه و تقویت هر چه بیشتر فرهنگ پدر سالار می شود و زنان ایران برای مقابله با فرهنگ پدر سالار و قوانین تبعیض آمیز ناشی از آن به هر شیوه ممکن در توانمند سازی خود و مقابله با وضعیت موجود کوشیده اند. زنان وقتی به قوانین تبعیض آمیز و ضد زن اعتراض می کنند، حکومت به قوانین شریعت استناد کرده و مخالفین را مرتد می داند.

بنا بر این زنها به دنبال راه حلی هستند که بدون آن که در معرض اتهام ارتداد قرار گیرند، به مبارزه با فرهنگ پدر سالار برخیزند. یکی از این راه حل ها پیروی از افراد یا گروههایی است که تفسیر ملایم و جدیدی از اسلام دارند و بدین گونه زنان خود را توانمند می سازند که در قبال حربه "ارتداد" حکومت ایستاده و ثابت کنند که با تفسیر درستی از اسلام می توان به وضعیت تبعیض آمیز زنان در قانون و در اجتماع پایان داد.

کتاب حاضر تحقیقی است جامع و مستند راجع به قسمتی از این گونه تلاش های زنان. با خواندن آن متوجه می شوید که چرا گروههای مختلف "عرفان" این چنین در مشرق زمین پر طرفدار هستند.

PREFACE

It was a big apartment with a nice garden in front of it: the hall was on the ground floor of the building. A crowd of people were chatting, standing all the way from the entrance of the building to the hall so that I could hardly pass them to reach the reception area. At the entrance of the hall, there was a table and two ladies were sitting behind it; they were checking everyone's membership cards to allow them permission to enter. After waiting in a long queue, I showed my card and went inside. At first glance, I saw a large number of people. All the seats (approximately 500) were taken and many people were sitting on the floor and near the walls. There was a small open kitchen in a corner of the hall, full of women. The hall was equipped with three roll-down projection screens allowing everyone to see and hear the speaker, Mr Taheri. I was surprised by what I was observing. Only the three back rows were occupied by men: all the other seats were taken by women. Women were more active in the class than men; they were enthusiastically sharing their experiences and asking Mr. Taheri questions. They were even talking openly about their families and private problems in front of others, which they were unlikely to do in other situations. At the end of the six hour class nobody seemed tired. It was late in the evening and women were still asking questions. I thought it was really intriguing that women were staying after the class and continuing the discussion; it seemed as though they were achieving something for themselves in a society where women are expected to put family or home first. I looked at all these women and asked myself, why are they all here? What are they looking for in a class like this on spirituality?

I encountered this scene in 2007, when I was visiting Iran for two weeks, and it sparked my curiosity and interest so much that it led me to the topic of my doctoral research and then this book. As I reflected on the scene, some questions began to occur to me: Why do some women choose to follow this spiritual movement, *Inter-universal Mysticism*, in Iran? What does spirituality mean to them? How is spirituality understood and experienced in their lives? To what extent and how does their participation in such a movement transform or change their lives? Is there any relationship between the remarkable number of women within this movement and feminism?

In order to understand the connection between spirituality and the high number of female participants in *Inter-universal Mysticism*, after a period of reading, planning and reflection, I planned and carried out a qualitative study of women of different ages and social backgrounds within this movement in three Iranian cities, Tehran, Yazd and Mashhad, between April and July 2010. As the research progressed, I became interested in expanding the study to investigate the relevance of feminism to these women's experiences. My aims at the beginning of the study were deliberately broad: to discover the connection between women's participation in this movement and feminism in Iran. Through further study, significant themes emerged and shaped my approach to exploring how, and to what extent, this spiritual movement might change an Iranian woman's life.

My own life story and route to my book are relevant to this project. I was born in 1981, two years after the Islamic revolution, in Tehran, the capital city of Iran. Like many women born since 1979 I grew up in a world where, on the one hand, there are diverse modern opportunities but where, on the other hand, Iranians must deal with the constricting and intrusive official interference of the Islamic regime. I was raised in a very modern and westernised family which was at odds with what seemed, to me, a restrictive Islamic official culture: a challenging experience for me as I matured. For example, I used to attend private dance classes and mixed parties without wearing a hijab, yet our religious teachers at school told us that if we listened to music our ears would be burned in hell, or that if we showed one strand of hair we would be hanged by that in hell. This contradictory experience is one which I share with many of the women I interviewed for this study. As a result of these conflicting messages, like some of the women in my study I began to question the life I was living and started to ask myself: Who am I? What is the purpose of my life? What is my mission in this world? These questions led me to search within different religions and spiritual movements, until eventually I learnt about *Inter-universal Mysticism*.

When I joined *Inter-universal Mysticism* in 2005, it was a relatively new public movement. Although founded in Iran by Mohammad Ali Taheri thirty years ago, Taheri had only been teaching public classes for a couple of years and the movement was not as well-known as others, such as meditation and reiki which had been introduced to Iran in the 1990s. I heard about *Inter-universal Mysticism* from one of my close and pious Muslim friends with a similar interest as myself in the path of *erfan*/mysticism. The popularity of *Inter-universal Mysticism* developed through word of mouth, and the majority of the women in my study heard about it from family members, relatives or friends. At first, I thought *Inter-universal Mysticism* was intended for groups of people to discuss matters of Shia Muslim doctrine, ritual and practices, but I then discovered that it

is a modern religious or spiritual movement which has a relationship to the
traditional path of *erfan*, but which goes beyond those understandings.
Interestingly, I later found that my perceptions were common to many
women in my study, who also did not initially realise that *Inter-universal
Mysticism* is about *erfan*/mysticism; most of my interviewees, particularly
in Yazd, assumed at first that it was about healing, calling it *faradarmani*/
the spiritual healing on this path. Although I had some initial doubts which
made me cautious about progressing within the movement, I eventually
became a Master[1] in *Inter-universal Mysticism* after one year of study. In
2006, I came to the UK to undertake post-graduate study in human rights.
At that point I thought of *erfan* or spirituality as a personal interest, little
imagining that one day I might teach it or conduct academic research and
eventually write a book in the field.

After living in the UK for a year and half, I travelled back to Iran for a
brief visit in winter 2007. I was looking forward to meeting Mr Taheri and
my friends in the *Inter-universal Mysticism* movement. I had heard that
because of the increase in the number of participants, the classes had been
relocated from a room in an office in one of the less affluent areas of
Tehran to a big hall in a more expensive area of the city. The event I
described above took place on a day when I decided to go to one of the
highest-level classes (Level eight) to visit Mr Taheri and some of my
friends. I mention which level of the class I was attending because it is
important to note the large number of women who reached this high stage
on the path. In contrast to my previous experiences of class attendance,
when there were just 20 participants in the class with approximately equal
numbers of men and women, all of whom were well-educated and mostly
pious Muslims, this time I noticed a large increase in the overall number of
participants and a much higher proportion of women. It should be noted
that I observed men and women sitting separately even if they were
related, with women wearing Islamic hijabs. On previous occasions when I
had attended these classes, women wore loose scarves and sat next to men
and the atmosphere was relaxed. The more recent session was formal in
other ways: the teacher, Mr. Taheri, used technology including PowerPoint
and the class was more like a formal seminar than a spiritual class. Recent
restrictions on spiritual movements suggest a clear reason why the
informal atmosphere of these classes has changed into a more formal
academic style. This prompted me to consider the changes that had

---

[1] Master is a title given to anyone who has passed six levels in *Inter-universal
Mysticism* and becomes qualified to teach its lessons to others.

occurred in the last two years. How had *erfan* become so popular, particularly among women? Drawing on my own experience, I began to consider both the gendering of spirituality in Iran and, in particular, the predominance of women on the *Inter-universal Mysticism* path in the second decade of the twenty-first century: these became the central concerns of my study. This short autobiography reveals how my own experience places me in a position where I can comment on, and empathise with the situations of the women I have studied. Both I and the women I interviewed are Iranian women with shared experience, language and ideas who have followed the same mystical or spiritual path. While my own understanding and lived experience as a Master on this path give me important insights, my understanding of how to conduct academic feminist research and my experience of living outside Iran allows me to use those perceptions reflexively and to comment as an outsider.

Here I should acknowledge that this study is the first academic study on *Inter-universal Mysticism* itself not its healing and is only about women inside the path and I did not expect these women's stories to all be so positive. Although I could have interviewed women who were not interested in joining the movement but were practicing its spirituality, I was not able to find any woman who had left the path, and therefore there may have been more critical stories which are not reflected here. Yet, my intention is not to construct a pro-*Inter-universal Mysticism* argument, but to study the experiences of women within *Inter-universal Mysticism* through a feminist lens.

In short, this qualitative study endeavours to broaden discourses about women in Iran by examining the link between spirituality, coping, and meaning-making in the lives of a sample of women involved with *Inter-universal Mysticism*. The novel contribution of the study is not simply to extend the range of contexts in which gender can be analysed but rather, through the lens of feminism, to demonstrate the significance of women's choice of spirituality as an investigative issue which can elucidate women's wider social, cultural and political processes in contemporary Iran. My main objective in studying women on the path of *Inter-universal Mysticism* is to demonstrate how spirituality rather than religion (Shia Islam) affects women's lives and self-empowerment. Analysis of my data revealed convergences between the practice of *Inter-universal Mysticism* and women's self-empowerment, or rather their movement towards what they experience as greater authenticity or a more authentic self. This aspect of women's lives has not been studied yet and in this way my approach differs from existing work on Iranian women's lives after the Islamic revolution. In other words, understandings of the spiritual lives of

Iranian women are limited in current studies on Iran, and that this study therefore offers a new and original contribution to the existing scholarship on women in Iran and to spirituality studies.[2]

---

[2] This study is about the everyday lives of women in Iran who have understandings of spirituality in a very different context to most of the other studies, which are mainly about spirituality in the west.

ACKNOWLEDGEMENTS

I must acknowledge that many people have contributed to the writing of this study, from initial conception through to completion. Most significantly, it has been primarily shaped by the participants – the women who gave up their time to talk with me and share their experiences and stories. I am very grateful to them all for their contributions.

A great deal of thanks is also due to Nahid, one of the most dedicated Masters of *Inter-universal Mysticism* who provided me with extensive help and support in carrying out my field work during such a strict political situation. She has been encouraging and for that I am eternally thankful.

The enthusiasm of two people, my inspiring supervisors Dr Joanna de Groot and Dr Ann Kaloski Naylor, have not only kept the whole process going, but also made it rewarding and enjoyable. They have advised, supported and guided me throughout and I am very thankful for having had them as my mentors.

I am also indebted to my parents for their kindness and invaluable supports both financially and emotionally. Thank you both for being persistent and encouraging, for believing in me, and for the many precious lessons you thought me along the way.

Finally, I could never have embarked upon this book, or kept going, without the love, help and care of my wonderful husband, Amirhossein SadrFaridpour – you are the best.

INTRODUCTION

It is striking that women in Iran are increasingly choosing to follow spiritual paths which differ from conventional Iranian Shia Islam. Although there is no written or other accessible evidence to support this statement, due to censorship and restrictions on unofficial movements, my recent experience of urban life in Iran and my conversations with other Iranians has led me to think that there is an increasing interest in spirituality, at least in bigger cities, particularly among young people and women. Young people are increasingly joining different schools of *erfan*/mysticism, one of which is *Inter-universal Mysticism*, because on such paths they can find a greater freedom to form their own way of life and belief. In her 2006 BBC News report, "Growing popularity of Sufism in Iran", Saberi states that "nowadays, hundreds of young Iranians are increasingly joining *erfani* groups… because Official religion has a series of limitations, and its limitations are much stricter than *erfan*"[3]. However, mainstream media, both online and in print, such as newspapers, magazines and weblogs, are not allowed to mention this growing movement because, in the government's view, it constitutes evil thought and is anti-Islamic. The purpose of my research was to investigate the self-perception of Iranian women involved in one of the most recognised of these movements in Iran, known as *Inter-universal Mysticism*. I contend that it is so well-known not only because of its large numbers of followers but also because it has been the target of public attack by the government, which has increased public awareness of *Inter-universal Mysticism*.

This book deals with women's subjective evaluations of their situation in Iran following their choice to participate in *Inter-universal Mysticism* since 2002. In this book, I present the findings of my study and evaluate 55 women's narratives of their experiences inside this movement: stories which reflect their desire for change in their lives. Along with the interview material I include observations of meetings, and ideas gleaned from four discussion groups I organised, in three cities in Iran – Tehran, Yazd and Mashhad – in which women discussed the influence of this movement in their lives. Throughout this book I argue that women's participation within *Inter-universal Mysticism* creates spaces to deal with

---

[3] Saberi, 2006, n.p.

their life experiences in current Iranian society, to cope with the difficulties they encounter, and to resist the limitations placed upon them. The women's narratives here are analysed in relation to a framework of feminist ideas, which interprets their ideas and experiences within a wider theoretical context. I have tried to articulate women's own interpretations of spirituality in their lives, and to understand their beliefs and actions in relation to *Inter-universal Mysticism*. My feminist approach allows for a fuller understanding of these Iranian women's realities, which are complex and sometimes contradictory.

I offer a narrative of Iranian society and its gender ideology after the Islamic revolution, which helps to demonstrate how Taheri's movement has developed with a particularly large number of women as its followers. In fact, any study of women living in Iran in the last 35 years, not just the ones I studied, requires an understanding of the ambiguities in the position of women. The revolution's impact on women in particular has been paradoxical, as it has both opened up new possibilities for them and at the same time instituted the most repressive controls on their lives. Women from various classes were active participants in the events leading to the overthrow of the Pahlavi regime in 1979. They joined the revolutionary (anti-shah) movements for a variety of reasons, religious and secular, economic and political, in the expectation that the revolution would not only defeat the Shah[4], but also would lead to the growth and development of women's status and opportunities[5]. But they soon discovered that the Islamic regime had its own agenda for women.

The situation of women in post-1979 Iran is rather contradictory: on the one hand, they have to cope with a regime which has a political gender agenda that is very powerful and constraining, part of which is reinforced by tradition and existing practices; on the other hand, it is a regime that set women up as part of its own constituency, since it celebrated the role of women in the revolution and changing the regime, and used women's skills and labour in periods of war. The new Islamic regime has involved itself in creative practices in which it has opened up spaces for women's religious education and education more generally. The women, who appear in this study like other Iranian women, are women who are constantly negotiating these contradictions. Most Iranian women, whether or not they participate in *Inter-universal Mysticism*, have been picking their way through this contradictory environment either by negotiation or resistance. I show how women have created spaces or negotiated different

---

[4] Shah is the title given to kings of Iran.
[5] Esfandiari, 1997.

outcomes from the ones the regime might have intended. I conclude that the development of spiritual paths like *Inter-universal Mysticism* after the Islamic revolution provides insights into a society that is complex and disillusioned with unfulfilled religious revolutionary goals. Women's choice of this movement is one of the ways in which women, as both social and political actors, express their critical dissatisfaction with the regime and challenge patriarchal and gendered relations in Iran in both the public and the private spheres.

The paradoxical situation of women in Iran since the Islamic revolution has inspired much research on the diversity of Iranian women's lives and struggles. On the one hand, these studies represent the lives of Iranian women as shaped by adversity and on the other, they look at how women challenge the current official Islamic gender ideology. Women in Iran employ myriad strategies to cope, to resist and to defeat the impact of the official Islamic norms imposed upon them, including their dress, work and public presence. However, despite considerable evidence regarding the commanding roles of spiritual practices (e.g. prayer) and spirituality in the lives of Iranian women, explorations of the spiritual lives of women in Iran remain limited. Much has been written on the experience or participation of men in Sufism and the path of *erfan*/mysticism, but women's spiritual activities in Iran have not received the attention they deserve: this is the main focus of this study. Those studies that do consider women and religion are primarily concerned with the history or the social and political functions of Islam and discuss women's roles or ideologies as projected or reproduced in religious contexts, rather than being concerned with women's spirituality as an analytic category in the sense undertaken here.

My approach differs significantly from that of existing scholarship on women in Iran. Scholars such as Friedl (1989) in *Women of Deh Koh: lives in an Iranian village*, and Torab (2006) in *Performing Islam: gender and ritual in Iran,* adopt anthropological approaches to women, religion and spirituality but, although I have used participant observation, my overall approach is different due to my distinctive insider-outsider position. In this study spirituality and religion are understood as overlapping but distinct categories of analysis and experience. Religion is conceptualized as an organized socio-cultural-historical system with rules, doctrines and practices, while spirituality is understood as an individual's personal quest to experience a close relationship with a higher power (e.g. God), seeking a meaningful life and a feeling of interconnectedness with the whole world. I examine spirituality within a particular school of thought – *Inter-universal Mysticism* – within which spirituality and religious belief can be interrelated. Spirituality, which is the achievement of *kamal*/perfection and fulfilment on this path, can be combined with religion "if the beliefs and experiences that are considered to be an aspect of traditional religion like prayer or reading holy books"[6], are linked to an individual's search for the divine or ultimate truth. My study also suggests that spirituality takes on a different sense when the lived experiences of women are in conflict with powerfully gendered religious ideologies in Iran. The spirituality of women in the *Inter-universal Mysticism* movement is associated with self-awareness, self-defined identity, inner strength, peace, and the clarification of core values and beliefs. It seems that it is the spirituality in this movement, rather than their Islamic religion, which has enabled these women to manage and negotiate the relationship between their personal aspirations and needs, cultural and family influences, and official religious demands and pressures.

In this study, I combine my personal interest in the lives of women in Iran, and the particular lives of women on the path of *Inter-universal Mysticism*, with an intellectual understanding of women's involvement in this spiritual movement. As King (1993) argues, while feminism is an important social and political movement, spirituality has a long history as a human quest to seek fulfilment, liberation and achieve perfection. I further seek to explore the relationship between spirituality and women's life transformations in Iran from a feminist viewpoint. For these purposes, I define feminism as the concern for the welfare and autonomy of women, which implies a principle relevant to all feminisms. My own feminism urges me to question the difficulties and disadvantages which women in Iran currently face, and "to interpret women's experiences in relation to patriarchy, men, and other women"[7]. I use feminism as an intellectual framework for analysing how the lives of Iranian women involved in *Inter-universal Mysticism* have changed. Feminism is important here because feminism provides "an ideological basis for change on every level of human existence, from intimate behaviour to transforming patriarchy and its core values of dominance and control"[8]. Moreover, using feminist tools helps to reveal how, by choosing to participate in this movement, these women confront "the everyday realities of male privilege and the oppression of women"[9] in Iran. Although the women I interviewed do not wish to be called feminist and reject the term feminism, they share

---

[6] Hill et al., 2001, p. 71.
[7] Meyers, 2002, p. 2.
[8] Johnson, 2005, p. 102.
[9] Ibid.

reactions to and critiques of their world which can be understood in "feminist" terms. In other words, while these women distance themselves from feminism, it is nonetheless possible to find an illuminating feminist way of reading, respecting, commenting on and valuing their words, which draws out feminist implications in their stories. My feminist perspective enables a better understanding of these women and allows women to narrate their own lives and to become valued analysts and commentators on their lives.

One of the key features of this study is that it explores women's agency, choices and autonomy, as well as their negotiations and strategies for a better life. I focus on women's agency in its various manifestations and, to determine the meaning of concepts such as identity, autonomy, and agency, I have used feminist theories – in particular Kabeer (1999), Meyers (2002), Isaac (2002) and Eisenstein (2004) – in analysing the experiences of women on this spiritual path. The women's narratives from this feminist perspective revealed interrelated themes relevant to women's choice of this particular form of spirituality over other ways of resisting restrictions and shifting attitudes both at home, in relation to male relatives, and more widely in relation to patriarchal practices and institutions. My study shows how this spiritual movement allows women either to create greater autonomy in changing their lives, or to negotiate and manage their lives in ways which are more satisfying for them. Close reading of their narratives reveals why women participate in this movement in present day Iran when there are simultaneously many opportunities and many restrictions for women because of the political situation there.

The women's narratives provide glimpses into their lives as they represent their struggles, achievements, and certainties as well as uncertainties. Their stories reveal the layered and complex experiences of women living in Shia Muslim Iran at the present time. During the course of my study, participants commented on how they dealt with patriarchal institutions and a patriarchal regime; the power of these particular ideologies of the regime is currently enforced by the national political situation in which the Iranian regime uses violence and discrimination against women. I should note that there is a recognisable term for "patriarchy" in Farsi which is مردسالاری/mard-salari. In Iran, mard-salari is a social system in which men appropriate most, if not all, of the dominant social roles and keep women in subordinate positions. The main argument for using this term here is that patriarchy in Iran supports gender inequality and the subordination of women within and beyond the household. Using feminist ideas in the reading and analysis of women's stories helped to show that as women proceed along this spiritual path, not only do they achieve self-determination and agency, but they also challenge patriarchy through the shifting of gendered power relations at home: for example, they treat their husbands differently; at the centre of these themes and ideas are strategies for developing the self and performing an authentic identity. Women's participation in the *Inter-universal Mysticism* movement has become a site for negotiating relationships between self, society, politics and the transcendent. It has created an opportunity for women to engage with critical reflections of themselves, and endeavour to widen their discussions to influence change in Iran's social and political systems. Ultimately, their narratives create much needed knowledge and context required to contemplate the interrelationships between women's choice, spirituality and feminism in Iran.

However, I have found that there is a gap between the understanding of feminism and of spirituality in Iran, a place with a considerable history of spirituality and mysticism (*erfan*). Most work on feminism and spirituality since the 1970s has been carried out by writers from western countries prompting the question: why have women in Iran not considered spirituality in their feminist movements? Or, if such arguments around feminism and spirituality do exist in Iran, why have we not heard them? Scholars who have investigated feminism in Iran have looked at it either as a rather secular tradition, or have focused only on women who very explicitly use Shia Islam; they have not thought about other aspects and experiences of religious life including the kind of spirituality associated with *Inter-universal Mysticism*. In other words, the studies that focus on feminism in Iran are mainly concerned with women's political and legal status, roles, or gender relations, based either on "Islam" or "secular human rights".

For example, Mir-Hosseini in *Stretching the limits: a feminist reading of the Sharia in post-Khomeini Iran* (1996), and Moghadam in *Islamic feminism: its discontents and its prospects* (2002), focus on Islamic feminists in Iran who, despite their respect for the Qu'ranic laws which define gender roles and the structure of the family and community, develop modern readings of the sharia and re-read the Qu'ran, Hadith, and Islamic history. Such feminists use their re-readings "to implement reforms with a view to facilitating women's access to the public sphere, thereby overcoming gender stratification"[10]. The focus of such studies is on elite women such as: Shahla Shirkat, the editor of *Zanan* magazine;

---

[10] Kian, 1995, p. 408.

Mahbubeh Ummi and Ma'sumeh Ibtikar, the editors of *Farzaneh*;
Tayyibeh Iskandari, the new editor of *Zan-I Ruz* magazine; and Faezeh
Hashemi, a journalist and former member of the Iranian parliament. These
women all participated in a movement known as Islamic feminism,
challenging the reduction in women's rights and the strict limits placed on
women by the Islamic government.

By contrast, in their studies, Rostami Povey, in *Feminist contestations
of institutional domains in Iran* (2001), and Ahmed-ghosh in *Dilemmas of
Islamic and secular feminists and feminisms* (2008) analyse the complex
relationship between gender, institutions, feminisms and democracy in
Iran. They discuss secular feminists in Iran, for example: Mehrangiz Kar, a
legal attorney; Shirin Ebadi, a former judge and winner of the Nobel Peace
Prize; Nahid Musavi, a journalist; and Zhaleh Shaditalab, a sociology
professor; "base their rationale for women's rights on a human rights
discourse which enables and empowers the individual in a secular
democracy to create a civil society"[11]. In their view, although religious
reform is helpful and necessary, the recognition of its limitations is very
important. Such feminists consider that "secular democracy is the
prerequisite for demands for individual rights based on a system of
fairness and justice, thus ensuring women a way to claim those rights"[12].

In their challenging of longstanding and conventional patriarchal
frameworks that affect the lives of Iranian women, none of the feminist
studies on Iran have considered the role of spirituality or spiritual
movements. This study addresses this gap. It is also interesting that
women who campaign for women's rights and interests in Iran have not
considered engaging with women who are neither conventional Muslims
nor strongly secular, but who explore other aspects of religion and
spirituality. Women in my study identify themselves as believers in God,
but they have different views of religion; some wish to be called religious
but do not follow the official Islamic Shia and have their own way of
being a good Muslim, while some think of spirituality as their religion and
call themselves spiritual. Scholarship on women in Iran has not yet taken
this approach or considered women's interests in spirituality over or with
religion; this preference is central to my study as I examine the potential
feminist implications of women's involvement in *Inter-universal
Mysticism* and its emancipatory potential and feminist capabilities for
women. My argument is that feminist spirituality is an expression of
women's power to identify, explore, and assess their own spiritual

[11] Ahmed-Ghosh, 2008, p. 106.
[12] Ibid.

experiences to construct their sense of self and transform their lives. The reasons that I am able to develop this discussion are twofold. First, *Inter-universal Mysticism* as a movement has established an innovative relationship between religion and spirituality as both distinct and overlapping categories. Second, my close analysis of women's explanations of what spirituality on this path means to them indicates that there is an open and flexible relationship between religion and spirituality. They have recognised spirituality as something distinct in its own right but not necessarily or completely detached from their traditional religion of Shia Islam.

Given the lack of research on women and spirituality in Iran and the absence of any cohesive and empirically developed frameworks in the literature on Iranian women in this area, it was necessary for me to undertake this study at an exploratory level. Feminist-inspired scholarship on women and spirituality in western countries has provided a useful basis for my research and offered some valuable insights into the role of spirituality in women's lives. These studies were particularly useful in suggesting a wider range of contexts where women's choices, ideas and relations are questioned and shaped within a spiritual framework. In particular, they helped me to scrutinize spirituality in women's everyday lives. For example, in studies of African American women's spirituality, Mattis takes a similar approach to mine. Studying the subjective experiences and perspectives of African American women, she identifies the distinctions that these women make between religiosity and spirituality in their understanding of spirituality. Tisdell's work on women's spirituality and emancipatory adult education for social change is also relevant, as she examines the influence of spirituality in the lives of a group of women adult educators and its connection to emancipatory education. She investigates the particular religious traditions in which her respondents grew up and then assesses their renegotiations towards a more "adult" spirituality.

However, while these studies are useful, limitations remain, mainly because they study women and spirituality in other belief systems and cultures rather than women whose spiritual experiences and activities are embedded in Iranian Islamic culture. The spiritual experiences of women in my study are heavily influenced by the tradition of Shia Islam even while they remain critical of it. As studies such as *Islam in practice* by Loeffler (1988), *Women of Deh Koh* by Friedl (1989) and *Performing Islam* by Torab (2006) show, within popular Shia Muslim practice, the recitation of Qu'ranic verses or the repetition of prayer are meaningful and valuable for many Iranians. In fact, there is a rich texture of religious culture over and above the official Islam in Iran. The belief in the importance of reciting Qu'ranic verses is one part of practicing traditional Shia Islam which has been developed over many years by ordinary people. Indeed, repeating prayers is an important part of daily life for most Iranians. For example, during my field work I spent time observing women on public transportation and in public places, including two pilgrimage centres that I visited to learn more about the lives of women in contemporary Iran. Interestingly, I witnessed many women on public transportation practicing some kind of spirituality, for example by whispering verses of the Qu'ran for various reasons. These included young girls on their way to their exams, women with economic problems such as an inability to pay bills, and many women who whispered verses for their own or family illnesses. I also saw men acting in this way; for example, I saw a man in Mashhad driving illegally and whispering a verse, hoping that the police would not catch and fine him. In shrines in Tehran and Mashhad, I noticed that the number of female visitors was considerably higher than male visitors. In hairdressers I heard women, especially young ones, referring to fortune tellers and those who write special verses of the Qu'ran for solving life problems: substantial amounts of money are paid for these services. It seems that looking for a spiritual, mystical or supernatural source of help for various problems has an important role in daily life for many Iranians. While such a conclusion is supported by my observations, my interviews and discussions with women involved in *Inter-universal Mysticism* led me to deeper insights to explain why spirituality and following such paths could have meaning in an Iranian woman's life.

My analytical approach to my research findings in this book is formed of two stages. The first stage is about reporting and contextualising the meanings which the women themselves attribute to their experience. In other words, I read women's narratives in a way that allows them to speak the meaning of their own experiences as far as is possible. The second stage is my own commentary and added reflections on those narratives and meanings. Importantly, women's narratives are used to ground my findings in women's own experiences. This study has a distinctly feminist focus as a consequence of my own interest in the quality of women's lives despite the fact that this movement, *Inter-universal Mysticism,* considers itself to be gender neutral, with human beings understood as beyond gender. I present and analyse the words of 55 women inside this movement who volunteered their ideas, opinions and stories within the framework of my enquiry.

SUMMARY OF THE CHAPTERS

In chapter one, "An introduction to *Inter-universal Mysticism*", I give a brief overview of *Inter-universal Mysticism* in order to introduce the reader to the history, aims and structure of the movement. Chapter two, "Setting the Scene: concepts, methods, and fieldwork", establishes a context for this book by explaining the processes by which my research developed from its original aims to its final analysis, detailing how the research was carried out and why the selected combination of methods (one-to-one semi-structured interviews, focus/discussion groups and participant observation) was chosen.

The following four chapters describe and examine the findings of my research. In chapter four, "Iranian women's choice of *Inter-universal Mysticism*: the personal and social motivations", I talk about women's accounts of *Inter-universal Mysticism* and their reasons for joining and following this movement. I identify five themes from women's stories of choosing and joining this movement: how women found out about the path; their religious conflicts and opposition to official Islam; patriarchy and social pressure; the spiritual healing of *Inter-universal Mysticism* called *faradarmani*; and women's desire for self-improvement. However, as I argue, the real experiences of the women I interviewed were various and demonstrate combinations of these themes: I separate the themes in order to facilitate investigation rather than because they operate independently.

Chapter five, "Engaging spirituality: women's perceptions and experiences", examines women's perceptions of being spiritual on this mystical path. Here, spirituality is theorised as a way of approaching life. By assessing women's relationships with their spirituality, I discuss how the spiritual and the material interact. The chapter identifies three different perspectives of spirituality among the women: those who think spirituality is separate from religion; those who believe in spirituality within religion; and those who think both religion and spirituality offer the same kind of resources. I argue that the beliefs, worldviews, and values of religious traditions and spirituality for women from all three perspectives provide the context in which they can generate "a sense of meaning, order, and place in the world"[13] that is central to their definition of spirituality.

---

[13] King et al., 2011, p. 173.

In chapter six, "Transforming lives: challenging everyday patriarchy through *Inter-universal Mysticism*", I analyse women's views of how involvement in *Inter-universal Mysticism* in Iran may change a woman's life. I argue that joining *Inter-universal Mysticism* has affected women in different ways and, for some of them, has changed their everyday lives. The agency, autonomy and self-confidence that women learn inside the movement give them new tools, resources and insights which they can use to change their lives or, if they are living the same life they had before joining this path, to find strategies for greater happiness.

Chapter seven, "The relationship between feminism and women's achievements in *Inter-universal Mysticism*", considers the extent to which women, in any way, connect their views and behaviours with feminism. I also attempt to show how women's achievements on this path–redefining themselves as confident women, able to challenge obstacles such as social structure or personal difficulties, and being able to search for *kamal*/fulfilment–can be read in a feminist way. My analysis show that these women distance themselves from what they understand as feminism for two main reasons, which I consider further by examining the influence of social and cultural assumptions and of *Inter-universal Mysticism* on women's insights. Finally, I argue that there are feminist implications in these women's own words which lead to the articulation of the relationship between feminism and these women's experiences on this spiritual path.

My conclusion suggests that women activists in Iran may want to think about an alternative strategy in their campaigning through considering the experience of women on the path of *Inter-universal Mysticism*. The application of feminist analysis to my interviews and the study of women's own understanding of themselves allow me to propose a particular way or relationship between spirituality and feminism in Iran. One possibility is that what I call feminist spirituality among women in *Inter-universal Mysticism* may open a dialogue between Islamic and secular feminists in Iran to find common ground which is as much a matter of practice as theory.

CHAPTER ONE

AN INTRODUCTION TO INTER-UNIVERSAL MYSTICISM

In order to make sense of the experiences of the women inside this path, I will introduce the reader to *Inter-universal Mysticism*. This short chapter presents a general introduction to the movement, describing how it has developed over the last thirty years, outlining its key tenets, and offering a snapshot of its important practices. You can read further about the significance of the *Inter-universal Mysticism* and how it differs from other spiritual movements in its place throughout the rest chapters.

The Development of Inter-universal Mysticism

In Iran, there is a rich tradition of mystical endeavour, thought and practice, some of which has echoes in *Inter-universal Mysticism*. To explore the mystical culture within which this movement has developed, I start with a brief history of *erfan*. *Erfan*, which in Farsi literally means "knowing", is similar to the Greco-Christian concept of *gnosis*. Taheri suggests that "the term is used to refer both to Islamic mysticism as well as the attainment of spiritual knowledge springing from direct insight"[1]. *Erfan* overlaps considerably with Sufism and is understood in two ways; as a part or element of Islamic religion which is called Sufism, and/or "as a process or way of life which is an attempt to express and seek a direct consciousness of the presence of God"[2]. The purpose of *erfan* is to achieve *kamal*, which in Farsi means the attainment of perfection, fulfilment or completeness. *Erfan* consists of "a variety of mystical paths that are designed to ascertain the nature of humanity and of God and to facilitate the experience of the presence of divine love and wisdom in the world"[3]. It is an aspect of Islamic belief and practice through which Iranians find a

---

[1] Taheri, 2008, p. 16.
[2] McGinn, 2002, p. xvi.
[3] The New Encyclopaedia Britannica, 1989, p. 355.

direct personal experience of God in which they seek the truth of divine love and knowledge. As such, *erfan* has developed a rich variety of forms, practices and institutions since its emergence in the tenth and eleventh centuries.[4]

Erfan was established in Iran by the eleventh century and was flourishing by the fourteenth century. In the following years, a number of Iranian thinkers and poets contributed to *erfan*. Of particular note are two *arefs*[5] who have profoundly affected Iranian life and culture and have enjoyed enduring popularity and influence: Jalal-al-din Rumi (1207–1273), known as Mowlana, and Khawjah Shams al-din Muhammad Hafez-e Shiraz (1325-1389), known as Hafez. Mowlana was the founder of the Mevlevi Sufi order, known to westerners as whirling dervishes, and the search for God passes to his followers through music or dance which they believe transcends thought. Hafez's influence on the lives of Iranians is maintained by *fale-e Hafez*/Hafez readings.[6] His collected poetry (*Divan-i Hafez*) can be found in the homes of most Farsi speakers who learn his poems by heart, and even non-literate Iranians use his writings as proverbs and sayings to this day. The tradition continued in Iran in the nineteenth and twentieth centuries, and, for many Iranians, *erfan* is an expression of personal religion. Some people practice both *erfan* and Islam simultaneously while for some *erfan* refers to a personal relation with God: a sense of self and a search for meaning and purpose in life outside of Islam.

Erfan Keyhani (*Halgheh*) or *Inter-universal Mysticism* (*Circle*) is based on the intuitions and revelations of Mohammad Ali Taheri and was founded by him thirty years ago.[7] Taheri was born in 1956 in Kermanshah, Iran and trained as a mechanical engineer before discovering *Inter-universal Mysticism.* He believes that the principles of his understandings are compatible with Iranian mysticism or, rather, that its insights are deeply embedded in the Iranian mystical tradition of Sufism, Persian poetry and Abrahamic or monotheistic faiths. In an interview on 14 September 2010, Taheri said that his mysticism is based on discoveries

---

[4] For a general schema of different modes of *erfan* and its development see Trimingham, 1998.

[5] The precise word for 'master in *erfan*' or an *erfan* master. Also sometimes called Sufi, Dervish or Pir.

[6] 'For centuries, it has been a Persian tradition to open Hafez when confronted with a difficult decision or choice. When used in divination, it is widely believed that Hafez's poetry will reveal the answer to your destiny' (Samipersia, 2007, n.p).

[7] Taheri has never mentioned an exact date or year of founding for this path but has simply said it is thirty years old.

that have been made of past mystical content, such as the path of *erfan* and Sufism.[8] However, its creative development of mystical practice and reflection makes *Inter-universal Mysticism* a new and distinctive movement, going beyond existing traditions. The term 'inter-universal', as Taheri puts it, refers to a kind of mystical thought and suggests:

> [T]he promotion of human beings' level of thinking to the level of the world of existence. In this regard, humans think beyond the sectarian, tribal, racial, national, etc. and through the perception of the general divine compassion they can understand the world of existence. On this path, it is believed that without perception of the whole, man cannot properly plan the course of perfection.[9]

In another, more biographical interview in January 2008, Taheri recounted that since his childhood he had been extremely curious about the universe, the secret of creation and human existence.[10] He strongly asserted that he had never followed any particular religious or Sufi path and did not have greater religious knowledge than a typical Iranian growing up in a traditional Islamic culture. Therefore, to find answers to his questions he studied relevant books and documents and meditated deeply. He insisted that because of his great desire to find the truth of life he started receiving intuitions that amazed him and which then took him ten years to explore and reflect upon.

Taheri (2008) stated that his mystical movement has developed over the last three decades without any influence from other similar paths or movements. He recalled that in the first decade he rationalized and tried to understand all the intuitions he received. In the second decade he started to work on these intuitions and to test them out in practice. He began by teaching his knowledge and cognitions to his family and friends in private and using the healing, which he later called *faradarmani*, on different types of diseases. At that time, Taheri started to compare his newly understood principles with those expounded in the Holy Qu'ran, the Bible, including the Old Testament, Islamic literature and Sufism. He suggested that while the broad theories of *Inter-universal Mysticism* are universal and compatible, for example with the two fundamental doctrines in other

---

[8] This is one of the interviews published by the *Inter-universal Mysticism* institution that does not contain details of the interviewers: it is titled simply 'Question and Answer'.

[9] Taheri, 2008, p. 130.

[10] Some of Taheri's recorded interviews that I collected during my field work did not contain the name of the interviewer (probably for safety reasons) or exact date information: only a given month and year was mentioned.

mystical traditions of the Transcendent Unity of Being and the Universal or Perfect Man, its practice is different.

Taheri argues that *Inter-universal Mysticism* reveals the mysteries hidden in the Holy Qu'ran and in Persian poetry written by classic poets such as Hafez and Mowlana whose work explores creation and human existence. In his view, such mystical books and poems provide a source of exoteric and perceptible knowledge that must be studied and explored for inner meaning. Taheri further differentiates *Inter-universal Mysticism* from traditional Sufi and mystical schools of thought, such as that of the Shah Nematollah[11], which he suggests are more theoretical and generalized than practical and specific.

I would argue that *Inter-universal Mysticism* is a modern spiritual movement which, while strongly rooted in certain Iranian traditions of *erfan* and religious thought and practice, is very much a product of Taheri's understanding of his intuitions as an educated man living in modern Iran. In a sense he has developed a very original and a very contemporary way of exploring spirituality. *Inter-universal Mysticism* is synchronized with the path of *erfan* and in some ways, certainly, Islam, as Taheri refers extensively to both in his teachings. It is also compatible with the mainstream of Muslim tradition within which Iranians are very skilled. Although he indicated that he was not part of any kind of *erfan* path, Taheri has obviously reflected deeply on spiritual matters within a modern context, and in this climate drew from many beliefs and practices–especially those related to the psychological and the psychic–alongside modern understandings of spirituality and religion. I suggest that it is one of the distinctive features of *Inter-universal Mysticism* that it synthesises traditional Iranian mysticism with modern global spiritual practices.

In the same January 2008 interview, Taheri also indicated that all his studies and experiences during the second decade of his work supported the truth of what he realised through his reflections. Consequently, in the third decade of developing *Inter-universal Mysticism* he publicized his knowledge by teaching it through structured lessons; first in a small class room with a few students, then progressing to run an official institution in 2001 and teach at one of the top universities in Iran, Tehran University, at a more professional level. At the same time he was participating in radio programs and journal interviews. *Inter-universal Mysticism* was initially designed by Taheri to be studied at six core levels, and he later added two more levels (seven and eight) and *Psymentology*.[12] Each level lasts six

---

[11] He was a Sufi Master and poet from the fourteenth and fifteenth centuries.

[12] *Psymentology* is one of the two Iranian complementary and alternative medicines founded by Taheri, which considers the treatment of disorders in the

weeks and teaching consists of one four-hour session each week. To participate on the path, each participant must register their name, pay the enrolment fee for each level and sign a letter provided by Taheri affirming that it is the responsibility of each person to make sure that he or she is practicing this mysticism in favour of God and goodwill towards others.[13]

The whole journey begins at level one with *faradarmani*, the spiritual healing in *Inter-universal Mysticism*. *Faradarmani* is a complementary treatment whose nature, in the view of Taheri and his followers, is mystical and is considered a branch of *Inter-universal Mysticism*. *Faradarmani* considers the treatment of diseases which are categorized in the field of medicine.[14] However, the purpose of *faradarmani* is to gain a practical acquaintance with divine intelligence. From this point of view, healing is a means to help mankind move onto the path of *Kamal*/perfection and is not a goal in itself: it is part of a larger process. In the structure Taheri designed to teach *Inter-universal Mysticism*, *faradarmani* or healing is the first step of spiritual development on this path. Many people's initial interest in *Inter-universal Mysticism* is in this healing process, through which not only do their mental and physical problems receive healing but, through practical experience, they also become familiar with the nature of the movement, from which they can go forward to further spiritual development. In 2006 Taheri trained all those who had reached level six to become Masters in order to be qualified to teach *Inter-universal Mysticism* to others. Consequently, he could develop his movement faster in many parts of Iran, Europe and America. He (2010) stated in his resume that before its closing the institution registered about 20,000 trainers, who are teaching the concepts of this pathway worldwide.

---

field of Psychiatry (Taheri, 2010). This is also one of the areas of work that Taheri has developed recently and, in my view, is not relevant to my study; therefore I am not going to consider it further.

[13] The fee was £26 for each six week term. There were various arguments around this issue; while some thought that it was a reasonable cost for such classes, some thought that it was expensive and not affordable for everyone. There were also people who disagreed with the enrolment fee and argued that spiritual classes should be free. In this regard, Taheri stated that the reason behind the fee was people's commitment to attend classes regularly; based on his experience of providing free classes in the past, Taheri argued that people do not care about attending classes as much when they are free as they do when they pay for it.

[14] *Faradarmani* has been discussed in several specialized editions of medical magazines, such as *Danesh Pezeshki* and *Tebe Kol Negar* in Iran.

Inter-universal Mysticism in Theory

In this section, by way of an introduction, I have chosen to concentrate on those theories of *Inter-universal Mysticism* which will best help contextualize the narratives of women's stories in my study. They also support my argument about why *Inter-universal Mysticism* is particularly relevant to women.

The purpose of this mystical practice is to help humans to reach *kamal* or, in other words, to achieve perfection and transcendence. The term *kamal*, as Taheri describes it, literally means "completeness and refers to the human's spiritual growth toward completion (perfection) and includes self-realization and self-awareness: clarity of vision about the universe"[15]. It is concerned with learning things which can be transferred to the afterlife and includes concepts such as unity, the magnificence of God and the perception of his presence. To clarify, *Inter-universal Mysticism* is characterised by a movement from the world of plurality to the world of unity through which one comes to understand the concept of the unified body in the world. The world of unity is the world where all component parts are considered the manifestations of God. In this movement "humans find themselves interacted and unified with all the constituents of the world of existence"[16]. This aspect of *Inter-universal Mysticism* is very important for understanding women's views on feminism and why they say gender does not matter, and I will return to this idea later.

Erfan Keyhani (Halgheh)/Inter-universal Mysticism (Circle) examines mystical concepts both in theory and in practice. Since it includes all human beings, Taheri (2008) argues that "everybody, regardless of their religion and personal beliefs, can accept its theories and experiences and make use of its practical aspects"[17]. Its theories are monotheistic and, as mentioned above, *Inter-universal Mysticism* considers that there are no differences within the original doctrines of Abrahamic religions, which all claim that there is only one God: the creator. This theory is in alignment with the teachings of Hazrat Salaheddin Ali Nader Angha, a famous Islamic Sufi Master, who says that

> [T]he words and the teachings of the prophets such as Moses, Jesus, and Mohammad are in accordance with one another. They all guide souls to the cognition of God and to the ultimate level of divine unity. There are no

---

[15] Taheri, 2008, p. 14.
[16] Ibid, p. 15.
[17] Ibid, p. 21.

differences within the original doctrines of the different monotheist religions.[18]

Therefore, in *Inter-universal Mysticism* too "the seeker of the truth seeks oneness with the divine. Through the ecstasy of love the barrier between God and his creatures gradually breaks down, resulting in divine unity"[19]. The goal is union with the beloved, a notion which is also found in Judaism, Islam and Christianity.

Spiritual experience on this path, then, is directly connected to submission to the divine mercy of God as the main source of knowledge. Later, I show how women with different religious beliefs (Sunni or Shia Islam and Christianity) develop on this path and can strengthen their faith without encountering any conflict. While Taheri respects religious rituals and commandments, he does not insist on or interfere in any religion and does not identify any one religion as the best spiritual way of life. As he argues, his mysticism relies solely on a direct relationship with the divine and with God himself or on the universal view of the deepest layer of monotheistic mysticism[20]. In this regard, he quotes the Holy Qu'ran that says:

> *Say we believe in God and in what has been revealed to us. And in what was revealed to Abraham, Ishmael, Isaac, Jacob and the tribes. And in what is given to Moses, Jesus and the prophets from their lord. We make no distinction between one and another among them and to God do we bow our will.*[21]

This emphasis and insistence on personal experience and knowledge of God and the connections with Inter-universal intelligence which assist humans in the path toward this goal is the structure which makes *Inter-universal Mysticism* the bridge between one's inner being and the real world. In other words, with its universal doctrine and method *Inter-universal Mysticism* contains within itself the possibility of being practiced in any circumstance in which one finds oneself in the spiritual world as well as the material one: one lives in the world without being seduced by it. Likewise it is also a means to integrate the active and contemplative lives so that a person is able to remain inwardly receptive to the influences of his or her spiritual experience, while remaining most active in the real

---

[18] Angha, 2012, n.p.
[19] Ibid.
[20] Taheri, 2010.
[21] Holy Qur'an, surah 3, verse 84.

world. This is one of the significant features of this movement that attracts more women compared to other mystical paths in which men are dominant and where it is believed that in order to reach perfection one should abandon a material life. I mean that the practical expectations of other mystical paths (for instance making a pilgrimage) makes it difficult for many women, whereas the spiritual practice in *Inter-universal Mysticism* can be maintained while being fully involved in everyday life.

Inter-universal Mysticism in Practice

Inter-universal Mysticism's practice is based on the linkage to several *halgheh*/circles of Inter-universal consciousness, which is "the collection of consciousness, wisdom or the intelligence governing the world which is also called awareness and is one of the three existing elements[22] in the universe"[23]. Taheri argues that "divine grace flows in different forms through various *halgheh* and these *halghehs* are the same as 'divine communal mercy' which can be applied and utilized in practice"[24]. In Taheri's view, all human beings, regardless of their race, nationality, sex, age, education and knowledge, individual talent and capability, religion, sinfulness or chastity, purity or impurity, can benefit from divine mercifulness.[25] The entire transformation and exploration on this path, then, is made possible through different *halghehs*.

In order to benefit from this practical part of *Inter-universal Mysticism* there is a need to establish *ettisal*/connection with the various *halgheh*/circles of the Inter-universal consciousness. *Ettisal* literally means connection or link. In *Inter-universal Mysticism*,

> *Ettisal* is establishing a form of communication or connection or a link to Inter-universal consciousness; which there is no accurate definition for, because *ettisal* is taking place in a world that is free of device/material, hence we can only study the effects and influences of *ettisal* and not the nature of *ettisal* itself.[26]

Put simply, *ettisal* is the practice of becoming aware of divine communal mercy and meditating upon it. The concept of *halgheh*, which is the concept of a circuit or circle, and of *ettisal*, which is the concept of

---

[22] These elements are matter, energy and awareness.
[23] Taheri, 2008, p. 26.
[24] Ibid, p. 19.
[25] Ibid, p. 22.
[26] Ibid, p. 111.

connection, are both used to describe how it is possible to become aware of and benefit from an understanding of personal connection to the divine communal mercy within *Inter-universal Mysticism*. However, both concepts are used to express different aspects of that connection. This is consistent with what Persian mystical poets say in their poems and what Taheri has discovered from their inner meanings. For example, Attar (1142-1220), a Persian Sufi Poet, says:

> *You are hidden from yourself, if you finally become visible*
> *The hidden treasure inside your soul will appear.*[27]

In fact, in the world of *erfan*/mysticism the circle (*halgheh*) has been repeatedly mentioned with different names and descriptions. For instance, Saadi (1213-1291), one of the major Persian poets, says:

> *The alluring chain of the beloved's hair is formed of circles which keep*
> *away the troubles*
> *The one out of this chain (halgheh's) that is not connected to beloved by*
> *this chain is disengaged from all these ventures.*[28]

Regarding the *ettisal* between humans and God, Mowlana says:

> *A simple measureless ettisal, is between God of people and the heart of*
> *people*
> *An ettisal which words can't bear*
> *But its utterance to you is a 'must' that's all*[29]

Taheri (2008) argues that there are many different *halgheh*/circles for those who are on this path, each dealing with a particular issue.[30] For example, *halgheh faradarmani* is used for health issues and healing. Each *halgheh*/circle of Inter-universal consciousness provides a distinctive facility and, in *Inter-universal Mysticism*, with the aid of such circles one can take a spiritual journey for self-exploration. Simply put, I would say that the particular processes of making *ettisal*/connection to divine

---

[27] Translated by myself.

[28] Translated by Dr. Homayounfar, in Taheri, 2008, p.114.

[29] Ibid, p.115.

[30] In general, there are two major *halghehs*/circles recognized in *Inter-Universal Mysticism*: one, circles that may be established for the benefit of others by the one who is already eligible in the cycle; and two, circles that do not require the presence of the eligible person. In such a case, everyone can use and take advantage of the circle independently, as soon as the cycle is shaping.

communal mercy through different *halgheh* serve various purposes: one is healing, but others are more spiritual and mystical in order to achieve perfection and transcendence. Understanding the distinctive practice of *Inter-universal Mysticism* is important because my interviews show that women's perceptions of changes either in their own selves (e.g. self-confidence and agency), or their lives (e.g. making better relationships), occur mainly through their experience of this practice along with the insights they received on the path. Therefore, an awareness of *ettisal* is critical for this study.

Taheri (2008) suggests that there are two general types of *ettisal*/connection to the Inter-universal consciousness. An individual way–which Taheri himself experienced thirty years ago–occurs when a person, by means of considerable eagerness and enthusiasm, becomes connected to the Inter-universal consciousness without the help of an instructor or any guidance. To establish such *ettisal*/connection an extraordinary amount of *eshtiyagh* (meaning 'enthusiasm' in Farsi) is necessary. The other way is collective where, with the assistance of an individual who serves as a connector, one becomes present in the circle. In this way, each *halgheh*/circle has three members: the Inter-universal consciousness; the person who serves as a connector; and the person who is about to be connected. Upon the formation of the *halgheh*/circle, divine grace immediately flows through it. For *halgheh* to take place the presence of the so-called three members is enough, and the fourth member is always Allah or God.

Inter-universal Mysticism establishes the *ettisal* based on a collective connection. This collective way of experiencing spirituality on this path indicates the importance of my argument that women's empowerment and agency on this path do not happen in isolation and that we should consider women's agency of self-in-relation to understand the changes they make in their lives. This practice not only rejects a focus on self as an individual in a mystical journey, but also sees it as an obstruction to spiritual growth which must be avoided. The figures below show both types of *ettisal*/connection to the Inter-universal consciousness: the individual way (A) and the collective way (B).[31]

---

[31] These figures are provided by Taheri in class at level one and are also published in his book, *Human from another look*, 2008.

Figure 1: Two types of *ettisal*/connection to the Inter-universal consciousness[32]

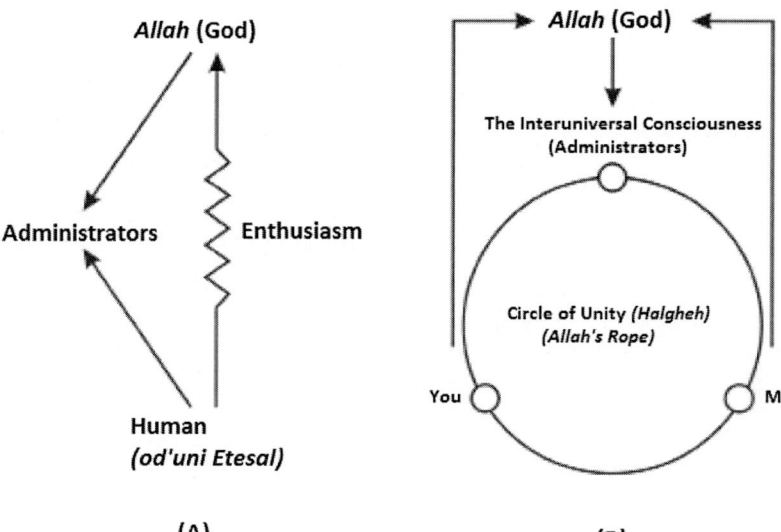

(A)   (B)

Based on my own knowledge as a Master on this path, I consider that the best way to explain the notion of *ettisal*, as developed in *Inter-universal Mysticism*, is the following. To practice *ettisal*, people usually close their eyes and, regardless of external events, should observe, notice or pay attention to themselves and their self-being. This observation and attention makes people aware of their entire being with impartiality and open-mindedness. The only condition for establishing the connection and being present in the *halgheh*/cycle is being an "impartial observer": there is no need for any relevant faith. Impartial observance means to be an open-minded observer or to surrender and remain impartial all the way, and not to make use of fantasy, imagination, or interpretation, since these will divert attention from simple observation. It suffices for the involved person to observe the presence of the cycle without pre-judgment and to be present in the moment. The person may take part in the cycle as soon as he or she can obtain the status of impartial, open minded observance: the connection with universal intelligence would therefore start at this stage.

All interested persons can take advantage of *ettisal* at any time or in any place. Closing the eyes helps to avoid distraction, but there is no

---

[32] Source: Taheri, 2008, p. 114.

specific need to do this. Everyone, at any time and in any condition (lying down, seated, busy at work, with opened or closed eyes), can step into the cycle and take advantage of its special results. One other point is that in order to step into the cycle there is no need to utter any special phrase, such as "In The Name of God": the link is established as soon as the person willingly chooses to enter the cycle. Each person's experience of *ettisal* is as unique as fingerprints, although they can attain similar effects: for example, healing in the *faradarmani* cycle.

Ettisal can be practiced both directly and indirectly. The direct use of *ettisal* is practiced by those who are already inside the path for their own benefit. The indirect use of *ettisal*, on the other hand, can be practiced by followers of *Inter-universal Mysticism* on others who are outside of the path, in order to help them benefit from the effects of *Inter-universal Mysticism*. Through this indirect type of connection people can gain some of the advantages of *Inter-universal Mysticism* in the same way that followers do. For example, in the *faradarmani* cycle anyone, regardless of whether they are practicing it through direct or indirect *ettisal*, can experience healing. To establish such an indirect connection the practitioner must have some knowledge of the person–the person's name, a photograph or a familiarity with the person–on the part of the practitioner this will be enough to establish the connection and the practitioner just keeps the person in mind or holds the person's name in his or her thoughts. In this way, a person is admitted to the inter-universal common sense network: at this stage the practitioner does not need to do anything more than submit and leave the treatment to the network.

Taheri holds honorary degrees, certificates and gold medals from Belgium, Romania, Russia and South Korea for the founding of this mystical practice, in particular for its spiritual therapeutic approaches to complementary medicine. He has published five books three of which– *Erfan-e-Keyhani (Halqeh), 2006; Human from another outlook, 2008;* and *The human comprehensive view on the world, 2010*–were published in Iran, and two of his recent books–*Non-organic creatures, 2011;* and *Human and awareness, 2011*–were printed in Armenia. At least 25 articles are waiting publication pending licensing from the Iranian government. Despite his achievements, Taheri has been attacked by Islamic extremists as "the head of the deviated *halgheh* cult and also been accused, detained, arrested and jailed on numerous counts by the government"[33]. In 2010, after four court hearings in which he defended himself, he was sentenced to five years imprisonment by the Tehran Public and Revolutionary Court

---

[33] Burke, 2012, n.p.

on charges of making statements that he had no speciality in and claiming to receive divine inspiration and knowledge and presenting these to others. He was also sentenced to 74 lashes for treating patients without a medical license.[34] Human rights groups have condemned Taheri's capture and demanded that the government release him. All *Inter-universal Mysticism*'s classes, taught by Masters in all parts of Iran, have been officially cancelled since 31 July 2010 and any action in support of this movement has been forbidden. It should be noted that while classes were formally cancelled by the government, many Masters are still teaching in their private houses and there are many accessible websites that teach *Inter-universal Mysticism*'s lessons online.

To sum up, it would help the reader to understanding the following chapters if they bear in mind these significant aspects of *Inter-universal Mysticism*: 1. it has a monotheistic viewpoint and its fundamental doctrines are universal; 2. the spirituality on this path can be practised by anyone regardless of their faith or religious view; 3. its aim is the pursuit of achieving communion with (or conscious awareness of) spiritual truth, ultimate reality, or God which is made possible through direct experience, intuition, or insight in the practice of *ettisal*; 4. *ettisal* can be practiced both directly by its followers and indirectly by those who are not inside the path via someone already on the path; 5. its spiritual practice is collective and considering the self as individual is an obstruction to its spiritual growth. Mysticism, here, means the creation of unity and an understanding of the concept of the unified body in the world.

---

[34] This was reported on the state-run website *Tabnak* and in the state-run daily newspaper *Mashreq* on 13 February 2011.

CHAPTER TWO

SETTING THE SCENE:
CONCEPTS, METHODS AND FIELDWORK

In this chapter I address my research strategy and methods. I present my approach to this study as a sequence of decision making stages. The first stage is about embedding my research in a set of feminist practices and theories, opting for a feminist methodological framework. The second stage gives a fully reflective consideration of what it means to be both an insider and an outsider in this research. The third stage moves on to the methods I deployed both during the fieldwork and the data processing. I explore the values and limitations of my choices both in the field and when analysing this material. Having detailed the theoretical and methodological underpinnings of my research, the final stage concentrates on the practical details of my fieldwork: "telling the story" of gathering and generating data via observation, focus groups and interviews. The value of this structure, with section three (data processing) coming before section four (fieldwork), is that the reader becomes familiar with the procedure of the research on a step-by-step basis before dealing with the real picture in practice.

Feminist Theories

Part of my feminist approach to this study was to recognise and give full expression to women's own understanding of their experiences; "women" here refers to women following *Inter-universal Mysticism*–in particular the 55 women I interviewed–augmented by four focus group discussions, observations at *Inter-universal Mysticism* meetings and letters and other personal documents sourced from *Inter-universal Mysticism* resources. The women I listened to came from various social and family backgrounds (most of my interviewees were reasonably well-educated and urban) and were at different stages of development on this path, and I am very grateful to them for volunteering their ideas, opinions and stories. My analysis is indebted to their thoughtfulness and insight, and the conceptual framework I have developed draws on their everyday theorisation and my own autobiographical understandings of the path, as well as on academic research and understandings.

In order to develop a gendered perspective, which maximizes my ability to explore the experiences of women inside *Inter-universal Mysticism,* I have made use of various elements of feminist thought. I adopted a feminist perspective which recognises that women are able to conceptualize and analyse their own situations; the perceptions and words of women participants were both the empirical reality and part of the analytical framework for the research. I drew feminist methodological understandings and criteria from various theoretical traditions, including theories of women's empowerment, agency and autonomy, insider–outsider positions and reflexivity. These were appropriate both for the nature of my research itself and for my own position as a feminist researcher.

Feminist Theories of Empowerment

My findings indicate that the way in which women are socialized in Iran and their negotiation of social relationships in a patriarchal culture constrains their capacities for autonomy and self-conception. This underpinned my investigation of the relationship between *Inter-universal Mysticism* and women's empowerment and feelings of self-worth and self-determination. In order to analyse women's empowerment in this particular context, I drew on Kabeer's (1999) theory to argue that women's empowerment is a cyclical rather than a linear process, through which women attain agency, autonomy or self-construction. I also used Carr's (2003) concept of empowerment as an "inherently interpersonal process in which individuals collectively define and activate strategies to gain access to knowledge and power. As such, empowerment is praxis, a cyclical process of collective dialogue and social action that is meant to effect positive change"[1]. Women's empowerment on this path does not happen in isolation, and I found both Isaacs's theory of "self-in-relation agency" and Eisenstein's notions of choices, self and others very useful. Isaac (2003) has focused on the possibilities for action that being a self-in-relation creates, and thoughts of agency which are less individualistic. Likewise, Eisenstein's (2004) argument, like mine, endorses the view that one can choose to act as an individual while recognizing the sense of self as both interconnected with others and also autonomous. Both of these

---

[1] Carr, 2003, p. 18.

theories helped to understand how my participants rethought the "self" in ways which affected their relationships with "others".

I understand women's self-construction as becoming aware of one's self, one's self-conception and one's strength or vulnerability in relation to others, which are all socially and culturally shaped, notably by gender. This awareness allows women not only to change or improve their vision of self, but also gives them the ability to reinterpret, resist, or replace the conditioned vision of a woman in Iranian society. In this respect, I found Meyers' (2002) theory of "autonomy competency" useful as it concerns the autonomy-impairing effects of oppressive socialization. She also suggests that the fact that "women's identities are gendered in patriarchal cultures does impede women's ability to function as self-determining agents"[2]. My use of the concept of agency is broadly similar to that of Mahmood (2001), who draws attention to the specific ways in which "one performs a certain number of operations on one's thoughts, body, conduct, and ways of being, in order to attain a certain kind of state of happiness, purity, wisdom, perfection, or immortality"[3]. The experience of *Inter-universal Mysticism* has enabled women to make sense of their lives. It has offered them a method for reviewing and interpreting their life events, developing their sense of integrity and coming to terms with their identity as humans. Therefore, while women's agency does not always enable women to make changes, it does allow them to find potency and effectiveness in negotiating, managing or coping with their difficult situations. As a result, they can also act differently in the world.

Insider-Outsider Position and Reflexivity

My feminist approach to research enables me to come to terms with the fact that I am both "inside" and "outside" of *Inter-universal Mysticism*, and that I have needed to develop strategies to deal with this position in the course of my work. I critically reflect on my role, noting that my own identity as an Iranian woman on this path situates me as an insider, but that I am also positioning myself as an outsider by undertaking academic research about *Inter-universal Mysticism* and by my awareness that my ability to do research stems from my academic choices (such as having a higher education and living in the UK rather than in Iran). I also take the view that it is possible to discuss *Inter-universal Mysticism* as a commentator and analyst not just as a participant or supporter.

---

[2] Meyers, 2002, p.3.
[3] Mahmood, 2001, p. 210.

My status as an insider carried both advantages and disadvantages. Both myself and the women participants are Iranian women with some common experiences, language and ideas, who also share the same spiritual path. There were also some participants with whom I shared similar class and educational backgrounds. Sharing religion, gender, ethnicity and nationality with these women, in addition to our shared involvement in *Inter-universal Mysticism,* eased the establishment of equal communication between us. I believe the issue of power inequality was reduced, if not overcome, through my relationship with *Inter-universal Mysticism* so that all respondents seemed to feel very comfortable sharing their ideas and stories with me. Similarly, being an insider means that I have a full understanding of this movement and what is like to be inside this mystical path, and of the relations that women have and activities they follow within it. Although I considered this insider position to have benefits for my research, I took heed of Brannick and Coghlan's (2007) warning that insiders are "perceived to be prone to charges of being too close, and thereby of not attaining the distance and objectivity deemed to be necessary for valid research"[4]. There are feminist scholars (e.g. Alvesson, 2003) who see insider research as problematic because it can be seen as not conforming to appropriate standards of intellectual rigour. They think that "insider researchers have a personal stake and substantive emotional investment"[5] and are thus insufficiently critical. In their view, insider researchers might seek to persuade readers of the value of their study rather than offering a more analytical perspective.

To overcome this problem, I have tried to be reflexive and to be aware that my beliefs, background, feelings, experiences and perspectives, which are part of the process of my knowledge construction, influence the research process and outcome. For example, reviewing my interviewees' interpretation of spirituality, I was reflecting on my own understanding of religion and spirituality since I was nine, questioning how growing up in Iran has affected my perceptions of these terms. Paradoxically, having insights from my own understandings and lived experiences as a Master on this path enabled me to be reflexive in my work. For example, while I was reading my interviewees' stories about the difficulty of explaining *Inter-universal Mysticism* to others, I was reflecting on my own challenging experience of teaching new students about this path. Through writing and reflection on my own relevant thoughts, experiences and emotions, and through discussing them, I have engaged in critical

---

[4] Brannick and Coghlan, 2007, P. 60.
[5] Ibid.

understanding. I am therefore aware of the strengths and limitations of my empirical and theoretical understanding of *Inter-universal Mysticism*. Taking a critical, inward look at my own lived reality and experiences, particularly my experiences of being inside *Inter-universal Mysticism*, has been extremely helpful in the research process. During the field work in Iran when I was talking with women and listening to them, I tried my best not to impose my own assumptions born of similar or shared experiences. Similarly, I was also aware of the assumptions they may have made about me. For instance, I decided not to let my interviewees know at the start of the interview that I was a Master of *Inter-universal Mysticism* in order to enable them to speak freely about the movement. As Yung (2002) argues, in this case "they could have omitted certain ideas or experiences believing that, as an insider, such things would already be apparent to me"[6]. I also encouraged my interviewees to ask if there was anything they wanted to know about me, whether they felt uneasy about anything, or if they disagreed with what I was saying at any point.

By contrast, taking an "outsider" position helped me to combat the imbalance in power relations between me, as the researcher, and the women participants. Letting women know about my research, undertaken in a foreign country, and explaining my reasons for the study allowed women the space to critically assess their experience of being inside this path. It potentially gave women, as Brayton (1997) put it, "the opportunity to safely criticize"[7] this movement without fear of being heard either by other advocates or government officials. Adopting an outsider status also helped me to be less subjective, or at least to look at these women critically. This does not mean that I ignored the importance of being simultaneously subjective; such a relationship between me as the researcher and the women as the objects of my study is evident in my reflexivity. Looking in from the outside also allowed me to appear more impartial to my respondents and encouraged me to ask questions, e.g. about their experience of *ettisal* (the spiritual practice in *Inter-universal Mysticism*), which I might otherwise have taken for granted as shared knowledge: I could discover the unique perspectives my respondents have on a particular issue. For example, while I had knowledge of the indirect use of *Inter-universal Mysticism* on others outside of the path, I asked my interviewees about the effects it might have on their family members and friends.

---

[6] Yung, 2002, p. 88.
[7] Brayton, 1997, n.p.

My outsider position helped me to reflect as accurately as possible on these women's experiences and choices and to avoid making assumptions about the understandings they had throughout their journey on this path. Thus, whilst recognising the impact of my insider position and reflecting on my own privilege as a researcher, I was also committed to conveying these women's understanding of their own experience. In addition, I did not have any fixed perspective on the research and my viewpoints were either shifted or developed in new ways over time as I progressed with the research. Interestingly, I had some preconceived ideas which were challenged. For example, I was surprised, when listening to my interviewees' stories of suggesting *Inter-universal Mysticism* to other women, that they claimed gender does not matter to them and rejected a feminist label. Although I am familiar with this movement and its insights that people are "beyond gender", I had expected to find accounts of how women on this path had seen the influence of this movement on women's lives in Iran. Nonetheless, by analysing these stories from their perspective, I began to understand that these women had tried their own method of negotiating gender through the experience of being a woman on this path and feeling that women, more than men, need to participate in *Inter-universal Mysticism*. I have reviewed my own experiences both before and after joining this movement and my shift from thinking only about women's issues earlier in my life to later thinking beyond gender. This gave me a basis for understanding women's rejection of the term feminism but also enabled me to see the feminist implications in their stories through a process of analysis. As such, I learned to reflect on my feelings, thoughts and perceptions throughout the research process.

Research Methods

My research used a combination of the following methods: 1) one-to-one semi-structured interviews; 2) focus and discussion groups; 3) participant observation. Each method looks at my research questions from a different angle or from its own distinct perspective[8], and I used them as a means of comparison and contrast. These methods were complementary in order to help uncover different aspects of the reality under investigation which, when put together, maximised the strengths and minimised the weaknesses of each approach to expand the depth of my research. I am going to outline my research participants in more detail, and explain how each of these three methods specifically helped me to collect data during the fieldwork.

---

[8] Denscombre, 1998, p. 84.

Research Participants

It had been my aim, before starting fieldwork, to select women at various stages on the path of *Inter-universal Mysticism* for interview and to find women who were diverse in terms of their religious views, family background, class, marital status, education and age. Women progress on this path either through attending classes or by being Masters and teaching others. Some finish the classes and do not teach. I intended to have participants from each of these groups. I was able to gain access to women since I am in the path myself and I am familiar with the *Inter-universal Mysticism* institutions and classes around Iran. This helped me gain access to 55 women in three different cities: Tehran, Yazd, and Mashhad. It is worth mentioning that *Inter-universal Mysticism* is essentially an urban movement, and although I am aware of a few groups of women in small towns who are practicing it, at the time I did my fieldwork I did not visit any villages. I chose these three particular cities in Iran for two main reasons, one analytical and the other practical: the three cities are different from each other and therefore could offer the opportunity to access a variety of women; and these were the cities I was practically able to visit.

Tehran is the capital and largest city in Iran. It is a complex metropolitan urban centre with lots of inward migration. I chose Tehran because it was here that the movement was founded and developed by Mohammad Ali Taheri and the city has the highest number of followers of any other city, many of whom are women. Tehran is also my home city and I learned about the movement here in 2004, so it was my first choice of location to start this study. Yazd is a small provincial city in the centre of Iran. I chose Yazd from many other smaller cities in which this movement is developing for two reasons. First, because it is one of the traditional cities in which women have run the movement themselves without the involvement of Taheri or the main institution in Tehran, although they are in contact with them; and second, I have family and friends in Yazd who supported me when I was conducting my fieldwork. Mashhad is one of the holiest cities in the Shia Muslim world. It is known as the resting place of the Imam Reza, the eighth Shia Imam. People practise Islam strictly and women mostly wear the chador in public. As in Yazd, the followers were mainly women and have run the movement there themselves. At this point, I should say that my initial intention was to choose Tabriz, the city with the second highest number of followers of this movement after Tehran, but because of the political situation during the time I was in Iran for my fieldwork (April–July 2010) it was very risky to travel and to conduct interviews there, so I looked for a safer place and chose the religious city of Mashhad.

Table 1: Number of participants in each city

Name of city	Number of participants	Interview participants	Focus/discussion group participants	Participants in both
Tehran	20	11	7	2
Yazd	8	8	0	0
Mashhad	27	10	11	6

In addition to diversity of background, I also intended to access women with a range of experiences of the path. As long as they were accessible to me, I tried to interview women mainly at levels one (primary) and six (becoming Master), with some in between. My main reason was that women at the first level are at an early stage on this path and are close to their initial decision to choose it, a situation which may help them recall fairly clearly how and why they came to the path. By talking to participants at level six or higher, I found out more about the extent to which their lives had been transformed by following the path this far. It was also interesting to compare how each group talks about the term feminism and why they reject it when they reach higher levels.

The second table shows certain patterns. Three-quarters of the women participants are under 50 which reflect the youthful demographic age profile of the Iranian population[9], rather than indicating a skewed sample. More than 50% of these women have a university education, which indicates that the women I interviewed on the whole have a relevantly high level of education. It is also noticeable that 43 women out of a total of 55 are or have been married, which reflects cultural patterns or social practices and norms whereby most women marry relatively early. While the age range is broader than the educational range, the average participant could be described as a university-educated, middle-aged woman who stays at home and takes care of her children. However, to generalise is also to reduce; there are also participants who are young, educated to a higher level and who work full-time out of the house, a pattern which reflects the social patterns of many Iranian women in urban areas. As previously discussed, participant diversity was necessary to gain a deeper insight and,

---

[9] Based on the Iran Demographics Profile 2013, 89.1 % of the population are under 54, 44.4 % are between 25-54 years, 20.8% are between 15-24 years, and 23.9% are between 0-14 years.

Chapter Two

Table 2: Commonalities & variations of participant backgrounds

Level of the path		Age range		Education		Family/Household circumstances		Work	
Primary (1)	13	20 – 35 years	19	School	1	Single	12	Full-time in house	2
Middle (2-5)	25	36 – 50 years	29	Diploma[1]	24	Single (widow or divorcee) + Child	3	Full-time out of house	19
Final (6-8)	17	51 – 65 years	5	University graduate	28	Married	4	Part-time	3
Total participants	55	Over 66 years	2	University student	2	Married + Child	36	Housewife/Retired/ Student	31

[1] The Iranian education system has three cycles: primary, intermediate, and secondary (or high school). 'The five-year primary cycle covers grades 1-5 for children 6 to 11 years old. The three-year intermediate cycle covers grades 6 to 8 for children 11 to 13 years old. The secondary education cycle is a four-year stage which covers grade 9 to Grade 12, from age 14 to 17' (*Education System in Iran*). After finishing secondary education at the age of 18, students gain a diploma and become eligible to go to university.

in terms of the demographics of followers of this movement, was an important element to reflect upon.

One-to-one Semi-structured Interviews

At the centre of my research was an interest in the knowledge, views, understandings, interpretations, experiences and interactions of women involved in *Inter-universal Mysticism*. Thus, I conducted what are termed by researchers as semi-structured interviews. I chose this type of interviewing because, in contrast to the rigidity of structured interviews, in a semi-structured interview I could rely on my own interview guide while also allowing myself the flexibility to explore issues that came up in individual interviews.

Neither did I want to make the interviews completely unstructured by, for instance, simply asking women to talk about *Inter-universal Mysticism*. I had some specific ideas that I wanted to explore with the women which were related to my three main research questions. There were thus topics which were important that I introduced, in various ways, in all the interviews as questions similar to the following:

1. How did you find out about this path?
2. What were your initial assumptions about it?
3. Why do you think you need such spiritual paths? What does spirituality mean to you? What are the benefits?
4. What have you got out of this movement? To what extent do you think this path affects both your personal and social life as a woman?

(I was also curious to know if the path did not work for them or what aspects they were not happy with and to let the conversation move towards discussing these ideas, so whenever I got a chance I also asked about critical views.)

5. Would you recommend this path to other women? If yes, why and how/what do you say?

Before the interviews, participants knew only that the general theme of the research was their experiences of being on a path called *Inter-universal Mysticism*. I hoped that revealing minimal information about the study would allow them to express their own ideas spontaneously, with a minimum of influence from me or from others with whom they may have discussed such subjects. I let the women take their own time to prepare which would have allowed them to think more deeply and provide me with their considered understandings.

During the interviews, I tried to go with the flow of the conversation within the context of my skeleton set of questions. Sometimes my questions were in response to what they told me or I asked for clarification of one of their answers. I started my interviews by asking questions designed to establish some trust between myself and each of them. For example, I told them that I was a PhD student in Women's Studies at the University of York in England, and gave them information regarding the aims of this research with my contact details in case they required further information. I also told them that all information provided would remain confidential and that their identities and responses would be completely anonymised. Then I asked them to tell me more about themselves. In this way, I allowed them to speak about what they thought was important and to express their feelings about seeking such a spiritual path. In order to accurately record data, I used a small digital dictaphone in conjunction with note taking. I started recording as early as possible during a meeting with a participant after I had asked permission to record and then continued with casual conversation. The notes I took on paper were kept as brief as possible. The interviews were more like a "conversation with a purpose"[1] than a question and answer session. Therefore, such interviews were useful for understanding how these women make sense of and justify their choice of being inside this movement. I could also gain an insight into these individual women's visions, imaginings, hopes, expectations and critiques of the present and future of this movement. On the whole, I did not have any difficult interviews and discovered more than I had initially expected and for this I am thankful to all the women who were very enthusiastic about discussing their participation in this movement.

Focus / Discussion Group Interviews

I used focus groups and group discussion techniques in order to gain information about attitudes, thoughts, feelings and personal experiences from a range of women respondents at the same time by observing the interplay of diverse perspectives on a subject. Through analysing "the operation of, for instance, consensus and dissent and examining different types of narratives being used within the group"[2] I could identify shared and common knowledge. I also wanted to explore the extent to which these women thought that this movement might change a woman's life in Iran, and decided that raising this subject in a group would create a good

---

[1] Burgess, 1984, p. 102.
[2] Kitzinger, 1995, n.p.

opportunity for discussion, where some women's ideas could stimulate responses and discussion among others who may not know what to say at first. I set up four focus groups in which I opened up discussion about the extent to which this path may influence a woman's life in Iran. I managed separate groups of women at level one and level six and some in the middle levels, e.g. levels three and four. I intended to have a maximum of seven women in each group but in one group I could only gather five women. Equally, in the two groups in Mashhad there were more than seven women in each group. I chose some group participants from amongst those who agreed to participate in my research after I initially contacted them, and some women came of their own volition when they heard about the discussions.

Finding a location in which to conduct these groups was a difficult matter, since it was very dangerous to hold such gatherings due to the tense political situation in Iran at the time. It had been announced by the government that they would inspect and arrest groups that they suspected were related to this movement. I held two groups in Tehran in one of the Masters' private houses where women feel safe. In Mashhad the situation was less risky and we had our group discussions in a public park. We gathered as a group of friends who came to the park to have fun and chat. We started our discussion and acted just like women who are chatting in a park. Fortunately, we did not draw any attention to ourselves and could have a relaxed discussion. In each group, I started recording as early as possible, once all the participants had gathered and I had asked permission to record, and then continued our discussion.

The group dynamic had the effect of opening up conversation around this topic and producing important discussion, understanding and even debate among diverse or similar participants. However, I also found that sometimes group members could actually silence others in the group by dominating the conversation or making it difficult for others to express their own viewpoints comfortably. For example, there were two women in my discussion group with women at the first level of the path who talked more than the other five women. Therefore, I had to encourage other women to speak by asking for their opinions. I found that letting these two women continue their discussion would not allow other women to talk about their ideas. In order to avoid this happening I tried to act as a moderator; by controlling the conversation I ensured that each member was able to speak, asking those who were silent to talk about their own views on a matter that others were discussing.

Participant Observation

By using participant observation, I intended to watch these women's activities during the classes they attended to learn about *Inter-universal Mysticism*. The classes at each level consist of six four-hour sessions spread over six weeks. Sessions are in two parts: in the first part the teacher (Taheri or his Masters) asks participants to raise any issues or problems regarding the last session's lessons and their practice through the week; in the second part, new lessons are taught. Therefore, by attending classes and observing women during the first part of the session I gained information about the issues raised by women in class which I might not have come across in interviews or discussion groups.

I observed women in sessions designed for several different levels. By observing women at level one, I could learn more about their first reactions to this mysticism, and by observing women at higher levels I could find out what issues and concerns they discussed in the class after progressing further in the movement. As Taheri himself no longer teaches, I attended and observed the classes of one of his Masters, Nahid [3], who knows me as a Master. I informed her of my intentions and received permission to observe her classes. I was a covert observer, since no-one in the class except the teacher knew that I was a researcher. There is a rule in *Inter-universal Mysticism* that anyone who passes a particular level can freely attend lower level classes to repeat the lessons, therefore I could easily attend and observe these classes without generating comment. Importantly, I did not know the women in these classes and simply observed their activities regarding the issues they were raising in front of others in the class. I did not use any voice or video recording, which would have been disruptive, and just took notes on what I was observing.

Primary Textual Material

In addition to the data I gathered through my interviews, focus groups and observations, I had access to some primary sources. The first set of data was Taheri's books and written records of his interviews[4]. These helped me to learn more about his perception of himself as the founder of this movement, and about the purpose and principles of the path and how it has developed during the three decades after the victory of the Islamic Revolution. The second set of data consisted of some of the testimonies of

---

[3] I do not use the Masters' full names for their safety.
[4] Here I should note that because of safety reasons, there are some interviews which do not reveal interviewer details.

followers of this path that were provided to Taheri's solicitors to help him rebuff accusations made against him in court in 2010: his followers wrote these personal statements in support of Taheri. They are presented in different formats; some are written with a pen on small pieces of paper, some are typed on A4 paper and all are dated and signed with the authors' names. These statements detailed what had been learned on the path and what had been gained.

I should mention that in 2006 Taheri found himself in the same situation and his followers provided him with similar testimonies. However I could not gain access to these older testimonies as the institution where the testimonies are stored has been closed by the government. I was able to access copies of some recent testimonies from Nahid who had her students' permission to use these testimonies in favour of the movement and in support of Taheri. She allowed me to read the statements given at that time. Although these testimonies were written as court evidence in favour of *Inter-universal Mysticism*, the detail within them allowed me to supplement the information that I had gathered from participant interviewing. I also need to note that I did not overtly mention any of this information in my study, but have used them as background detail. For example, these testimonies were useful in learning the reasons for joining this movement (chapter three) and the influences of *Inter-universal Mysticism* in one's self and life (chapter five).

The Matter of Data Translation

The language I used during my fieldwork was Farsi. While coming from the same cultural background is of benefit to me in understanding the whole context of my data, there were some difficulties in translating from Farsi to English. Transcriptions were important and my understanding of English mattered at that stage, since it would affect the extent to which I was able to realize the differences of culture and context between languages.

My involvement in translation took place in three stages. First, I translated an outline of my research and my interview questions from English to Farsi. In relation to this first step, Birbili (2000) has suggested that it is worth pre-testing the research implement in the local culture. In order to gain "conceptual equivalence or comparability of meaning"[5], I tried to make my translation easily understandable to my interviewees. For instance, my familiarity with the spiritual culture in Iran and the concept

---

[5] Birbili, 2000, n.p.

of spirituality in *Inter-universal Mysticism* helped me to explain the aim of my research to the women participants. At the second stage, after transcribing my collected data in Farsi, I translated into English only the parts of the interviews that were especially relevant to my argument, attempting to convey the meaning of key concepts. Casagrande (1954) argues that "one does not translate languages, one translates cultures' because 'the attitudes and values, the experience and traditions of a people, inevitably become involved in the freight of meaning carried by a language"[6]. In this respect, to make clear some of the expressions that the women used, I tried to explain the cultural context as explicitly as possible, either in my comments or in the footnotes. In some cases where phrases or words have subtle distinctions not found in English, I have given the Farsi word in italics and then provided a translation (using a slash) or an explanation.

Moreover, as the women often talked informally or, in a few cases, used proverbs, at the second stage I tried to translate Farsi into simple sentences to allow the reader to understand them. However, I occasionally encountered some complexities about which I consulted others who know both languages. I gained much help from one of my supervisors, who is a native English speaker and who also knows Farsi, in finding equivalent phrases after I explained the meaning of Farsi phrases. For example, when translating the word "توانمندسازی/*tavanmandsazi*", I intended to use the English term "self-empowerment". But after learning more about the context of this term in English and consulting with my supervisors, I changed the translation to "agency" as the best term to describe these women's inspiration and growth. Another dimension of this process, the third stage, was translating my own thoughts and analysis from Farsi into English since I use to think and understand things in my mother language, Farsi. In short, as translation is a creative attempt to give meaning to another language, I have done my best to translate what these women say without distorting their meanings.

Interpretation and Analysis of Data

One aim of feminist research is to open up areas where women's experiences have been unidentified, ignored or silenced. However, in interpreting women's lived experiences through academic study we may inadvertently silence or denigrate the voices of research participants because of inequalities of knowledge between the researcher and the

---

[6] Casagrande, 1954, p. 338.

researched. When researching women's lives we need to take their experiences seriously, but we also need "to take our own theory seriously and "use the theory to make sense of ... the experience"[7]. To assess the complexity of women's experiences, my feminist research required me to go "beyond citing experience in order to make connections which may not be visible from the purely experiential level"[8]. This interpretative and synthesizing process helps make the connection between experience and understanding. Therefore, I analysed the participants' voices in the context of the conceptual framework of the research project.

I transcribed all 55 interviews and four discussion groups, and referred to women by their actual first name although in cases where respondents did not tell me their first name, I used their family name. I did not record their full names for anonymity.[9] During this process, I both highlighted and wrote short notes alongside the summaries I wrote during my interviews in order to make clear the specific context of any distinct sentences or statements made by interviewees. The analytical process was as follows: I went through each transcript and noted all the themes that emerged from interviews, focus groups, observations and my primary textual materials. I organized these themes into different sections and drew upon "different theories, using them when appropriate, ditching them when not, re-working them to construct explanatory frameworks"[10]. Then, by coding and then sorting and sifting them, I linked data and existing theories in order to make a dialogue. In other words, I conducted intensive data coding, highlighting groups using different colours, to create three different groups based on my three research questions. After sorting each group into smaller categories, which involved much trial, error and frustration, I identified how they best fitted together. I then compared and contrasted each group in order to consider similarities and differences and also to identify sequences and patterns.

For example, I chose the colour red to highlight women's responses to my question about what spirituality mean to them. When I compared these, I could categorise them into three smaller groups: their interpretation of spirituality separate from religion; within religion; and the same as religion. I then cut up each group into its constituent parts and started to find similarities and differences between them. When considering common themes, I went back to the individual interviews to

---

[7] Cain, 1994, cited in Maynard, 1994, p. 24.

[8] Maynard, 1994, p. 23.

[9] In Iran, people are officially known by their full first and family name plus the first name of their fathers.

[10] Skeggs, 1994, p. 82.

check specific quotes and collated these. The themes of each chapter were already set as they had been identified as the three main questions of this research. However, a number of other themes, for example the relationships between religion and spirituality, arose during the analysis of the data. When I started writing chapter drafts, each time I introduced specific quotes, I routinely contextualized them by providing a brief background account of the interviewee, e.g. their age, their home city, their marital status, the level of their education. By doing so, I have tried to realize what DeVault suggests: "reading a narrative account, placing oneself in the narrator's position and referring to an implied context from the story that is told"[11]. At the same time, I studied other comparable studies in order to cross-examine my interviewee's perception of spirituality and to understand the differences and similarities of their experience on this path.

However, I was aware that while this jigsaw puzzle approach to analysing data can be productive and fruitful, it also entails some risks and problems. For example, Wiseman, who also codes data, points out that "the simple act of breaking down data into its constituent parts can distort and mislead the analyst"[12]. To avoid this problem, I made three copies of my transcribed interviews and focus groups. Thus, when I highlighted, cut apart and affixed them by subject matter to sort them, I had two other intact copies from which to read the interviews or discussion groups in their entirety. For example, I highlighted five themes for the reasons behind women's choices to participate in *Inter-universal Mysticism*. I collated material relevant to each theme from my cut up transcripts in order to facilitate my analysis. Then, when I read the complete interviews, I found that, for some women, it was a combination of some of the themes that affected their decision to join the movement. By "working back and forth between the parts and the whole"[13] of my data, I tried my best not to destroy the totality of ideas as expressed by the women.

The Fieldwork

I now turn back to my fieldwork, and attempt to recount the story of how I gathered the data. I have chosen to leave this section until the end of the chapter because I intended to introduce the reader to my approach and to how I designed this research before I narrated my practical experience.

---

[11] DeVault, 1990, p.104.
[12] Wiseman, 1979, p. 278.
[13] Ibid.

As a result of the Iranian government's hostile position towards any religious or spiritual movements other than the official Islam and the increase in detention and condemning of the founders or leaders of such movements over the last five years, carrying out my fieldwork about *Inter-universal Mysticism* was slightly different and more perilous than I had expected before travelling to Iran. I planned to conduct this research in a particular way, but when I arrived in Iran circumstances had changed and therefore I had to find other ways to do my fieldwork and to locate my participants, because the main *Inter-universal Mysticism* institution had been closed. Since I was used to such political problems, I was not scared of doing my field work and could manage it carefully. It had been three years since Taheri had last taught, and in Tehran and in other cities Masters were doing the teaching. As a result, the enrolment forms in the central institution also included copies of the enrolment forms for each Master's students in different Iranian cities. As I could not access the enrolment forms in the central institution in Tehran, I had to consult copies of enrolment forms which were kept by Masters themselves. Consequently, I talked to one of the oldest Masters in Tehran, Nahid, whom I have known for many years, to see if I could recruit my participants from among her students and she willingly accepted and welcomed me into her house. She was teaching in her house during the day, as there was less risk of being traced and closed by the government. In the first week, I did three of my observations there and also looked through the forms to make a list of women–in different levels of the path and from different social backgrounds and education levels–whom I then contacted to ask for their participation in my research. Although I did not ask her to, Nahid, also talked about me and my research in her classes and asked students to participate if they were interested. Thus, I sourced some of my women participants from among these volunteers. I was fortunate that the women who came forward as participants were from diverse backgrounds and ages, perhaps reflecting the larger demographic of followers. Most of my interviews and discussions in Tehran took place in a room in Nahid's house as I found it was a convenient place for women to come and talk about their ideas and understandings of this path. This was how my fieldwork in Iran began in April 2010.

As I have mentioned, the government was very sensitive to any movement that went against their rules and was tracing all phone communications, texts and even emails, so I had to be very careful. This meant that my contact with women asking them to participate was very dangerous, so when communicating via phone I tried not to use the name of the movement or mention the fact that I had come from the UK. I gave participants more information at the time of our interview than on the phone. Since all of the followers of this path knew about the political situation I did not encounter any issues with this and they accepted that they would have to ask their questions when they met me rather than in advance. Over the phone I simply said:

> This is Tina Eftekhar, a PhD student researching on women's empowerment in spirituality. I got your number from Nahid and would like to interview you. I will explain more about my research and why I am doing it when we meet, so would you please let me know when is possible for you if you are happy to do that. It is also possible to meet in her house before or after your class if you like.

Nahid was these women's Master and so using her name meant both that women would know that I am not someone from the government checking on them and also that I did not need to say the name of the movement as by hearing her name they would immediately understand what I was talking about. I was fortunate that none of the women I called refused: in five cases women said they would call me back as soon as they could and three of them did so. I should make it clear that except Nahid and four other women in Tehran, I did not previously know any of the women in this study and gained their names and contact details from the enrolment forms. Furthermore, as I have mentioned, there were some women who volunteered and contacted me themselves to participate in my study.

My work in Yazd was difficult because women in Yazd were much more cautious and doubtful about participating in interviews compared with women in Tehran. Some women in Yazd decided to have *Inter-universal Mysticism* classes there, so they invited Nahid to teach them. Nahid used to travel to Yazd two days a week and, based on her experience, her classes there were much more challenging due to being more biased religious people there with many questions, who come to these classes for diverse reasons that I will discuss in following chapter. A week before I travelled to Yazd, the moral police warned Nahid that she should not teach anything other than Islamic mysticism: she signed a paper making this commitment and had to stop teaching in Yazd for a while. I had to be very careful not to arouse suspicion. For this reason I asked Nahid to contact women in Yazd instead of me, choosing women whom she knew would be discreet and asking them to contact me if they wanted to participate in this research. Finally, thirteen women contacted me and one of them offered her house as a place to hold my interviews. I conducted three interviews at her house, four in my own place in Yazd and one in a public hospital's waiting room. I conducted this interview in hospital simply because it was convenient for the interviewee to do the interview while she was waiting for her medical test results. We were sitting in the waiting room and talking as two friends without drawing attention to ourselves. I did not use my recorder as I did not want anyone to know I was conducting an interview and just wrote down notes while she was talking. Immediately after I finished my interview with her and left the hospital I sat down and wrote down whatever I could remember that I did not already have in my notes. The remaining five women who contacted me did not come for interview: one of them could not manage to find time for me; three said they needed more time to think and offered to contact me again to arrange a time, but did not call again; and the last one was a young girl who was so unsure it seemed that while she was willing to do the interview, she was scared of her parents' assertion that if she did this interview she might be arrested. After calling me three times and asking different questions about my research, she said she would let me know when it would be possible for her to come and then never called again. Therefore, overall I conducted eight interviews in Yazd.

Before my journey to Yazd, I heard that the situation in Tabriz was too risky to carry out such interviews so I had to reconsider my plans. At that time, my father- and mother-in-law were going to Mashhad on pilgrimage so I decided to go with them and conduct my interviews there instead of Tabriz. To locate participants in Mashhad I needed to identify one of the Masters there in order to find women participants from among their students. The problem was that the central institution had been closed and I did not have access to their numbers, so I looked for other options. Luckily, I procured the contact number of Mr Azarmi, a Master in Mashhad, from one of the women I interviewed in Yazd. I contacted him and, after introducing myself and my research, he welcomed me and said I did not need to worry as the situation was still fine in Mashhad and he was there to help me in any matter I needed. When I arrived in Mashhad he gave me the address of a two-floor private house in which he had an office and taught classes. He also offered me a room there for carrying out my interviews as I did not know Mashhad at all and, based on my experience, the majority of women prefer to come to the place of their classes rather than to conduct interviews in their homes or in a public place, and I was always open to their suggestions for the time and place of their interviews. I gained access to enrolment forms, which were only for three levels as it had not been long since Mr Azarmi had started these classes in Mashhad.

After making my list I started contacting women and was able to schedule a time for interviews with some of them: the rest told me they would contact me later but only two of them called me back. One said her parents would not allow her to come for an interview and the other said she could only answer my questions over the phone. In the meantime, a woman contacted me and introduced herself as one of the Masters[14] in Mashhad: Arezoo. She had heard about me and my research through one of the women I had contacted and wanted to cooperate by letting me source some of my participants from among her students. I thanked her and informed her that I needed participants from the final levels for interview. Then, for the last two days of my stay in Mashhad, in the mornings, she gathered more than ten women from different levels of the path who I met in a big public park. Instead of having individual interviews, which would have been impossible in two days, I decided to conduct discussion groups instead. So, on each day that these women gathered I introduced myself and my research and explained that my time there was limited so I could not interview each of them individually and suggested that we have a discussion group instead, to which they all agreed. I also did two interviews each evening on those two days, again in a room that was provided for me, with two women who could not attend the discussion groups in the mornings.

In conclusion, I should say that although I carried out my fieldwork in a very risky and critical situation, I was able to gather good and useful information from the most ardent advocates of this movement. In the following chapters, I explore the participants' stories in the context of the theoretical framework discussed in this chapter. I try to cautiously articulate women's own interpretations of spirituality in their lives and to understand their beliefs and actions in relation to *Inter-universal Mysticism*. I hope that this research practice and experience of analysis will add to methodological understandings of conducting feminist research as an insider-outsider, and also illuminate some of the issues raised by doing qualitative research on women's spirituality.

---

[14] Later I found out that there were ten active Masters in Mashhad at that time.

CHAPTER THREE

IRANIAN WOMEN'S CHOICE OF INTER-UNIVERSAL MYSTICISM: THE PERSONAL AND SOCIAL MOTIVATIONS

To explore women's reasons for embarking on the path of *Inter-universal Mysticism*, in this chapter, I examine women's narratives of their early relationship with the movement, focusing particularly on the stories women told in the interviews and focus groups I conducted. In order to understand their relationship with the movement more fully, I also contextualize their accounts by introducing my own observations of *Inter-universal Mysticism* group meetings and an appreciation of the broader social, political and religious situations the women live in. I discuss five main themes which I argue are important for understanding the personal and social motivations of women's decisions to participate in the *Inter-universal Mysticism* movement. While women had different reasons for joining the movement, these five themes were common among them.

In the first section, I discuss how these women talked about their initial encounters with the movement. I reveal that there is an important connection between the reasons why women choose to follow this path and how they find out about it. I argue that it is because they mostly learn about this path from those who are both connected to them (family members and friends) and who are considered to be trustworthy. I also talk about these women's initial anxieties as a result of lacking enough knowledge about the path. Second, I explore the conflict my respondents experienced with the very particular, ideological version of Shia Islam within the Islamic Republic of Iran. I argue that these women have a deep desire to be spiritual and religious but that they are critical of the official version of Islam promoted by the regime. They are therefore attracted to *Inter-universal Mysticism* because it offers something spiritual which is perceived to be modern and rational and which also allows them to practice their religion as they wish. The third section, developing the argument of the second section, deals with the patriarchal attitudes and practices that govern the lives and life-options of many women in Iran, particularly after the Islamic revolution. I explore the experiences of these women in relation to their suffering under patriarchy and the social pressures in their lives and consider how such experiences influenced them to choose to participate in this movement, both as a social support and as a sustaining resource in helping them to get out of their difficult situations.

There is a particular connection between the fourth and fifth sections, as I discuss opportunities such as healing and self-improvement which this movement has offered to women. While, in earlier sections, I consider women's problems and life difficulties as motives in their choice, in the fourth and fifth sections I examine how the ability to receive healing for both physical and mental illnesses, followed by self-improvement and changes in their lives, have encouraged many of these women to choose to be involved with this spiritual path. Finally, I conclude that investigating these women's understandings of their spiritual concerns and their life choices is important for three main reasons: first, it indicates the existing burden of internal social tensions currently present in Iran; second, it suggests dissatisfaction with the prominence and organizational form of official Islamic religion in modern Iran; and third, it reflects the nature of women's self-identity in the context of modernity.

Women Finding out About the Path

Despite the fact that any advertisement of spiritual movements is restricted, *Inter-universal Mysticism* has been developing quickly in most parts of Iran entirely through word of mouth. Since the movement is not officially approved, it is not easy to find out about it in bookshops or through general notice boards through which women might ordinarily find out about such activities. The reason behind women's initial fears about joining the movement is that there is not enough information about it. Ironically, since Mr Taheri was taken into custody in 2010 and his path was publically declared illegal *Inter-universal Mysticism* has become more widely known. The progress and development of the movement during the last decade is notable in the remarkable increase in its followers, most of whom are women. Because of governmental pressures and restrictions, many masters are now teaching the path in private. Therefore, there is no exact figure for how many women and men are followers of this movement. However, based on the enrolment forms collected from the *Inter-universal Mysticism* Institution in Tehran before it was closed and those that I studied during my field work, women make up approximately 70% of followers. The ways in which women found out about this movement and decided to join are important. In this section I will discuss the significance of how women learn about this spiritual path from people they know and trust and then assess their anxiety and fears about participating in the movement.

It is important to understand what this movement means to the women I interviewed and to realize that they come to it mainly through people who are part of their existing social or family networks. Here, I should note that life in Iran operates through networks of family and friends rather than through work colleagues. While most Iranians are suffering both from the economic crisis and the extreme socio-political impact of the Islamic government, getting together with family and friends appears to be one of the most valued ways of spending time, even if it is not always enjoyable. For example, even if a woman does not get on with her mother-in-law she would still regularly visit her. This is the way people manage their lives in Iran; indeed, one could go so far as to say that for many Iranians the tradition of family networks are sites of resistance or at least support against external pressures. Reliance on these networks is an established social pattern which has long been part of Iranian culture and has been strengthened since the emergence of the Islamic Republic. I would also argue that because of the political situation over the past thirty years, particularly in recent years, people are more distrustful of others and prefer to remain within their network of family and close friends. Therefore, women are very likely to hear about *Inter-universal Mysticism* from a friend or relative, as is evident in these women's stories. The majority of the women I interviewed –50 of the 55–learned about *Inter-universal Mysticism* from a trusted friend or relative whose recommendations were considered honest and reliable. Here, trust is an affective attitude: it is an attitude of self-belief about someone's goodwill which provides a confident expectation. A vivid example is given by Afrooz, a 34 year-old university student, divorced, and working full-time as a teacher in Tehran. She said:

> *I came to these classes just because he* (the oldest and the most trustworthy and knowledgeable man in her family) *told us, I would not accept it if it was anyone except him.*[1]

When Afrooz wanted to divorce her second husband, she consulted one of her older relatives, who in her opinion, was honourable. This man suggested that Afrooz and her husband participate in *Inter-universal Mysticism* classes before making any decision about their divorce. She had faith in him and did what he suggested. The important point here is that she did

---

[1] Afrooz, (2010). Personal interview. Tehran, at Nahid's house. 15 April 2010.

not trust all of her family members or friends. Certainly, this man's good reputation in their family was an important factor in his being trusted, which was similarly the case for the majority of the women. For example, Nahid, aged 43 with a high school diploma, a housewife and a Master in Tehran and Yazd, said:

> *My husband allowed me to come to these classes because the woman who*
> *suggested this path to me is a religious woman with a good hijab who has*
> *a good reputation among our friends.*[2]

Good reputation plays a significant role in these women's decisions to trust friends or family members. It also helped women to persuade their husbands and families to overcome their misgivings about their participation in this movement, as it helped Nahid to secure her husband's agreement. In fact, reputation is deeply rooted in Iranian culture: it is called *khoshnami* in Farsi and is a powerful social influence. Being *khoshnam* or having a good reputation in both society and amongst family and friends is very important for Iranians. If someone applies for a job or wants to get married, they will be asked about his or her reputation before any further consideration. For example, all parents investigate the reputation of their daughters' suitors before giving their approval. Therefore, there is an important connection between *khoshnami* and trusting someone's recommendation.

For a small number of women–6 out of the 55–the matter of trust was less important or was replaced by what I term reliance. I distinguish between trust and reliance because here we are "led to focus on the disposition of cared-about objects rather than on attitudes toward a person"[3]. The difference between trust and reliance is that trust involves something like a "reactive attitude"[4] towards the person we are trusting. For these women, who are very different from each other in age, education, social status, and family background, reliance on acquired direct and indirect evidence was an important factor in their choice. These 6 women witnessed the effectiveness of the spiritual healing called *faradarmani*. They relied on the effectiveness of the path on some people they knew, not trusting that the path would always be effective. Here there is a difference between the matters of trust and reliance: if they trusted *Inter-universal Mysticism* and it was not effective they would be disappointed; but in the matter of reliance, they would just not choose it.

---

[2] Nahid, (2010). Personal interview. Tehran, at her house. 8 May 2010.

[3] Jones, 1996, p. 19.

[4] Strawson, 1974.

For example, Pasyar, aged 38, married and a nurse from Tehran, told me that she chose to follow this path because she witnessed one of the patients in the hospital being cured by this spiritual healing. She said:

> *One of the Masters came to our hospital and practiced faradarmani on one of our patients. I witnessed the patient's health improvement. So I felt that it can be good for me and through it I can help others. I also thought in this way, I can know God better because the knowledge I had about him was all what my parents told me, so I liked to learn more about him.*[5]

Similarly, for Maryam, aged 32, married, and a doctor/homoeopathist from Yazd, hearing from her colleague of the effectiveness of this healing was reason enough to go and learn more about it.[6] For women like Maryam and Pasyar, who both have a medical background, the nature of their occupations as nurse and doctor made them particularly interested in the health aspect of this path.

In contrast for others like Fatemeh, aged 68, a widow, with a primary education from Mashhad, life circumstances were the main motivation for joining the movement. Fatemeh met a woman in the city of Lahijan who was a follower of this path and was cured of her cancer by *fardarmani*. At the time, Fatemeh's daughter in Tehran was suffering from a serious disease so she asked this woman to practice *fardarmani* on her daughter from a distance and, unbelievably for Fatemeh, her daughter was healed.[7] Fatemeh was herself suffering from various illnesses and had had a difficult life facing financial pressures; therefore she decided to participate in the movement in order to improve her own life. Another three women said that they heard about this path by accident: one at a women's social gathering; one in her Qu'ran class; and one in her Yoga class. From their stories we understand how long-term issues and life situations come together in the specific moment that they hear about this spiritual path: at a different moment they might not have paid attention to such information.

Nearly half of the women affirmed that they had experienced resistance from their family or husbands to their participation in the movement. Therefore, they had to negotiate and compromise in order to be able to follow their choices. They used different strategies; for example Sara, aged 32 from Tehran, single and a university lecturer, tried to

---

[5] Pasyar, (2010). Personal interview. Tehran, at Nahid.'s house. 12 May 2010.

[6] Maryam, (2010). Personal interview. Yazd, at one of the women's/Hamideh's house which was kindly offered by her and was a safe place to conduct the interview. 3 May 2010.

[7] Fatemeh, (2010). Personal interview. Mashhad, at Mellat public park. 24 May 2010.

arrange a few meetings at her house with her parents and someone already on this path.[8] Finally, her mother gave her permission and accompanied her to the first level of classes to ensure that it was not harmful for her. Zahra, aged 38 from Mashhad, a housewife and unhappy in her marriage, recounted that her husband, when faced with her bad temper, concluded that it was better to allow her to go to these classes than that she should continue to be in a bad mood.[9] Zahra grew up in an illiterate family and at the age of 14 was forced into marriage with a man 15 years her senior. She could not continue her education at school until her two children grew up. She then decided to finish high school, received her diploma, and now runs a dressmaking shop. Her husband knew that she was not happy with him and feared that she might leave him, so he finally listened to her and allowed her to participate in this movement. Similarly Nastaran, a 41 year-old legal advisor from Mashhad, negotiated with her husband for nearly five months to convince him that her participation in *Inter-universal Mysticism* was a good idea.[10] In waiting for his permission she missed three beginners' enrolment sessions. On the other hand, there were women among my interviewees who told me that they made their choice regardless of any disagreement and perceived that later on they could show their husbands and family that the movement is a great opportunity for them. This was possible as a result of the beneficial changes they could make for themselves through the lessons they received on the path.

Further evidence on this issue comes from Nahid, the Master of many of my respondents, who told me that she received many calls from women who would not join the movement unless she provided them with single sex classes, or at the least did not record their names.[11] They asked to remain anonymous so that nobody would find out about their participation in the movement. She told the story of a mother and her daughter who used to come separately to classes once a week in secret. They attended without the awareness of their husband or and father, because he would not allow them to attend any classes and wanted them to stay at home to take care of the household and of his mother. Therefore, this mother and daughter used to take care of his mother separately, pretending that they were going shopping or see a neighbour in order to attend the classes. Nahid also mentioned that in her own case her husband had only recently discovered her involvement in this movement and had previously thought

[8] Sara, (2010). Personal interview. Tehran, at her house. 10 April 2010.
[9] Zahra, (2010). Personal interview. Mashhad, at Ghazaleh's house. 23 May 2010.
[10] Nastaran, (2010). Personal interview. Mashhad, at Ghazaleh's house. 23 May 2010.
[11] Nahid, (2010). Personal interview. Tehran, at her house. 8 May 2010.

that her classes were on medical therapy, taught by a female teacher, not about a spiritual path, taught by a male teacher. Nahid married when she was just 17 and had a difficult life both financially and in her relationship with her dogmatic husband and his traditional family. She said that she could not do whatever she wanted until she found the opportunity to join *Inter-universal Mysticism*. She said she did her best not to give her husband any reason to suspect, which might have prevented her from attending these classes. It was only after she became an active Master on this path that her husband found about her involvement in this movement. I do not know how her husband reacted, but it appears he was convinced that it had benefits for Nahid and for their children, as he allowed her to extend her involvement in the movement and teach in their home.[12]

We can see how these women negotiate with their husbands and, in some cases, even tell lies in order to participate in *Inter-universal Mysticism*. They needed to find a way both to pursue *Inter-universal Mysticism* and to maintain workable family relationships. While joining the movement is something that women wanted to do for themselves, they did not want to upset their families or husbands. Their negotiations indicate that these women wanted to maintain good relationships in order to get on with their lives and not simply because their husbands were oppressive. In this way, not only could they please their families and husbands, but they could also please or protect themselves in assuring that their husbands were not critical of their choices. Even if these women's freedom of choice was restricted, ultimately they could make their own decisions and find ways to participate in the movement.

I move now to the second aspect of women joining the path: their anxiety about taking it further. Despite the fact that these women eagerly made the final decision to follow this path, I found that they still had some uncertainties, hesitations and even fears when they first came to the class. From my observations I noticed physical signs, such as women's facial expressions or gestures, which showed their fear. In the introductory session[13] I observed on 9 April 2010 at Nahid's house in Tehran, there were 25 new participants (5 men and 20 women). I found that although all

---

[12] Nahid transformed one of the rooms in her house into a classroom and held two classes daily: one in the morning and one in the afternoon. As I noted in chapter one, I conducted my focus groups, observations and most of my interviews in Tehran in her house.

[13] In the introductory sessions given by Mr Taheri himself or any of his Masters, basic information about *Inter-universal Mysticism* is given to anyone in attendance. These sessions are free for anyone who wants to learn more about the path before deciding to follow it or not.

of them had heard about this path from their families or friends, they displayed uncertainties and doubts; they looked around the house and, when meeting Nahid, it was evident that they did not know much about this movement as they continuously asked questions such as: what is *Inter-universal Mysticism*? What does *faradarmani* mean? Does it really work?

These women's trust in their family members or their friends induced them to take the first step in gaining information about the movement, but it did not mean that they would necessarily follow the path to the next stage. This might be as a result of not having enough information about this very new and recent movement in Iran. Understanding the movement is difficult, even for those who are on this path. When I asked participants how they explained this path to others outside *Inter-universal Mysticism* they responded that it is difficult for them to explain it because it is something very new and there is nothing similar to it. Therefore, they usually suggest that others come to classes to experience it for themselves: in some cases they may offer them relevant literature. For example, Nooshin, a 41 year-old housewife from Yazd with a high school diploma, said:

> I do not talk about it with everyone as it is something difficult to explain and is still vague and not understandable for many people, and they think it is not real and is our imagination. Even if I myself would not see its effectiveness on my own daughter, I might have the same opinion as them and could not believe it. If you do not go to the classes you will not understand it. But as I have a good reputation among my relatives and friends, they believe me. So I just talk about it to those I already know, not strangers.[14]

Indeed, getting a clear explanation about this path from a person who is not qualified to teach it is difficult, because *Inter-universal Mysticism* is 80% practical and everyone needs to experience it personally in order to find out what it really is.

Interestingly, I found that a considerable number of women who joined this movement in Yazd did not know the name of the path as *Inter-universal Mysticism* at the beginning. This path was introduced to these women as an alternative therapy called *faradarmani* from a homeopath, Maryam. Maryam was the main advertiser of this movement in Yazd and used the name *faradarmani*/healing, in order to recommend it to her patients as a complementary treatment. This is another example of the

---

[14] Nooshin, (2010). Personal interview. Yazd, at my cousin's house in Yazd. 3 May 2010.

matter of trust: doctors are trusted by their patients so patients believe that whatever they suggest is good for them. Many of the women in Yazd found out about the real nature of this movement, as a type of Iranian mysticism, only when they attended an introductory session. As a consequence I was not surprised that many women were nervous and curious about this movement at the beginning of their decision making. During the introductory session that I observed, nearly half of the participants could not make a decision and left the class, four participants seemed to be sure of their choice, and the rest chose to take a chance and joined the movement mainly because they trusted their families or friends who had suggested the movement.

In interviews, women often mentioned their fear of joining the movement. Of the 55 women I interviewed, only 5 explicitly discussed feeling fears at this first step but at least 20 women implied nervousness through their comments. Shahla, a 47 year-old widow with a high school diploma from Tehran, who is now one of the Masters in Karaj, feared that while joining the movement might help her to overcome her depression and other pressures in her life, it might also add to her problems.[15] There were three factors which enabled Shahla to overcome her hesitation. First, her initial assumptions were overturned when she saw that those who were practising and working on this path were ordinary people like herself and did not appear strange. Second, they conducted themselves well, treating her well and putting her at ease. Third, the people practising this spiritual healing, *faradarmani*, were doing it in their offices in the evenings which, in her opinion, was a convenient and safe place. Likewise Aram, a 29 year-old housewife with a diploma from Tehran, clearly explained how she experienced fear and hesitation when she had no knowledge about the path itself, the Master, or the place she was going to for the first time.

When I went there for the first time, I went with my husband. My friend who introduced Inter-universal Mysticism to me was supposed to come but she did not which made me wonder whether it might be a bad place otherwise why did she not come and said you go alone... when we arrived my husband said ok you go I will wait for you here. It was a private house; I could not see the light switch so I had to go up on stairs in darkness which scared me more. I got strange doubts and it was interesting that the house number was 13 so all those negative thoughts and superstitions came to my mind to stop me from going further. Then when I saw her (the Master, Nahid) in front of the door, I said hello, please let me call my

---

[15] Shahla, (2010). Personal interview. Tehran, at Nahid's house. 17 April 2010.

*husband. I was stressed and had no idea where I was but when I entered
and saw that it was her private house with her children, I was relieved.[16]*

Like Shahla, Aram was anxious about where she was going, particularly
when she found that her friend, whom she trusted, would not accompany
her. Her doubts increased when she discovered that it was a private house.
But when she saw Nahid in front of the door and realized that her children
were there in the house she overcame her fears. Women's stories, like
those of Aram and Shahla, indicate that the appearance of the Masters and
the safety of the place where classes were held influenced many women in
their decision to take part in this movement. As I said earlier, this
movement is not officially approved, so there is a risk to followers of
being prosecuted by the government. Therefore, these women needed to be
assured that the location of their classes was safe enough in order to avoid
being tracked by the government. Later, I found that private houses were
the most convenient places for most of these women to attend meetings. In
short, lack of adequate information or any clear explanation about the
movement was the main reason why many women hesitated or were
anxious about their initial decisions. However, their fears could be
lessened by encouragement from someone whom they trusted.

Religious Conflict and Opposition

Since the Islamic revolution thirty years ago, Iran has become a place
where religion is prominent in many areas of life. Although Shia Islam has
been a powerful and strong tradition in Iran since the Safavid period, the
current version of Islam in the Islamic Republic of Iran is a very
ideological understanding of Shia which is officially and forcefully
promoted by the regime. On the one hand, there is a very powerful official
ideology and constitution which confirms that the state promotes a
favourable environment for the official version of Shia Islam and places
the highest executive authority in representatives of the Shi'ite *ulama*.
There is thus virtually no aspect of the culture and customs of Iran–be it
law, social customs, education, dress or food–which lacks an official
religious dimension. For example, Islamic religious lessons are
compulsory in schools and universities. On the other hand, there are
several debates about different ways of practising Islam along with
multiple traditions inherited from the past. Hence, Shi'ism, the established
form of Islam in Iran, and its several forms of expression are used in

---

[16] Aram, (2010). Personal interview. Tehran, at Nahid's house. 8 April 2010.

different ways by different *ulama*. Although there has long been a diversity within Shia Islam in Iranian culture, in recent years this diversity been reduced and Shia Islam has become much more limited. The disparities between *maraji-'i taqlids'* interpretation of religious rules in society and in the education system has created confusion and conflict for many Iranians. Some may argue that this is a plurality that allows for more choices for followers of Islamic religion, but the tension which arose after the Islamic revolution derives not from plurality but from the regime's attempts to enforce a single official version of Islam and of being a good Muslim. Therefore, the government has restricted people's choices of practising their religion in the way that they prefer. As a consequence, in order to fulfil their spiritual needs, a considerable number of people inevitably choose to follow a spiritual path other than their conventional religion.

Of the women I interviewed individually, 27 talked about how they were struggling with the religious belief systems of society and of their families. The prevalence of religious conflict for these women emerges from the duality of norms in the family and those they must follow in the public sphere, as well as from the contrast between the more or less egalitarian Islamic education they receive and the inferiority they experience through social segregation because of official Islamic obligations in Iran. In other words, half of the women I interviewed believe that a spiritual path like *Inter-universal Mysticism* meets their religious and spiritual needs more than the narrow, dogmatic and assertive version of Islam enforced by the regime. Maryam, from Yazd, described how the disparities between people's religious beliefs and what she learned in religious schools in the city of Qom scared her away from religion and compelled her to look for an alternative approach to her beliefs and to her life.

I am not from a religious family but I was always interested to learn more about religion. I went to university and saw every single person had different ideas about such matters. So I decided to go to the city of Qom where I thought I could study theology and learn more to answer my questions. Not only did I get something useful, but I also got a strange fear of religion that I was afraid for my child to be born and have the same experience as me... until I found about this path and it has changed my worldview.[17]

---

[17] Maryam, (2010). Personal interview. Yazd, at one of the women's/Hamideh's house which was kindly offered as a safe place to conduct the interview. 3 May 2010.

The interesting point here is Maryam's use of the word "strange" to describe her fear of religion. My point about the disparities between the teachings and interpretations of Islam among *ulama* is a good explanation of her feelings here. Maryam was not able to find consistent responses to her religious questions and, because of this lack of consistency she found religion so confusing that she did not want her child to experience it. In contrast, *Inter-universal Mysticism*–with its easily understood spiritual teachings–could be a clear pathway for Maryam, and worked as an alternative to fulfil her religious and spiritual needs.

In addition, the training of female religious leaders is regarded as important by the Islamic Republic. Therefore, many opportunities were provided for women to obtain religious training. Islamic leaders encouraged religious higher education for women as soon as they established their regime. They opened access to theological schools and religious seminaries, providing "unprecedented opportunities for women to gain positions of religious leadership, authority, preaching and privileges traditionally reserved for men"[18]. In fact education, in particular, is used by the Islamic Republic "as a tool of politicization, Islamisation, and socialization in training the New Muslim Woman to serve and struggle for the Islamic government"[19]. Advanced religious education went hand in hand with religious activism in both private and public meetings. However, "there was a limit to the status women could attain as a Shi'i scholar. Islam did not allow a *mojtahed* woman to issue religious decrees and if she did they could not be binding"[20]. Although this religious education was under the control of the regime, for example in the content of its lessons and the level women could attain, such an education created opportunities for feminist thought which was far from what the regime would have expected.

In her study on the politicization of women's religious circles in post-revolutionary Iran, Torab (2002) found that there was an astonishing increase in female preachers with large numbers of followers in women's interlocking religious circles. The main concerns of these gatherings, despite their diversity, were internal social and political issues such as developing new understandings of religious texts. In accordance, Osanloo (2009) stated "the women's Qu'ranic meeting is an indispensable component of the emerging sites that contribute to the forging of dialogue within Iran today"[21]. In Tehran and in other Iranian cities, women were

---

[18] Torab, 2006, p. 6.
[19] Afary, 2009, p. 304.
[20] Paidar, 1995, p. 308.
[21] Osanloo, 2009, p. 75.

gathering at Qu'ranic meetings (jalaseh-ye Qur'an) and, by reading the Qu'ran, asking questions and familiarizing themselves with what Islam as a whole offers them. These kinds of gatherings, however, are not new to Iranians in general. In fact, women from urbanized classes in particular, held the same kinds of meetings even before the 1979 revolution and the establishment of a theocratic government. There is a long tradition of women having shared religious or spiritual activities, such as visits to cemeteries and attending female gatherings of *rowzeh* and *sofreh*, which were as much about ritual and activity as about studying Islamic texts and discipline. So what seems to have happened from the 1970s onward is those women's gatherings became much more focused on studying Islamic texts and discussing Islamic doctrines. Women were determining and defining how, why, and to what extent Islamic principles affected their rights and roles.

For some women struggling with such religious belief systems, religious activities had been part of their home lives since childhood or were part of their devout life. Despite attending Qu'ranic meetings of *jalaseh* (pious gatherings of women), they maintained that they could not find convincing responses to their search for religious meaning in those practices. They continually felt that there were many contradictions in the sayings and practices of those who called themselves religious. These women thus sought a spiritual alternative. Nastaran, a 41 year-old legal advisor from Mashhad, heard about *Inter-universal Mysticism* from another woman in her Qu'ran class. At the time of my interview with her she was at her first level on this path and was not sure how it could help her. But being disappointed with what she had experienced of religion, she said she was more determined to experience the spirituality on this path than to continue with her previous religious practices.[22]

Some criticisms of the Islamic religion in Iran are based on a critique of traditional religious practices, which certain people think of as irrational beliefs or superstitions. These traditional religious practices–like tying a green ribbon or cloth to the holy shrines for a wish–are sanctioned by custom. This means that people do it because their ancestors did it in that way. Although some may call these habits 'superstitions', for many they are desirable religious practices in which they truly believe. For instance, prayer beads are used daily by many people in Iran and there are a number of auspicious elements for everyday situations and health matters. Friedl (1989), relating the stories of rural women living in Deh Koh, a small

---

[22] Nastaran, (2010). Personal interview. Mashhad, at Ghazaleh's house. 23 May 2010.

village in Iran, shows how the thread of such beliefs, activities and traditions have run through Islamic history. Narrating Huri's story about the belief in beads, Friedl wrote:

> Beads are powerful. Like talk, like words, they have to be used with care. Treated with respect, they help a woman do what she is supposed to do: protect herself and her children. But mullahs say the beads are superstition and one should only trust in God. Still, I say: God made those beads and God gave them their power... it is a matter of knowledge: some women know, and therefore can keep their children healthy and themselves strong. And some women do not, or they are too? lazy to do what is necessary, and then their children die, and they themselves are weak and cannot work.[23]

The women in my study (most of whom had been to university) talked, directly or indirectly, about these customary religious practices and all criticized them. For instance, Marjan, a single 28 year-old with an MA degree from Mashhad, said:

> *To learn more about God, I have taken an interest in religion since I was 13. Not only have I never received any answers to my questions, but also it stricken me by contradictions with God. I was seeing my mum's vows to God whenever we had problems and they did not help her much. When I saw these bargains I thought because I pray on time and have good hijab, I am a very good person so I will never have a problem while it was not like that...I like the Qu'ran but I had a lot of disagreements with what I thought about religion.[24]*

As is evident from Marjan's words, not only she is criticizing her mother's practice of making vows with God for solving their problems, but she also clearly names them as 'bargains'. Since Marjan gained nothing from the deal, she faced contradictions between her beliefs and the realities of her life. This caused her to look for an alternative in spirituality.

Being critical of and dissatisfied with both official Islam and with some traditional religious practices these women, rather than simply rejecting or giving up on religion, chose to seek a form of spirituality. They found that this spirituality met their needs in a way that the official version of Islam did not. Thus, we encounter an interesting connection between two concepts: religion and spirituality. There are two perspectives on spirituality with an important distinction between them: "spirituality in

---

[23] Friedl, 1989, pp. 219-220.

[24] Marjan, (2010). Personal interview. Mashhad, at Mellat public park. 24 May 2010.

religion" and "spirituality as opposed to religion". In the first perspective, spirituality can be a central and essential function of religion: in other words, spirituality and religiousness are interrelated and can co-occur. Based on the teachings of *Inter-universal Mysticism*, spirituality can occur with religiousness if "the beliefs and experiences that are considered to be an aspect of traditional religiousness, like prayer, reading holy books, etc., are triggered by an individual's search for the sacred"[25]. Put simply, the view of *Inter-universal Mysticism* on the relationship between religion and spirituality is that, if a person's aim in his or her religious practices is connection with a higher power, i.e. God, he or she is more likely to have a spiritual experience than if they were just doing them as part of their daily religious routines.

By contrast, the second perspective considers that religion and spirituality can be both contrasted and paralleled in the specific ways that each pursues the quest for the sacred. In this view, then, the spiritual is associated with "the personal, the intimate, the interior and the experiential, contrasted with religion, which is associated with the official, the external and the institutional, often picking up negative connotations of the hierarchical and patriarchal along the way"[26]. In recent years, there have been arguments put forward by scholars, e.g. Roof (1999) and Veries (2007) that spirituality is more open to new ideas and influences than religion, and is more pluralistic than the faiths of mature religions. However, the concepts of religion and spirituality can be so varied in interpretation that it is difficult to achieve an agreed common ground, particularly when the word "religion" can be applied with equal ease to a much wider range of activities than just the so-called mainstream religions. Here, spirituality is understood as a communion with the divine that provides its seekers with a meaning and orientation for living life: these notions can be found in the two perspectives on religion and spirituality discussed above. This language of spirituality is the one used in discussions within the *Inter-universal Mysticism* movement and in accounts of what attracted these women to the movement: a focus on inner-transformation and the holistic, spiritual healing of the self. *Inter-universal Mysticism* is not a new religion but a new spirituality in which one can either maintain one's own religion or not while following the path. For example, followers of the old established tradition of Muslim spirituality can move to *Inter-universal Mysticism* because it is about the spiritual side of belief and leaves untouched what each person practises.

---

[25] Hill et al., 2001, p. 71.

[26] Heelas, 2002; cited in Guest, 2009, p. 181.

These women's criticism or rejection of the way Islamic religion is practiced in Iran has coincided with a revival of spirituality as a profoundly personal quest for enlightenment and meaning. Along with many other ways of being spiritual, they are attracted to *Inter-universal Mysticism* because it not only offers them a modern spiritual experience, along with rational explanations, but it also allows them to maintain their own religious beliefs and practices. As I mentioned above, some women found out about this spiritual path in their Qu'ran class which shows that there is no intrinsic barrier to practising both *Inter-universal Mysticism* and Islamic religion simultaneously. While some women followed the path to enhance their religious practices, the majority of women preferred spirituality over religion, and few of them even said that they did not wish to hear anything about religion or to attend any religious events or classes. From both my individual interviews and the observations I carried out in the classes, I found that whereas some people enjoyed hearing examples from the Qu'ran during *Inter-universal Mysticism* lessons, some complained about such referencing of the Qu'ran or of other religious holy books. In this regard, I argue that some people's aversion to religion occurs mainly as a result of huge contradictions in the sayings and practices of those who call themselves *mazhabi* in Iranian Islamic society. The word *mazhabi* could be translated as 'religious' in English, but in Farsi the word *din* is used for religion. So there is a difference between *mazhab* and *din*: *mezhab* is a creed or sect, a Muslim school of law or *fiqh* (religious jurisprudence), while *din* is religion in general. Takaloo, a 43 year-old housewife with a high school diploma from Mashhad, described this difference. She used to attend Qu'ran classes and was offended by the way other women there used to look at her because her appearance and hijab was different from theirs. In those women's views, she did not have a good hijab. She also found it hurtful to see that after they finished reading the Qu'ran, these *mazhabi* women would start talking behind other people's backs. This was what urged her to follow the spiritual path of *Inter-universal Mysticism*.[27]

My argument here is that spirituality has been invoked in this way to articulate the dissatisfaction of these women with the official Islamic tradition in Iran and to indicate an attempt to move beyond its limitations and inconsistencies. In other words, whereas official Islamic ideology argues that it possesses the absolute truth and that Islam is the only way to get closer to God, on this spiritual path people find that there are many

---

[27] Takaloo, (2010). Personal interview. Mashhad, at Mellat public park. 24 May 2010.

ways to approach God, and that "meaning and identity can be derived from an internal source"[28]. In my focus groups, women discussed their faith in God and love of the Qu'ran, both of which are a common part of Iranian identity and culture. However, they argued that they did not wish to follow what they had learned about religion, particularly what they knew of the official Shia Islamic teachings and ideologies. The women in my second discussion group argued that:

> *religion talks about rules, if you do this or that you will go to hell...The religion we learned about is like a bargain with God,... its beliefs are dogmatic and mostly forceful which also limits us in our lives.*[29]

These ideas indicate that these women contrast the rules and dogmas drawn from Shia Islam, which are predominant in present day Iran, with the personal and spiritual rewards of *Inter-universal Mysticism*'s path. They argued that this path provides them with the spirituality that they could not experience in their religious practices. They commonly agreed that their prayers are now fulfilled by spirituality and that they are now eager to pray as it is led by an inner love of God rather than a duty or a fear of God's anger, which religion had previously taught them.

Furthermore, as Watt points out, "women often turn to spiritual belief to cope with everyday struggles which arise with living in the socially and politically oppressive system"[30]. For these women, spirituality includes a search for ways through which they can self-describe their identities and cope with the negative messages they receive from their Iranian Islamic society. Violations of women's human rights in Iran range from arrests for immoral behaviour or dress to sexual assault, all in the service of brutal social and political control. A 2009 report by Gender Across Borders on the "Sexual and reproductive health and rights situation in Iran" indicates that

> While the detaining of women for inappropriate dress is itself a violation, it also goes beyond moral police to the widespread and purposeful intimidation of women and the use of their sexuality as a weapon against them. The same goes for teenagers who may be beaten for such moral offenses as an overly revealing veil.[31]

---

[28] Houtman and Aupers, 2008, p. 109.
[29] Second discussion/focus group conducted by myself on 12 May 2010 with women in the early stage of the path in Tehran, at Nahid's house.
[30] Watt, 2003, p. 29.
[31] Heroy, 2009, n.p.

It is evident that women's identity and status are undermined in the Islamic Republic of Iran. Farnaz, a 29 year-old computer engineer from Tehran, expressed this point as follows:

> *In fact, an Iranian woman has never had self-confidence and self-determination especially today, when they humiliate women. For example, in the morning a woman goes to work and certainly has this satisfaction with herself that she is a wife of a man and is useful for both her society and her children. But when she wants to return home in the evening she is stopped or arrested by moral police and is humiliated and insulted for her hijab. So all her satisfaction about herself is destroyed. Once she thought she could find solutions in religion, but when she saw much discrimination she preferred spirituality.*[32]

Here, spirituality, while located in various contexts, is increasingly associated with the experiential, the interior, and, generally as Guest argues, "the subjective dimensions of personal identity"[33]. Discussions in my focus groups and individual interviews with women like Farnaz revealed that these contemporary Iranian women were looking for the cultivation of their subjective self–the intuitive, interior dimensions of identity–through spirituality because of patriarchy and cruel gender discrimination which exists in the official Islamic ideology in Iran.

Linda Woodhead offers an interesting parallel in her sociological examination of the predominance of British women within holistic spirituality movements and cultures, arguing that women are denied public recognition in the world of work and leisure, and often feel alien in the face of perceived notions of masculine hegemony. They thus need spaces for both the self-questioning and the healing that holistic spirituality supplies. Since women in Iran have been particularly subjected to the male authority of Islamic religion it is thus not surprising that women are at the forefront of developing postmodern discourses of spirituality and that some experience these new discourses as liberating. I would now like to develop these ideas of patriarchy and spirituality and in the next section I discuss the patriarchal tradition in Iran and its consequences for women's search for support and meaning in their lives.

---

[32] Farnaz, (2010). Personal interview. At her house in Tehran. 6 May 2010.
[33] Guest, 2009, p. 181.

The Effect of Patriarchy and Social Pressure on Women

Women's respect and dignity are not considered in our society. Most women cannot fight the discriminatory laws and patriarchy we have both in our society and home. For example, when a woman wants to speak she will be told to shut her mouth otherwise she will lose her husband, her children and even her life. Therefore, women look for some superhuman power in order to help and support them in such culture and society. In fact, they need such extraordinary support as they could find none from either humans or legislation, so because of this I think women chose to be on this path more than men. (Maryam, a 39 year-old architect working part-time from Mashhad).[34]

I start with this quotation from Maryam as this is an intense and powerful example of how women not only describe but also analyse their lives, and offers an insight into women's perceptions of their situation. Of the women I interviewed, 24 (out of 55) were overtly concerned about patriarchy and the concomitant social pressure in relation to their participation in the movement. In addition, women in my discussion groups recognized that factors present in both the public and private spheres–such as social controls over women's sexuality, the undervaluation of women's work, violence against women, and sexual segregation–have resulted in women feeling frustrated and unhappy with their lives.

In the view of many pious Muslim people, the Islamic gender ideology would bring back Iranian women's dignity which had been damaged under the previous regime. This idea was associated with the premise that "because women were both vulnerable to non- and anti-Islamic influences and a potential source of moral decay, they would have to conform to strict rules regarding dress, comportment, and access to public space"[35]. In fact, the Islamic Republic's ideal of women's domesticity was based on the idea of immutable gender differences between men and women in their social and intellectual capacities, which mean they have complementary sex roles in both the family and in society. The emphasis on women's domesticity and difference is illustrative of the extraordinary ideological pressures of family attachment, domesticity, marriage, and motherhood[36]. As a consequence in many Iranian families, as is evident in my interviewees' stories, there have been more restrictions on women and girls compared with men or boys with respect to individual freedoms,

---

[34] Maryam, (2010). Personal interview. Mashhad, at Mellat public park. 25 May 2010.

[35] Mir-hosseini, 2000, p. 54.

[36] Moghadam, 2003.

dress codes and relationships with the opposite sex. For instance, Iranian Islamic law says that the marriage of a virgin girl requires the permission of her father or paternal grandfather while a Muslim man is allowed to marry whomever he wishes at any time: even a non-Muslim woman.[37] A married or single man can have as many wives as he likes, while a woman is required to be unmarried before her wedding and can only be *sigheh*[38] to one man.

In fact, in Iran men legally and culturally have held more rights and privileges than women. Centuries of gender discrimination and the segregation of men and women have created distinct roles and codes of behaviour for both women and men. Price (2006) confirms that patriarchy has been a major institution in Iran for a significant period and is deeply rooted in religious, legal and cultural practices. However, the reproduction of patriarchy in Iran is closely associated with control of the family model by the state ideology: that is, the social construction of family through educational systems, the media, and religious institutions, particularly after the Islamisation of the state. Despite the fact that, historically, Iranian culture has been patriarchal, since the Islamic revolution a new version of patriarchy has been promoted and strengthened with enforced patriarchal practices, such as controlling female appearance and mobility. In an analysis of the Islamic Republic of Iran, Shahidian (2002) asserted that "the new regime sought to revive private patriarchy in all its tyrannical forms"[39]. The link between patriarchy and the new Islamic regime was examined further by Katouzian and Shahidi in their book, *Iran in the 21ˢᵗ Century: Politics, Economics and Conflict* (2008). Katouzian and Shahidi argue that "by implementing the Sharia and Islamizing the family institution, the political and religious elite attempted to reconcile society and the patriarchal state"[40]. Remarkably, a significant factor in the construction of gender ideology in Iran is a particular version of Islamic values and their impact on the everyday life of the people.

I define patriarchy as a social system in which dominant and privileged men appropriate most, if not all, of the social roles and keep women in subordinate positions. The main argument for using this term is that patriarchy leads to gender inequality and the subordination of women. Indeed, the subordination of women extends beyond the household in Iran. Most decisions relating to social relationships are made by fathers or

---

[37] Based on the law, a Muslim woman is not permitted to marry a non-Muslim man unless he converts to Islam.
[38] Temporary marriage; see glossary.
[39] Shahidian, 2002, p.3.
[40] Katouzian and Shahidi, 2008, p. 87.

husbands.[41] For example, a male relative can decide with whom women can be friends, and is able to regulate their social and educational activities (I discussed how some women had to negotiate with their husbands to gain permission to participate in this movement). Women, especially those who are widowed or single and are living without a male relative, are more likely to be subjected to harassment in society. A group of women consisting of middle-aged housewives in Mashhad argued that women are subordinate because they have learned to be submissive and obedient since their childhood. Women's brains are thus filled with ideas such as: *'You are going to be a housewife so you should learn to be obedient to your husband. You should do everything he wants in order to be satisfied by him and your mother-in-law.* Or when a little girl brings tea for others, women say: *inshallah* (hopefully) *you will be married and bring tea for your husband'.*[42]This group of women also mentioned that even if women are now more educated, the divorce rate is increasing. They said:

> *This is as a result of an increase in women's knowledge and awareness while men are the same as fifty years ago. It is only men's appearance that has changed; they look modern but they still think in the same way as fifty years ago and cannot accept women's liberation... If an Iranian man's wife does not listen to him, he will divorce her and will get two new wives.*[43]

Three important ideas are raised here: the relationship between the increase in women's knowledge and the divorce rate; men's rights in divorcing and getting more wives; and men's desire for their traditional power. In fact, the past decade has seen a threefold increase in the divorce rate in Iran.[44] According to an article in the Trend, "the rate of divorces in Iran has reached an alarming level, so that one in 5.2 marriages led to divorce in the past year, 2013" [45]. There is, however, only anecdotal evidence that women gaining higher education and an increased awareness of their rights are the main reasons for divorce; the reasons usually cited in

---

[41] For example, Erika Friedl's book (1989) on women's experiences in a village in Iran is an excellent account of the life of rural women which shows the internalization of patriarchal attitudes and behaviour at home and outside the home along with their negotiation and resistance.

[42] Fourth discussion/focus group conducted by myself on 25 May 2010 in Mashhad, at Mellat public Park.

[43] Ibid.

[44] Yong, 2010, n.p.

[45] Trend, 2013, n.p.

the media for dysfunctional marriages are connected to poverty, sexual dissatisfaction, and increasingly dishonest lifestyles or cheating.

It is evident that many men wish to enjoy their traditional power despite the practices of modern living. In their study on post-revolutionary marriage and family attitudes in Iran, Tashakori and Thompson (1988) found that "men were reluctant to give up their traditional power bases and privileges"[46] rooted in the patriarchal nature of Iranian culture. Indeed, they found that "modernity is more evident for females than for males on a number of issues such as opposition to polygamy and approval of women working outside the home, and that women are more likely to prefer social equality"[47]. But women do not have equal or even sufficient legal rights to complain about discrimination against them: these violations with devastating psychological repercussions continue to be seen as normal. One of the most palpable examples of such legal discrimination against women is polygamy, where women's complaints are seen as jealousy and not as men's violence against their wives or a discrimination of women's rights. Hence, one aspect I discovered in women's interest in spirituality is a response to forms of deprivation including gender inequality. "The proclamation that God loves every individual equally may be more immediately attractive to women, who are not accorded respect in family and society"[48]. On this matter, for example, Paygani, a 42 year-old married housewife with a high school diploma from Tehran, said:

> *I chose Inter-universal Mysticism because I felt so bad and depressed when I found my husband was having an affair with another woman.*[49]

Whereas some women in such situations adopt coping strategies such as shopping, sport, or drugs to manage their lives, other women chose to participate in the *Inter-universal Mysticism* movement as a form of support.

Yet the types of burden differ amongst these 24 women in relation to their social status, age range, education level, and marital status. There were women, all of whom are married housewives with lower education levels, who have received a high school diploma, with an average age of 43. These women talked about particular life difficulties – financial dependency and pressure; early marriages; divorce; traditional and cultural attitudes, such as the interventions of their husbands' family; *cheshm*

---

[46] Tashakori and Thompson, 1988, p. 19.

[47] Ibid, pp. 19-20.

[48] Walter and Davie, 1998, p. 645.

[49] Paygani, (2010). Personal interview. Tehran, at Nahid's house. 12 May 2010.

hamcheshmi (meaning herd mentality); their distinctive roles as wives and mothers; being lower status; and gaining fewer rights both in society and in their own homes–all of which had forced them to remain silent and tolerant for a long time. Lara, a 30 year-old housewife with a high school diploma from Tehran, talked about her difficult life after her husband's bankruptcy. She was in the late stages of pregnancy when she had to give up her house to creditors. Being financially dependent, she had no choice but to return to his father's house and live separately from her husband until he resolved his financial problems. She became very anxious and depressed by daily calls from creditors and from her family and friends asking her what had happened. She became anxious as a result of reputation which is very important for Iranians. After her daughter's birth, Lara could not keep the baby calm. It was at this point that she desperately looked for something to help her and heard about *Inter-universal Mysticism* from a friend.[50] Her story builds upon my earlier point that her life situation came together with the specific moment that she chose this spiritual path whereas previously, in different circumstances, she had not paid any attention to her friend's suggestions.

On the other hand, there were highly educated and employed women from Mashhad and Yazd who complained about discrimination against them and about people's religious and cultural beliefs. Particularly insightful views are given by Roya–31, with a BA degree, married and working full-time from Yazd–and Maryam–36 with a BA degree, married, working part-time for her husband from Mashhad.

Roya stated:

> *People here in Yazd are much closed minded; they talk behind others' back very much. I was always complaining about why we should live here in Yazd. I used to be scared of what people thought about me... it was how I grew up here in Yazd... when I wanted to get divorced, and was feeling so bad and depressed, I heard about this path. You know in bad situations you just look for a way to survive so my mother suggested that I ask a master in Tehran to come to our house in Yazd. This was how this movement has developed also here in Yazd.[51]*

Maryam said:

> *Here in Mashhad, the problem of men's prejudice is much more pronounced than other places like Kerman, where I am from. Here, if my husband comes home and does not see me there, it will cause a problem. I*

[50] Lara, (2010). Personal interview. Tehran, at Nahid's house. 14 April 2010.
[51] Roya, (2010). Personal interview. Yazd, at my cousin's house. 5 May 2010.

am not allowed to even study or read a book in front of him. Although my husband is highly educated (he has two university degrees), he and his family are very religious and sectarian. I do not think about myself, I am much more worried about my daughter who is restricted at home and is forced to wear hijab against her wishes ... my mother-in-law should not know about me coming to these classes.[52]

Several elements are woven into these stories. For most people, particularly in cities like Yazd and Mashhad, religious values and rituals have a moral and symbolic significance and function as a guide for families. Although such values have long been part of Iranian culture, in the modern era women like Roya criticize them for their discrimination against women. Roya talked about the religious and cultural attitudes of people in Yazd and described them as closed minded people, despite the fact that such practices are well established customs. For example, she said she could not dye her hair for thirteen years as she was scared of what people would think of her. By looking ordinary, Roya would not attract the attention of others and would be seen as a modest and good girl. She envied women in Tehran, the capital city, who, in her opinion, could live a modern life as they wished. In addition to dealing with these cultural forces she also had a difficult relationship with her husband. She finally reached a point where she could no longer tolerate the pressure and chose to participate in this movement to release herself.

On the other hand, Maryam talked about the patriarchal manners of her husband and his family, forcing her to be an obedient wife and mother. She compared men in Mashhad with men in her home city of Kerman to state that, as a woman, she had more freedom in her home city than in Mashhad, a very religious city. She described how she studied and gained her university degree but that she was not allowed to even read a book in front of her husband. Maryam worried about her daughter, who wanted to be like fashionable girls and to live a more modern life than the traditional one she was forced to lead. Quite the opposite of her daughter, Maryam said that her son is an extremist Muslim and criticized her following this path, calling it a heresy. Dealing with her critics, Maryam was determined to participate in this movement in order to help her daughter.

A different subject matter is the consciousness that goes with motherhood and with womanhood. The historical development of patriarchy in Iran has created a gender hierarchy and a sexual division. In particular, under Islamic ideology "women came to be viewed primarily, if

---

[52] Maryam, (2010). Personal interview. Mashhad, at Ghazaleh's house. 23 May 2010.

not exclusively, as mothers; and home as their main place"[53]. The customary roles played by women, in conjunction with their traditional duties at home, is another factor which can explain these women's frustration with their lives. In this respect, women's tasks are viewed as especially problematic for two main reasons. First, women experience more role conflict and overload as they attempt to meet the demands of both home and work. Second, regardless of employment status, women are held responsible for most of the household chores, including childcare. In their study "Predictors of life satisfaction among urban Iranian women: an exploratory analysis", Kousha and Mohseni (1997) found that "the more active women are the more satisfied they are in their marital relationships, but they exhibit less general satisfaction"[54]. This finding can be related to the ideology of motherhood and dominant gender roles. Kousha and Mohseni argued that as long as women perform their motherly duties and follow socially prescribed roles they experience a high degree of satisfaction as mothers and wives. However, the fact that the same factor reduces women's general satisfaction led them to conclude that

> Women see themselves as occupying different and, at times, opposing roles, i.e., that of a mother and wife and that of a person. As mothers and wives, women feel a high degree of satisfaction because they are performing what is expected of them. As individuals, however, their general satisfaction is lowered. This could be due to the "ethic of care"[55], i.e., women's needs become secondary to familial needs and expectations.[56]

The results of my discussion groups support this idea that women in Iran, especially mothers, subordinate their own needs and desires to the needs of other family members. Women in my focus groups described how the need to constantly think about housekeeping, cooking, nurturing children and pleasing their husbands did not leave any space for them to think about their own needs. For them, to be seen as good wives and mothers meant putting the comfort and wellbeing of others first. Therefore, as Kousha and Mohseni argue, "functioning under the guise of the ethic of care, women's needs and aspirations become secondary to those of family

---

[53] Jahanbegloo, 2004, p. 164.

[54] Kousha and Mohseni, 1997, p. 341.

[55] The concept of the ethic of care suggests that 'women tend to provide for the needs of others first and in the process their own needs become secondary. This ethic of care, as an integral part of women's moral development, is also linked to women's role as the primary care-giver in the family' (Kousha and Mohseni, 1997, p. 342).

[56] Kousha and Mohseni, 1997, p. 342.

members"[57]. Indeed, occupying different roles from those of a mother, wife and personal ones, has its own needs and expectations. I would argue that when these needs and expectations were not met by these women it resulted in an intolerable burden and huge amounts of pressure being placed upon them, so that they consequently chose *Inter-universal Mysticism* as a place to seek refuge and release themselves. To sum up, male power and patriarchal domination, socioeconomic pressures, and the distinctive role of women as wives, mothers and employees were what caused these women to be unhappy in their marriages and their lives. Despite their dissatisfaction they struggled against the morality that forces a woman to remain silent and be tolerant until they heard about *Inter-universal Mysticism*.

Spiritual Healing as a Contemporary Concern

Since an interest in alternative and complementary medicine has grown around the world, "the notion of linking religious and medical interventions has become widely popular"[58]. White (2006), in his study on spirituality in health care practice, explains how disillusionment with the medical model of health care is interconnected with a reawakening of interest in a holistic approach within more conventional medicine and spirituality. He states:

> [A]lternative therapies, eastern diets and meditation all appear to resonate with these themes to a greater degree than the concerns of conventional medicine ... spirituality emerges as a powerful coping force for cancer survivors; meditation and relaxation have become valued aspects of health care that affirm the spirit as well as the body; motivation, self-esteem and personality are recognized to affect health in addition to physical make-up.[59]

For many people, "religious and spiritual activities provide comfort in the face of illness"[60]. Certainly, health and well-being have been religious and spiritual concerns in various societies for a long time; a few examples across a variety of religions [61] are Lourdes, Mihaya, Santeria, Hindu, Buddhist, Shamanic, and conventions including Iranian religious traditions.

---

[57] Ibid.
[58] Sloan et al., 1999, p. 664.
[59] White, 2006, p. 15.
[60] Sloan et al., 1999, p. 664.
[61] For more information on spiritual healing around the world see Kluger, 2009.

In Iran in particular, many diverse religious and spiritual movements promoting spiritual healings have flourished during the last decades of the last century. Groups as diverse as traditional Islamic spirituality, Sufism and New Age groups and East Asian religions, now spreading around Iran, are encouraging holistic/non-medical approaches to health and healing. Javaheri (2006), in her study *Prayer healing: an experiential description of Iranian prayer healing*, has found that "despite the growth in scientific medicine traditional healing is alive and well and is a cultural way of coping with health problems"[62]. In *Inter-universal Mysticism* spiritual healing, as the main and first step on the path, is important because, in Taheri's (2008) view, it prepares the background for elevation of the individual and universal body of the society. This school of thought believes that spiritual healing on this path can upgrade a human and lessen his or her pain. Spiritual healing, called *Faradarmani* in this movement, is a complementary treatment whose nature is completely mystical and which is considered a branch of *Inter-universal Mysticism*. In treatment, the person is connected to the *Inter-universal* common sense network which is the system of intelligence and wisdom or common sense dominating the world of existence, by a *Faradarmani* practitioner (*Faradarmangar*) and is scanned. Scanning can be described as

> [P]utting the person's body and soul under a magnifying lens where records of previous and present problems, both physical and mental, become patent and the discharge starts. These files might be about the person's body, mind, or other component parts and he or she is required to let the discharge finish and through treatment be healed.[63]

In my study, I sought to find out if a desire for spiritual healing drew people to *Inter-universal Mysticism* and, if so, what women's understanding of spiritual healing was and how it influenced their decision to follow this path. Of the 55 women I interviewed, 23 tried this path because of its healing possibilities or, rather, because they thought or hoped that these opportunities would become available to them.

Some women, including: Banafsheh, aged 25, suffering with bone cancer, single with an advanced diploma from Tehran; Shahla, a 47 year-old self-employed widow with a high school diploma from Tehran suffering with depression; and Azam, suffering with lupus, aged 36, married with a BA degree and working full-time, from Yazd, said that they felt they had no other options or believed that other kinds of treatment

---

[62] Javaheri, 2006, p. 117.
[63] Taheri, 2008, pp. 91-93.

would not be successful before taking the healing opportunity on this path. For instance, Banafsheh said:

> *I did not come to this path because of its mysticism: its name was faradarmani. I was suffering badly from my bone cancer - I had really bad pains that none of my medications could help me with, particularly after my surgery. Then my friend suggested I try this healing... I had no other expectations, just healing. It was after I witnessed my healing progress that I found this path was much more than healing and that it was worthwhile to continue.*[64]

Medical approaches have done much to treat diseases yet they remain resistant to actual cure for many of them, as Banafsheh found. This failure, of course, has left space for another approach to health: a holistic approach for those people who are not satisfied with their medical treatment. The holistic approach affirms that wherever spirituality is neglected, health and well-being will be reduced. The view of *fardarmani* in *Inter-universal Mysticism* is that humans can enjoy a great range of spiritual abilities, one of which is the ability to cure. Through this healing, which is based on no techniques, expertise or method, the person creates a relationship between the self–how he/she makes sense of the purpose of life–and the natural world: a sense of wonder or oneness with the rhythms and joys of creation. These interpersonal relationships give the person confidence and encourage the effectiveness of the healing. In comparison with mainstream medicine, *faradarmani* for these women was associated with a desirable, spiritual experience. This may be a significant factor in directing people towards spiritual healing.

In addition to these women dissatisfied with their medical treatments, there were women who were persistently encouraged by their family or friends to experience this healing. For example, Maryam, a 37 year-old married woman with a high school diploma, working part time from Mashhad, explained how she was encouraged by her brother's wife to try *faradarmani* for her breast cancer. She did not know anything about *Inter-universal Mysticism* and its spiritual healing. Because of her brother's wife's persistence, she decided to postpone her operation for a month with the doctor's permission to try this healing. By the end of the month when she went for her test again, she surprisingly found her cancer was gone.[65] For Maryam, such a spiritual experience was a good reason to learn more

---

[64] Banafsheh, (2010). Personal interview. Tehran, at Nahid's house. 14 April 2010.
[65] Maryam, (2010). Personal interview. Mashhad, at Mellat public park. 25 May 2010.

about this path and, finally, to follow it. Another account is given by Fereshteh, a 37 year-old married housewife with a BA from Tehran. Fereshteh talked about her difficult life experiences dealing with the patriarchal attitude of her husband which contributed to her severe depression. She was forced to continually listen to her husband and forget about herself and her own desires because her husband thought that he knew what was best for her. She had to give up her professional job and her beautiful house to become a refugee in Europe, in keeping with her husband's wishes. Living as a refugee irreparably damaged her self-confidence. Moreover, she had to study what her husband thought was good for her and work in a retail shop. She wanted to have a baby and become a mother but her husband did not want that as he was not ready to become a father. Finally she ended up in a psychiatric hospital. After being confined there for four months, her sister suggested that she return to Iran and join *Inter-universal Mysticism*. Fereshteh said that she was very fortunate to hear about this healing. It was an opportunity to rescue herself from the darkness of living in that situation.[66] From her story, we see how the interaction of patriarchal attitudes and health issues were influential in Fereshteh's decision to join this movement.

In contrast, for some women their own health was not of significant concern, but learning about spiritual healing and becoming a healer was the reason why they wanted to try this way of healing. Two women, for instance, were medical doctors: Afsar, a GP from Mashhad, and Maryam, a homeopath from Yazd. Through their occupations, they were both interested in complementary therapies—such as traditional medicine and herbal therapies—as well as spiritual healings, for example, reiki. While, for the homeopath, *faradarmani* was something unique—completely different from other kinds of healings and much more than what she expected—for the GP, it was something similar to and in harmony with other spiritual healings. However these two doctors had different approaches to the use of *faradarmani* with their patients. Maryam, the homeopath, said:

> *I talk about this healing with many of my patients and suggest that they join the movement and experience the path themselves as it is not just about the healing that I do for them but it is also about the purpose of*

---

[66] Fereshteh, (2010). Personal interview. Tehran, at one of the follower's private house. 25 April 2010.

living, which everyone should find out about, something that they have lost.[67]

Unlike Marayam, Afsar did not yet want to talk openly about *faradarmani* with anyone and used it only indirectly.[68] Here, their different opinions regarding *faradarmani* could be based on the fact that Maryam had already progressed through to the final level of the path, while Afsar was only at a very early stage of the path, having attended just two sessions of the first level at the time of my interview with her, so her opinion may change in the future.

The interest in spiritual healing for some other women has its root in unfulfilled wishes. Two very different accounts were given by Malihe and Nahid. Malihe, a 70 year-old housewife with a high school diploma from Mashhad, talked about her grandmother being her role model.

> *My grandmother used to heal different diseases through her hands. Since my childhood, I wished to have the same power for healing. I used to go with her to the 8th imam's shrine. It was how I found my faith in Imam Reza.*[69]

There is a long history of visits to shrines for healing in Iran and the shrine of the 8th Imam in Mashhad, mentioned by Malihe, is considered an especially sacred place. Javaheri points out that "people bring their patients from across the country and reside in the shrine for days and even weeks while praying for their patients' healing"[70]. Malihe continues, stating:

> *For many years after my grandmother's death, I continued going to shrine and prayed to be like her, but it did not work. So I tried another spiritual path which was unsuccessful too. Until last year, when I heard about faradarmani from my daughter.*

Because she had been disappointed by her previous lack of success with spiritual healing, Malihe did not believe in *faradarmani* at the beginning

---

[67] Maryam, (2010). Personal interview. Yazd, at one of the women's/Hamideh's house which was kindly offered as a safe place to conduct the interview. 3 May 2010.

[68] *Faradarmani* can be used both directly and indirectly on others and its effects are the same. The only difference is the matter of awareness. When it is indirect, the person cannot find out exactly what was effective in the healing progress.

[69] Malihe, (2010). Personal interview. Mashhad, at Mellat public park. 25 May 2010.

[70] Javaheri, 2006, p. 173.

and asked her son to try it first before deciding to follow the path. Her son had a similar interest in the spiritual healing and accompanied her for many years. However, for Nahid, the story was different. She said that the chance of becoming a healer in *Inter-universal Mysticism* was a big opportunity in her life. She had always wanted to be a medical doctor but because of her parents' divorce and their remarriage she had had no other choice except to enter an early marriage at the age of 17. She could not continue her studies due to financial difficulties and the wishes of her dogmatic husband. Having three children and a difficult life meant that she did not have a chance to study. However, in hearing about this movement her wish to help others with their health problems was fulfilled.[71]

Returning to my former argument, today's spiritual healing movements are one expression of dissatisfaction not only with the limitations of conventional medicine, but also with its expense. In this regard, White (2006) states that "despite the increasing effectiveness of some medical treatments and public health measures, there was renewed interest in holistic approaches as the high cost, in both resources and side effects, of much modern medicine became clear"[72]. Likewise in Iran, in an online report published on the website *khabar* news on 18 April 2010, Dr Alireza Zali, the President of Shahid Beheshti University of Medical Sciences and chancellor of the Iran Medical Council, said:

> Unfortunately, at present 60% of medical costs are paid by people themselves so that with just the one operation and hospital expenses, many families in our society drop under the poverty line and now 3.5 to 4.5 percent of our people are in this condition.[73]

When Shahla's husband died, her life with two children became extremely difficult. Financially, she was under such enormous pressure that she gradually developed serious depression. She visited many psychologists and counsellors, read many relevant books and spent lots of money to try and get her strength back for the sake of her children, but nothing was useful. When I asked her why she joined this path she said:

> *As soon as I was introduced to faradarmani, I asked how much it costs and they said it is free. I could not believe that there can be such a free service for healing. Although financially it was very difficult for me, at that time I was ready to pay any cost just to become healed. I got the healing and my*

---

[71] Nahid, (2010). Personal interview. At her house in Tehran. 8 May 2010.
[72] White, 2006, p. 30.
[73] Zali, 2010, n.p.

primary intention was just to be healed although later I excitedly decided to follow it.[74]

Whereas some might use spiritual healing as a complementary healing activity that can be combined with their medical treatment, many in Iran welcome it because it is free of charge. In my focus groups, women argued that some wealthy people may not trust this healing because it is free. In contrast, those with financial problems are ready to try it even if they have doubts about its effectiveness. In brief, the fact that healthcare resources are not sufficient and cost a lot suggests, encouragingly, a shift towards self-help through spiritual healing, reflected in the considerable numbers of women who chose to try the healing of *Inter-universal Mysticism* either to be healed or to become a healer.

Women's Desire for Self-improvement

With a desire for personal identity, worth and entitlement–a challenging aspiration for women in the Islamic Republic of Iran–these women have not been fulfilled in the roles of wife, mother or employee and embarked upon deep quests of self-exploration and self-improvement in spirituality. Of my 55 interviewees, 31 hoped that following the path would bring them closer to God and give them an experience of self-understanding. They were looking for an insight into the world to explore who they are and what they want. The language of spirit, soul and core self are used interchangeably within *Inter-universal Mysticism* so that "no clear line is drawn between spiritual exploration and self-exploration"[75]. The movement was thus an opportunity for self-improvement for these women as they discovered the purpose of their creation.

Hamideh, a 36 year-old housewife with a BA from Yazd, told me that she had an ordinary life with no problems. But gradually she felt that there was something missing in her life. She had no self-confidence and therefore had many fears in her life. Her involvement with the movement allowed her to get to know herself better as well as to make changes in herself.[76] Women's stories, like Hamideh's, offer an interesting contrast to earlier discussions of women who chose this movement because of illness, social pressure or religious conflict. Questions of meaning and identity prompted these women to explore the depths of their souls. They were searching for answers to questions like: what is it that I really want? Is this

---

[74] Shahla, (2010). Personal interview. Tehran, at Nahid's house. 17 April 2010.
[75] Woodhead, 2009, p. 121.
[76] Hamideh, (2010). Personal interview. Yazd, at her house. 03 May 2010.

the sort of life I want to live? What sort of person am I, really? For instance, Zhaleh, a 43 year-old housewife with a high school diploma from Tehran, said:

> *I wanted to know who I am. I wanted to find myself and find where is God? What I should do? What is my responsibility? ... I thought: I do not have any authority. In our childhood, our parents have authority over us. Then when we marry, our husband and his family have this authority. So I thought we have no authority and identity for ourselves as a human being.*[77]

This is a remarkable view which defines a shift from authority imposed on women from the outside (defined in Zhaleh's words as parents, husbands or predefined gender roles), to authority derived from within. Houtman and Aupers (2008) call this process "detraditionalization": the turn to the self Their argument is that women in modern times are turning away from the traditional lives they were living, with objective roles, duties and obligations, and are instead looking for their own subjective experiences[78].The rise of post-Christian holistic spirituality in the West has been seen by many scholars as part of this process of detraditionalization: looking towards the self and experiencing one's own truth outside of predefined roles in society. Likewise, I perceive these women's decision to participate in this movement in Iran as a move "from home-making to self-making"[79] inspiring them to follow this path to cultivate self and spiritual care.

These women are involved with this holistic spirituality because of the confusing and contradictory changes that have occurred in women's lives since the Islamic revolution in 1979. However, the impact on women's lives of detraditionalization or modernity, whatever we call it, permeates into women's identities. Women strongly identify themselves with their function of providing care for others, partly because they are still expected to do so. Sharareh, a 49 year-old housewife with a high school diploma from Mashhad, said

> *I was very conformist and would do everything for others even if I did not like to do so. I always thought I should keep my family and husband happy and satisfied without paying attention to myself and what I want.*[80]

---

[77] Zhaleh, (2010). Personal interview. Tehran, at Nahid.'s house. 08 April 2010.
[78] Heelas and Woodhead, 2005.
[79] Marler, 2008, p.47.
[80] Sharareh, (2010). Personal interview. Mashhad, at Mellat public park. 25 May 2010.

This comment from Sharareh brings us directly to the heart of the matter. Whilst men can more freely construct their own identity, women still have to fight a contest between their personal wishes and the social expectations that are forced upon them, particularly by Islamic ideology, causing more stress in terms of a time burden and more identity problems. These women stated that since their participation in this movement their identities are no longer synonymous with their relationship with a husband or children: they can self-identify. Women have an opportunity on this path to create a life of their own, which no longer conflicts with their social and personal goals.

Significantly, *Inter-universal Mysticism* has been chosen by these women as a safe space in which women can deal with their feelings of worthlessness and low self-esteem relating to the placing of others' needs before their own in the Islamic Republic of Iran. Aram, a 29 year-old housewife with a high school diploma from Tehran, expressed the matter:

> *Many Iranian women feel they exist just to serve others... if women in Iran have many problems it is because they do not believe in themselves in the way they should do... they always worry about the day they may divorce because they do not believe they are perfect human beings.*[81]

For these women, who culturally and traditionally pay more attention to others than to themselves, getting the opportunity to take time for themselves on this spiritual path was an act of self-assertion and identity-construction. Aram's identification of women's fear of divorce indicates how pressure is placed upon women to seek the support offered by this path.

While interviewees identified women's desire for self-recognition and increasing their autonomy as reasons for joining *Inter-universal Mysticism*, the women in the discussion groups raised different issues. The reason, that certain topics came up in the group discussions but not in the interviews, is because of the difference in the dynamic. When women were in a group, they chose to talk about subjects appropriate for a semi-public discussion. It was also a space in which they could share their views about other women on the path, whereas in the interviews the focus was on the interviewee's own experience. In groups, participants argued that women take part in this movement in order to avoid staying stagnant and to make a change. When I mentioned the fact that more women than men follow this path they commonly agreed that women spend more of their time in domestic situations. Therefore, women have a stronger desire to

---

[81] Aram, (2010). Personal interview. Tehran, at Nahid's house. 08 April 2010.

widen their horizons, expressing their potential and getting out of the house. In their view, those women who are mainly housewives are looking for change by having new experiences and learning new things: they wish to improve themselves and their lives. For instance, one of the women in the group of beginners on the path in Tehran said

> *I am a housewife and my husband thinks that because I am in the house*
> *most of the time, my knowledge about outside of the house is less than his*
> *and he knows much more than me.[82]*

This comment indicates that women's secondary status is imposed by the patriarchal dominance of men, a situation which often results in women's lack of confidence. The official view of women as only care givers encouraged these women to not only increase their self-autonomy and independence, but also to develop their identities by participating in this spiritual movement.

My observations also indicated that some women did not join the path in order to learn about mysticism. For them, it was an opportunity for self-assertion and self-development through new experiences and meeting new people and not being restricted within the cult of domesticity. Indeed, most leisure activities in Iran are dominated by male interests and identities. Therefore, for women who are struggling to avoid submerging their identities into the traditional roles of care-giver and staying at home, there are not many opportunities. Consequently, women who are engaging "in a quest for greater personal fulfilment are likely to find ways to explore this within the spheres traditionally open to them"[83], such as classes on religion or spirituality, as well as female social networks centred on family members and friends. For instance, Yoga classes were very popular, first in Mashhad and then in Yazd. However, all my individual interviews, discussion groups and observations provided significant evidence to support the view that women chose to participate in this movement "to explore forms of identity through self-improvement which move beyond what are perceived to be the more damaging aspects of traditional domestic identities"[84]. What my findings suggest is that this path has been chosen by these women to either improve or construct a stronger sense of self by gaining insight into the world and discovering the purpose of their lives, which lies beyond conventional roles and performances.

---

[82] Second discussion/focus group conducted by myself on 12 May 2010 in Tehran, at Nahid's house.
[83] Woodhead, 2009, p. 120.
[84] Ibid, p. 121.

Conclusion

I have argued that there is a connection between the reasons why women choose to follow this path and how they find out about it. The majority learned about *Inter-universal Mysticism* from either family members or friends and chose to participate in the movement because they trusted particular people who had a good reputation. They hoped that this movement would solve their problems and it is, in effect, used as a form of support. However, their choice is not only largely affected by their life difficulties, it is also shaped by their personal motivations: a search for change; to improve things in more dynamic ways; to resist negative images of themselves, both in family and in society; and to gain self-identity and self-improvement. They found *Inter-universal Mysticism* to be an easily-accessed space in which their difficult life and health problems can be alleviated, and the conflicts they face in their religious beliefs and identity in late modernity can also be negotiated. Furthermore, they are attracted to this spiritual movement as women who want to explain life, death and creation: they are looking for an insight into the world. They found that *Inter-universal Mysticism* appeals to them because of the spiritual practices on this path: the connection to the numerous links of the *Inter-universal* common sense network and its spiritual healing has to do with self-construction for them.

CHAPTER FOUR

ENGAGING SPIRITUALITY:
WOMEN'S PERCEPTIONS AND EXPERIENCES

> The human being is not a creature that is left on earth, alone on his or her own. Considering that the plan of creation has been initiated based on an intelligent design and a systematic programme, it is impossible to assume that God would take action without a plan and purpose, or take pointless and futile actions.[1]

In this chapter I try to explore women's spirituality in everyday life, and to touch on explanations of difficult concepts of spirituality through careful attention to the words of the women I listened to. Indeed, spirituality is difficult to define. For the women in my study, the term relates to the process of achieving both communion with God and a sense of self, and is connected to how they think about their ultimate purpose in life. They rarely defined the term but, rather, talked about their experiences in a way which enabled me to realize how they understand spirituality in their daily lives. Their stories indicated that finding out who they are, why they are living and, in fact, the meaning of life, was a central component of their view of spirituality, as was having a closer relationship with God. They provided many examples of how "being spiritual" helps them to move through and beyond difficult situations. Therefore, spirituality is here not theorised via mysticism, but as a way of approaching life. By assessing women's understanding of their spirituality, I will discuss how the spiritual and the material can interact.

Despite definition being difficult, in my interviews I did ask all 55 women what spirituality (معنویت /manaviyat in Farsi) means to them. While 5 women had a clear definition for spirituality, I was able to infer women's perception of spirituality through the stories they told me about their spiritual experiences. Each woman had their own perception, but four key themes emerged: a primary concern with finding meaning in life; valuing interconnections between a closer relationship with God and being

---

[1] Taheri, 2008, p. 13.

a better person; the experience of peace and happiness; self-transcendence and preparation for life after death, which was the specific aspect acquired through their involvement with *Inter-universal Mysticism*. I argue that these women's conceptions and experiences of spirituality are greatly influenced by their religion, culture, family background and educational achievements. Their spirituality is rooted in a specific context–the Iranian Islamic cultural and religious tradition–which is very significant for them and, without exception, informs their self-described identity. Against this background, I wanted to establish how these women viewed the differences between their traditional religious views and their new ones and whether they still follow their religion: Shia Islam, Sunni Islam and Christianity. I asked them this question directly: 'what does spirituality mean to you?'. Their responses led them to consider the differences between old religion and new spirituality: 39 women distanced themselves from religion (Shia Islam) and considered spirituality as different from religion; 11 women practiced both spirituality and religion and thought that being on this spiritual path strengthened their religious beliefs; and 5 women saw no difference between spirituality and religion and considered them both as ways to guide human beings. For the majority of them, religion was associated with formal doctrines and rituals while spirituality was conceptualized as a personal and direct relationship with God, which is a common perception among Iranians.

The Concepts of Spirituality and Religiosity

Traditionally, the concept of spirituality is aligned with the empirical dimension of religion. This spiritual dimension exists in many religions of the world and is even distinct in sub traditions within each that emphasize religious experience or spirituality rather than doctrine. Some examples are Sufism or the path of *erfan* in Islam, Gnosticism in Christianity, Kabbalah in Judaism, and Tantra in Hinduism. Conventionally, social scientists and psychologists of religion have used the terms spirituality and religiosity interchangeably or have conjoined both constructs under the term religion. This practice, however, elides the separate beliefs, values and experiences of spirituality and religion. I agree with Zinnbauer et al. (1999) that "the meanings of the central constructs themselves, religiousness and spirituality, are subject to diverse interpretations"[2]. Like the term religion, spirituality can be used as a universal and multicultural concept that encompasses a great variety of traditions and practices. As

---

[2] Zinnbauer et al., 1999, p. 892.

such, there are a significant number of thinkers who distinguish religion from spirituality. According to this approach, religion is conceptualized as an organized socio-cultural-historical system while spirituality is understood as an individual's personal quest for meaning, for a relationship with a higher power (e.g. God), and for a feeling of interconnectedness with the whole world. Certainly, religion and spirituality are "multidimensional constructs with different cognitions, feelings, behaviours, experiences, and relationships that in multiple levels must be considered from both theoretical and methodological perspectives"[3]. A well-accepted definition for religion is given by Koenig et al., who refer to religion as:

> [A]n organized system of beliefs, practices, rituals, and symbols that serve (a) to facilitate individuals' closeness to the sacred or transcendent other (i.e., God, higher power, ultimate truth) and (b) to bring about an understanding of an individual's relationship and responsibility to others living together in community.[4]

This definition suggests that to be religious, one has to have a relationship with a particular religion as an institution with a set of doctrines about the 'ultimate reality'. For *mazhabi* (religious people) in Iran, this relationship focuses on their affiliation to official Shia Islam and their participation in prescribed Islamic rituals and practices, such as attending *namaz jomeh* (Friday prayer), fasting during the month of Ramadan, and their support of official Shia beliefs. By contrast, spirituality refers to an individual's personal experience of the divine, regardless of whether they are part of a religious tradition or not.

Over the past three decades, debates about differences between religion and spirituality have been heightened by suggestions that not only the concept but also the practice of religion has been displaced by spirituality. Many, such as Veries (2007), have argued that institutional religion has declined while expressions of spirituality have increased. In fact, the decline of many traditional religious institutions has led to "a proliferation in personalized and individualized forms of religious expression, and a culture of religious pluralism"[5]. In this context, there is a tendency among sociologists like Veries (2007) to associate contemporary (or what they call new age) spirituality with new religious movements or with privatizing religion in which there is no need for a church or mosque. Therefore, the dual construction of religion is divided into religiousness

---

[3] King et al., 2011, p. 169.
[4] Koenig et al., 2001, p. 18.
[5] Zinnbauer et al., 1999, p. 892.

and spirituality. While, in this contemporary understanding of spirituality, religiosity remains tied to binding doctrine and external conceptions of the sacred, modern-day spirituality is characterized by a release from those ties and bindings. There is a noticeable trend among urban educated people in Iran dissatisfied with the official Shia Islam to search for different spiritual paths, both western and eastern (e.g. Buddhism, Reiki, Yoga, Meditation, *Inter-universal Mysticism*), to fulfil their spiritual needs.

Yet, there are others, including some of the women I interviewed, who think that religion and spirituality are not separate and that through spirituality they enhance their religious beliefs and practices. In this respect, spiritual paths provide exactly what religion has always provided: that is "the possibility for ritually maintaining contact with a more general meta-empirical framework of meaning, in terms of which people give meaning to their experiences in daily life"[6]. The spiritual "dimension of life influences the ways people relate to each other, to God, and to the world around them"[7]. Furthermore, Pargament and Mahoney claim that "God is central to any understanding of spirituality"[8] and other scholars, such as Gilbert (2000), argue that spirituality and religiosity are interrelated and see spirituality as an internal expression of religiosity. Even though there are significant intersections between spiritual and religious experience, my empirical evidence suggests that many people make major distinctions between the two. During my field work in Iran, through my observations of religious places and spiritual meetings and classes, I found that substantial numbers of people differentiate spirituality from religion and perceive spirituality to be the more personalized aspect of their faith while considering official Islam to be more about the doctrines and creeds which provide perspectives on how one should behave. Nonetheless for many individuals, including some of my interviewees and for *mazhabi* people, Shia Islam is a source of spirituality and can act as a tool to develop spirituality. Loeffler (1988), in his study on *Islam in practice: religious beliefs in a Persian village*, showed that for many in Iran religion does not solely function as a set of doctrines, norms, and official precepts to be enacted by individuals but, as he argues, is a way in which they relate to these patterns and use them in their lives.

This exploration of what individuals make of their religion and how religion affects them is the same approach that underlies work on religion in Iran, such as Mottahadeh (1985), Friedl (1991), Fischer (2003) and

---

[6] Wouter, 1999, p. 152.

[7] Mattis, 2000, p. 104.

[8] Pargament and Mahoney, 2002, p. 649.

Torab (2007), although they take a different perspective in each case. For example, Torab argues that "women's ritual activities are particularly revealing of the complex relationship between so-called formal and informal religion... they may each experience and interpret them in different ways within a plurality of ideologies and power relations that informs their everyday lives"[9]. Here, I would add that there are features of religion for many Iranians that intersect with their definition of spirituality, such as a belief in God or a yearning for material as well as spiritual values like meaning and goodness. Therefore there can be both striking similarities and distinctions between definitions of spirituality and religion. To clarify further the relationship between religion and spirituality, I suggest that they are overlapping circles rather than linear areas of experience. Visualizing them in this way allows for an understanding of my later arguments about the perceptions of women about spirituality within religion and as a distinct category.

The word spirituality is derived from the Latin root "spiritus", meaning the breath of life.[10] In Farsi, the word معنویت/*manaviyat* is used to denote a similar meaning: it comes from the root معنوی /*manavi*, which refers to the soul, the heart and the purpose of the universe and human reality.[11] *Manaviyat* (spirituality) emphasises a belief in, or a relationship with, the highest power (God) which gives purpose, meaning, and direction to human life. Tisdell asserts that spirituality is "a personal belief and experience of a higher power or higher purpose"[12], whereas Baker (2003) describes spirituality as "the aspect of life that gives purpose, meaning and direction"[13]. Delgado extends Tisdel's and Baker's definitions and characterizes spirituality as "a search for meaning and purpose in life, a sense of connection with others, and a transcendence of self, resulting in a sense of inner peace and well-being"[14]. In his definition spirituality is associated with transcendent forces, life purpose and meaning, and core social values. He suggests that the relationships between one person to another, to God and to the whole world are affected by the awareness of a spiritual dimension of life if he or she wishes to live in peace. In *Inter-universal Mysticism*, Taheri (2010) identifies spirituality as a deep experience which provides a sense of relatedness or interconnectedness among humans, the universe and God, through which everyone can strike

---

[9] Torab, 2007, pp. 21-22.
[10] Baker, 2003; Kale, 2004.
[11] Persian Dictionary *Dehkoda*, 1955.
[12] Tisdell, 2000, p.309.
[13] Baker, 2003, p. 51.
[14] Delgado, 2005, p. 158.

a balance between his or her inner and outer self to find the purpose of creation. There is an agreement among all these ideas of spirituality that it is through spirituality that individuals perceive, interpret, and respond to the world and that spirituality provides them with a context to understand life and their relationships with others. This interpretation frames spirituality as a relationship or as the active presence of the divine in the lives of humans which gives meaning, purpose and a mission in life as well as material value.

The Spiritual/Mystical, Religious and Cultural Background in Iran

Religious beliefs, values, and norms can easily be characterized as part of Iranian culture; being born and growing up in a religious Islamic country has a direct effect on the particular forms of religiosity and spirituality which Iranians engage in. Therefore, in order to understand the spiritual experiences of these women and their perception of spirituality in *Inter-universal Mysticism*, it is necessary to learn more about the religious and spiritual traditions in Iran, particularly the path of *erfan*. In fact, Iran is an example of a society in which the link between culture, political structure, and Islamic religious development can be seen quite readily. By seeking to shape and control Shia Islam–the official state "belief"–the government has influenced religious and spiritual development among the people as well as limiting opportunities for spiritual or religious expression other than Shia Islam. The government socializes individuals into Shia Islamic beliefs and practices through different processes. For example, it has invented a special ceremony for girls called the "Celebration of Puberty" (*jashn-e taklif*) or "Celebration of Worship" (*jashn-e 'ebadat*), the titles of which are used interchangeably, to symbolically prepare nine year-old girls for puberty and to mark their transition into adulthood in Shia Islam. In her study *Performing Islam: gender and rituals in Iran* (2007), Torab vividly describes this event:

> Two years following the establishment of the Islamic Republic in 1979, a new ritual emerged specifically to mark the coming of age of girls at the age of nine. This ritual swiftly became a major public event... Central to the ceremony is the performance of the daily prayers, *namaz* (Arabic, *salat*) by the novice, who must also display competence in answering questions posed by adults on her religious duties. The official designation of the ceremony is "Celebration of Worship" (*jashn-e 'ebadat*), although people commonly also refer to it as "Celebration of Responsibility" (*jashn-e mas"uliyat*) and "Celebration of Puberty" (*jashn-e taklif*) ... The main

purpose of the ritual is to propagate Islamic values of simplicity and spirituality, likening it to a 'new birth' that marks the girl's awareness of her responsibilities.[15]

This example shows that, along with cultural and religious traditions, being a female also shapes "differences in the extent to which religious and spiritual beliefs are developed and the importance placed on those beliefs"[16]. During my field work in Iran, I observed that more women than men were likely to pray, to affiliate themselves with Qu'ran classes, religious circles, and shrines, and to describe themselves as either religious or spiritual. It was particularly evident, in my observations of Imam Reza's shrine in Mashhad and *Inter-universal Mysticism* classes in Tehran and Mashhad that many fewer men than women were praying in the shrine or asking religious or spiritual questions in class.

In addition, there are long established customs and rituals–dating back at least to the eighteenth century–which have been developed and practiced by Iranians within Shia Muslim tradition and belief, albeit with their own distinct characteristics, through which people express and experience spirituality in their lives. For example, there is a healing ritual, *majles-e do'a daramani*, held at a popular votive centre where an enterprising woman mediates curative vows to the saint Zeynab. As Javaheri (2006) confirms, "in the Shiite tradition praying to God is performed by invoking the Islamic holy leaders"[17]. People from across the country travel to and reside in shrines or sacred places for seeking religious or spiritual insight, healing and support. Indeed, most Iranians believe in the efficiency of unearthly and spiritual methods to overcome earthly problems and some of the ways people express this belief is through the *sufra* (ritual feasts) attended primarily by women to practice their vows, cure their illnesses and gain religious or spiritual experience.

On the whole, as Fischer (2003) points out, in Iran one can identify four main ways or expressions of using Shi'ism. First, there is the scholarly religion of the *maktabs/madrasehs* in which the religious leaders, *maraji-'i taqlid* and *ulama*, are trained in the holy city of Qom, which is one of the main centres for Shia scholarship in the world; second, are the religious beliefs and practices of ordinary lower and middle class rural and urban people; third, are the mystical paths of *erfan*; and fourth, is the *roshanfekr*/intellectual and ethical religion of middle and upper class people with a modern, largely, secular education. Among these four styles

---

[15] Torab, 2007, pp. 169-170.

[16] Barry et. al, 2010, p. 317.

[17] Javaheri, 2006, p. 173.

of Shiism, *erfan* is pervasive in several different forms of Iranian consciousness:

> [I]ts poetry [works] as constant epigrams to frame everyday life, its organized meetings (function) as a kind of social gatherings consciously apart from the religion of the *ulama*, its philosophy and cosmology [work] as a contemplative frame for the intelligentsia, and its psychology [functions] as a moral referent in a corrupt world.[18]

Here I argue that as with any religious tradition, Islamic religion and spirituality are embedded in wider Iranian culture as, for example, Christianity is in western culture. There are also different ways in which Iranians express their sense of being Muslim: for some it is through Islamic doctrine and ritual while for others it is via spirituality. Therefore, I say that religious and/or spiritual feeling remains relatively strong among many Iranians and is often expressed "through the language of *erfan* which talks about the beauty, value, and truth of Islam"[19]. *Erfan* is part of the rich spiritual heritage of Iranians and the term means "knowing" in Farsi and is used to refer both to Islamic mysticism and to the attainment of spiritual knowledge from direct insight. Through the path of *erfan* one asks questions about life and its meaning and searches for a close relationship to God, the achievement of perfection, as well as an understanding of the ultimate questions. Although there are many religious spiritual traditions in Iran, here I focus on *erfan* for two reasons: first, because it is one of the most popular spiritual traditions among Iranians; second, it has considerable influence in *Inter-universal Mysticism* and on the way many women understand spirituality.

Erfan usually overlaps with Sufism yet Sufism, or the Islamic Sufi tradition, cannot be equated simply with mysticism/*erfan*. Although both have the aim of seeking *haqiqah* (meaning ultimate truth), *erfan* refers to an intellectual discipline and a set of personal practices of a mystical nature through which an *aref*/mystic pursues spiritual goals. Sufism has an additional element which is a tradition of practice that has been institutionalized through the collective organisation of a *tariqah*, meaning pathway. Since the revolution, Iranian Sufis have experienced persecution by the *ulama*. *Erfan*, as Metz (1987) states, is "strongly dissociated from the popular Sufism of wandering dervishes, which is widely associated with anti-social behaviour, drug abuse and blasphemy"[20]. Certainly, such

---

[18] Fischer, 2003, p. 139.
[19] Ibid.
[20] Metz, 1987, p. 125.

distinctions were considered by the Shi`i *ulama* as they "felt simply that any claim to mystical insight, especially one originating from within an "order", was a dangerous heresy alien to Islam"[21]. Therefore, since the early nineteenth century the *ulama* in Iran, particularly the senior *ulama*, have consolidated their influence in both Iranian politics and society by adopting an anti-Sufi position.[22] Likewise, Nasr suggests:

> The rejection of Sufism by the Shi'ite hierarchy was a political phenomenon of the late Safavid period when the *ulama* reacted both to royal patronage of Sufis and to an increasing flood of charlatan mystics who claimed to be Sufis. The *ulama* then drew a sharp distinction between gnosticism or speculative mysticism (*erfan*), which was acceptable, and Sufism (*tasawwuf*), which was not, a distinction that holds to the present.[23]

A historical examination of the attitude of the *ulama* towards Sufism suggests a degree of variety in their critical opinion, and supports the hostility of the current regime towards it. For instance, recently 189 Sufis had been arrested and jailed. They were charged with disturbing public order and insulting the leader.[24] *Erfan*, on the other hand, as an intellectual endeavour, is a largely respectable phenomenon within Iranian Shi`ism in which Imam Khomeini and several others among the revolutionary *ulama* were also known to have been trained.

While both *ulama* and *urafa*/mystics address ideas of perfection and unity with the divine, their interpretations are different. For the *ulama* the law (shari'at) is indispensable and essential while for *urafa* the law is a mere basis to be transcended. Therefore, most of the teachings of the religious intellectual sciences like *erfan* in Iran are today performed outside formal institutions, in private classes. In the path of *erfan*, the *aref* talks about *baten* or the core and the essence of religious rules, as do most exponents of *erfan*. In an *aref*'s view, religion is both *zaher* (the outward, the manifest) and *baten* (the inward, the hidden), whereby mankind performs some formal rites in order to draw nearer to God. This nearness is achieved when one tries to realize the inner significance of these rites while maintaining their external form. An *aref* believes that "this way or road ends in truth, which is monotheism and it occurs after the mystic has ceased to exist as an independent entity"[25]. An *aref* aims to change the self

---

[21] Ibid.

[22] For further historical evidence see Abbas Amanat, 2009.

[23] Nasr, 1972, p. 118.

[24] Asemi, 2012.

[25] Safavi, 2010, n.p.

into a state of self at peace. The characteristic of the self at peace is that it merges into the divine will and attains cognition or reaches the station of truth. In this way, *erfan* has a family resemblance to other mystical traditions such as Judaism, Christianity, Yoga, Vedanta, or Zen. For example, Kabbalah in Judaism includes practical directions for the achievement of religious ecstasy; through the practice of *hesychasm* and other practices Christians use the repetition of the "Jesus prayer" or techniques of meditation to evoke a stillness in body and soul and invite divine revelation[26]; and Muslims explore the mystical implications of love through the poetry of Mowlana and Hafez, the two *arefs* who have profoundly affected Iranian life and culture. What all of these diverse traditions share is "an intense desire to experience the divine; a commitment to the pursuit of knowledge of God as the heart of religious experience and the very core of what it means to be human"[27]. The specific characteristic of *erfan* is that everything is discussed and viewed simultaneously at both levels of discourse: the level of empirical existence (*zaher*), and the level beyond reason (*baten*) of hidden or inner meaning and power.

I should mention here that the use of the word *erfan* has now changed among Iranians. Traditionally, *erfan* meant a very specific discipline within Islam, or was considered a form of religious expression within Islam. But now it is used for a whole range of spiritual insights and practices. Nowadays a number of Iranians, particularly young people, are increasingly joining different schools of *erfan*–one of which is *Inter-universal Mysticism*–because on such paths they can find a greater freedom to form their own way. *Erfan*, as a religious and spiritual pathway, offers them the chance to explore themselves in ways that are not offered by official Shia Islam, and it is also a low risk or a moderately safe form of dissidence. The growing popularity of *erfan* "has contributed to greater tensions between its practitioners and certain elements of the official Islamic regime"[28]. People's criticism and rejection of the way Islamic religion is practised in Iran has coincided with a revival of spirituality as a profoundly personal quest for enlightenment and meaning. Among many other ways of being spiritual many people, like the 55 women in my study, are attracted to *Inter-universal Mysticism* because it offers them something spiritual which is new, has reasoned explanations, and which allows them to maintain their existing religious beliefs and practices. In other words, it allows them to be spiritual (or religious) but to

---

[26] Johnson, 2008.

[27] Ibid, n.p.

[28] Saberi, 2006, n.p.

distance themselves from the dominant orthodoxy of present day Iranian Shi'ism.

How *Inter-universal Mysticism* Conceptualizes Spirituality

One, by his own effort, can reach nowhere
Unless your mercy lights up his way (Saadi)[29]

According to the *Inter-universal Mysticism* school of thought, the creation and evolution of a human being is designed to follow a grand purpose as part of the wider process of fulfilling a much higher objective. *Inter-universal Mysticism* maintains that the purpose of humanity is to attain *kamal*/perfection and for this movement to take place, certain directions have been divined for humans which can be considered in the context of Divine Communal Mercy[30]. *Inter-universal Mysticism* provides its seekers with a meaning and orientation for living. Spirituality on this path is felt through the feelings, thoughts and experiences–which in this path are achieved through connections with Inter-universal intelligence–that arise within a search for the ultimate truth: God. Thus, spirituality can either be a central and essential function of religion, or spirituality and religiousness are interrelated and can co-occur. The main point here is the 'willingness' for the sacred search. Taheri has a particular approach to religion. He symbolically defines religion "as a bird with two wings. One wing is a religious law (*Shariat*) and the other is mysticism (*erfan*)"[31]. He argues that religious law is about principles and rules to guide its followers, while *erfan* is about how to gain the knowledge underlying those principles.

Developing his intuitive perceptions, Taheri argues that humans constantly face two challenges: the sphere of *aql* (rational knowledge) and the sphere of *eshq* (love). *Aql* relates to "the world of expertise, method and technique, reason and reasoning, endeavour and effort, counsel and advice, whereas, *eshq* relates to the world of enthusiasm and zeal, ecstasy and bliss, amazement and wonder, attraction and self-sacrifice and affection"[32]. Taheri argues that *aql* is the basis for understanding *eshq*, through which all human perceptions take place and, since all conclusions

---

[29] A major Persian poet (1213-1291). Translated by Dr. Homayounfar, in Taheri 2008, p.14.
[30] Divine Communal Mercy is the general divine grace that includes all human beings without exception and makes the pathway toward *kamal* accessible to everyone (Taheri, 2008).
[31] Taheri, 2010, p. 5.
[32] Ibid, p. 75.

are based on *aql*, without it perfection cannot be achieved. In this way, the spheres of *aql* and *eshq* are interdependent: the wise fall in love and the lovers become wise. Taheri further argues that *erfan* means being within the sphere of love, achieving illumination, clear-sightedness and gaining insight into existence: it is the movement from appearance to essence. Consequently, based on his opinion, *erfan* can be divided into both the conceptual part, which can be discussed and examined through the realm of *aql* (this part is in need of clarification and must explain where it will lead the human), and the practical part, which lies in the realm of *eshq* which is expressed through feelings. Experiencing spirituality on this path, then, means being present in the realm of *eshq,* in order to reach "illumination, enlightenment, clarity of vision about the existence and universe; and this cannot be attained through the world of logic, science and knowledge"[33]. In this regard, Shah Nemat-Allah Wali, a great medieval *aref* (1330-1431) says

> *Those who see through the eyes of the* (logical) *mind*
> *Are in dream watching something illusory* (cannot see the truth behind the surface, can only touch the surface)
> *Although wisdom and intellect light the lantern to show the way*
> *However it can never reach to* (the height of) *moonlight* [34]

In brief, spirituality in *Inter-universal Mysticism* is both the perception and attainment of *kamal*/perfection or fulfilment. Through spirituality, humans study the different kinds of awareness which are transferable to life after death. Since spirituality is in the world of *eshq* it is not a place for exclusivity, it is a world which can accommodate all human beings and which considers everybody included within divine love.

Taheri offers a comprehensive definition of spirituality that attempts to distinguish this construct from religiosity, although he thinks they can be interrelated and co-occur in certain circumstances. He states that spirituality on his path is far from the hierarchical structure of organized religion. He understands spirituality as an essential part of human beings and argues that the substance and potential of living is revealed to us through spirituality. Through my interpretation of spirituality in *Inter-universal Mysticism*, I suggest that spirituality is what allows us to be self-motivating, self-directing and self-validating. Spirituality on this path allows anyone, regardless of having faith in a religion or not, to experience enthusiasm, inspiration, growth, and change. However, this spiritual

---

[33] Taheri, 2008, p. 89.
[34] Translated by Dr. Homayounfar, in Taheri, 2008, p. 84.

experience is not self-centered. Implicit in the spiritual practice of *ettisal*, spirituality is both an individual and a communal phenomenon. Taking a communal approach, Taheri argues that spirituality is not a selfish pursuit and should link individuals with others, not only their immediate community but people around the world. In this context, spirituality is consistent with many scholars' definitions of the term that suggest spirituality is relational and gives humans meaning and direction.

Spirituality in the Words and Experiences of Women

This chapter has so far explored the conceptual and theoretical distinctions and connections between spirituality and religion. I now move to examine in detail how women inside *Inter-universal Mysticism* conceptualised spirituality in their daily lives. Coming from Shia Iranian backgrounds, most of these women expressed, to varying extents, their involvement in Islamic religious traditions. More than half of the women said that their early adulthoods were characterized by a questioning of their childhood understandings of religion. Because of their cultural background, they had two alternative perceptions of religion and spirituality. In their view, religion is based on belief in doctrines and participation in practices and rituals: for 53 of the women these were practices of official Shia Islam, for one those of Sunni Islam, and for one other, practices of Christianity. On the other hand, spirituality, regardless of whether it is understood as within or separate from religion, involves life's deeper inspirations: a sense of meaning; finding out who they are and where they came from; understanding their mission in this worldly life; and forming a direct connection with God or making their relationship with God closer.

There was an interesting take on spirituality offered in my second focus group in Mashhad, where women associated spirituality specifically with an aspect of their femininity. They argued that '*spirituality is granted to women by God because of their motherhood*'.[35] This comment indicates that they are reading their femininity in a particular way. This is as a result of the importance of family and childrearing in Iranian culture which has influenced women to be attracted to spirituality and to attach it to their motherhood. Historically, the patriarchal culture and tradition in Iran has caused many women to turn to religion and spirituality as a form of support to help cope with a repressive situation, as was the case for some of the women I interviewed. Furthermore, the way women are socialized

---

[35] Fourth discussion/focus group conducted by myself on 25 May 2010 in Mashhad, at Mellat public Park .

in an Islamic country, also leads more women to be attracted to religion and spirituality. For example, comparing the women in my study with those in Friedl's (1988) and Torab's (2007) studies reveal that women in Iran find different ways to express their own religiosity, spirituality and agency. As Torab asserts:

> They consider their rituals as a source of joy and support outside the familial framework and as the means toward leading spiritually rich and rewarding lives. The rituals provide them with possibilities for social competence as sponsors and hostesses, as teachers, mentors or spiritual guides, or enable them to act as intermediaries between people and the supernatural agencies.[36]

In *Women of Deh Koh: Lives in an Iranian Village*, Freidl gives multiple examples of hardship and triumph for women. Each story indicates the strength of spirit with which those women who live within the confines of Iranian Islamic traditions manage their religion in different ways to approach the challenges of everyday life.

Among the 55 women in my study, 16 associated spirituality with life direction; for 27, spirituality was characterised as life purpose and meaning; 22 spoke of spirituality as an experience of peace and being closer to God; while only 2 described spirituality as a sense of positive feelings such as love and hope.[37] For all of them spirituality is the belief in God, life after death, and the existence and presence of a transcendent, nonmaterial dimension of life. Yet, in their perceptions of spirituality these women had different viewpoints: those who saw spirituality as separate from religion; those who located spirituality within religion; and those who saw spirituality and religion as the same resource.

Spirituality, Separate from Religion

The prevalence of conflict between these women's religious beliefs and what they see in practice is reinforced by the inferiority they experience due to the social segregation enforced by official Islamic obligations in Iran. In general, women's responses to the new Islamic Republic's gender codes, both in general and towards hijab in particular, varied by class and ideological orientation, ranging from passionate support to consent, indifference, and absolute resentment. In the case of hijab for instance, some women, in particular those from the upper middle classes, perceive

---

[36] Torab, 2007, p. 246.
[37] Ten of these women held more than one view on spirituality.

hijab as oppressive. Conversely, many women from traditional and pious Muslim families consider it to be empowering.

Since the first decade of the revolution, the impact of the new gender policies towards women has been varied. As Moghadam (2003) states, "there were pro-Khomeini and anti-Khomeini women, and even among Islamist women there were different perspectives on women's issues, including the hijab"[38]. For religious women, "who were practically banned from public engagement by their husbands or fathers during the Pahlavi period, their veiled public presence, something that the government was also interested in, was a symbol of liberation from social and spatial isolation"[39] and also of support for khomeimi, leading to a diversity of forms of hijab. Here, I should note that while hijab has a broader meaning than just head covering,[40] it exists in different styles. For example in Iran, some women wear a scarf, some a chador, and some a mixture of both. Even within ethnic communities women wear different forms of head covering, e.g. a combination of both a small hat and a scarf over their head. Therefore, hijab is not a single form of dress and there is room for women to manoeuvre. Typical choices are short tunics, tight jeans or leggings, colourful head scarves which reveal their hair, which is often dyed and fashionably cut, and the wearing of heavy makeup.

Ghazaleh from Mashhad, 39, married and self- employed with a high school diploma, vividly described her experience.

> *I am not religious and never go for it as I have been scared by religion since my childhood. I was told if I show my hair, I would go to hell and I used to be punished for that. I always was beaten to force me to do my prayers and because I did not have hijab, they did not accept me. They used to say wherever someone is without hijab, there is evil. But I was stubborn and did not listen to them.[41]*

Ghazaleh's story suggests that official religion and spirituality are not the same. Many of the women abandon or resist, as Ghazaleh did, the Islamic religion of their childhood primarily because as a result of rejecting the codified rules and regulations of the official Islamic regime, such as praying and hijab. In Ghazaleh's case, she joined the spiritual paths of

---

[38] Moghadam, 2003, p. 99.

[39] Mahdi, 2003, p. 11.

[40] In Islam, hijab is 'the principle of modesty and includes behaviour as well as dress for both males and females. For women, it refers to the complete covering of everything except the hands, face and feet in long, loose and non see-through garments' (BBC Religions, 2009, n.p.).

[41] Ghazaleh (2010). Personal interview. Mashhad, at her house. 25 May 2010.

Alanan[42] and *Inter-universal Mysticism* to help her cope with living with an alcohol-addicted husband. She lived fearfully, because of her former bad experiences with religion. Ghazaleh had always had problems with her family relating to religious matters and was also scared of getting divorced, living as a divorcee, and of being alone with no financial support. She tried different methods to overcome her marital problems, which were also affecting her daughters.[43] She did not believe in spiritual support and said that the only reason that she chose to try those spiritual paths was that she was frustrated with the ineffectiveness of other methods. Interestingly, she offered the use of her house in Mashhad to one of the Masters of *Inter-universal Mysticism*, who was a relative, to conduct classes. Although at the time of our interview she was still experiencing problems with her husband, she was surprised by the changes she found in herself, her children and her finances. After passing just three levels on the path, she said:

> *Since my participation on this path my life has been full of blessings... I work less but I earn more... I am more energetic... my daughters are more healthy and happy.*

In this sense, for Ghazaleh, spirituality is being in touch with her inner self: finding what her beliefs and values are, what her fears are and where they come from. Spirituality, for her and for some other women, is separate from their traditional religion and represents their individual relationship with God and their knowledge of themselves and its effect on their lives. As such, "self-knowledge was conceptualized as a dynamic and interdependent process"[44], which they experienced in the practice of *Inter-universal Mysticism*.

Another respondent, Roya from Yazd, 31, with BA, married, and working full-time, offered her thoughts on how participating in this spiritual movement has enabled her to reconcile her values, beliefs and identity by releasing her from traditional Islamic views on how a woman should behave.

> *Erfan has an important role in life. Not only I was not spiritual but also I was opposing my religion. I was opposed to hijab and our Islamic rules... I*

---

[42] *Alanan,* well-known as Iran Alcoholics Anonymous, is an organisation that helps alcoholics, drug addicts and their families through 12 spiritual steps. For further information see the organisation's website: http://aairan.org/en/home.html.

[43] For example, her eldest daughter became depressed and would scream and cry at night.

[44] Mattis, 2000, p. 116.

used to think that since I have a boyfriend I am committing a sin or if I talk
to some stranger I should be ready to die. But I found God on this path and
feel I am happier.[45]

Although she was not religious and is strongly opposed to Islam, living
and growing up in a traditional city, Yazd, has made Roya feel culturally
Muslim. As she points out, having a boyfriend caused her to fear being
accused of not being a good girl in her traditional society. It suggests that
how living in an Islamic religious culture which forces women to be
virtuous can affect women's perceptions of themselves and their actions.
In other words, the ways in which women construct knowledge of who
they are and how they make meaning from this, are part of how they are
socialised as Shia Muslims in Iran. It was Roya's strong aspiration that
provided coherence to her miscellaneous and rather conflicting identities.
In the following quotation, we see how her identity and religious beliefs
are reconstituted in spirituality when she invoked her identity as a woman
who lives in a religious city and–in a specific and significant act–had not
dyed her hair for years. Dying hair here is an indication of how, through
spirituality, Roya gained the courage to be the person who she always
wanted to be and to overcome her restrictive religious dogmas.

Now I dye my hair. I always feared what others might think about me, that
[they would think] I am a bad girl. Before, I wanted to go somewhere to
not see anyone or talk to anyone. Now, after 13 years, I am dying my hair
and I do not mind how others may look at me. This path has changed my
insight and given me peace of mind.

Here, I should note that dying hair is an established cosmetic practice for
Iranian women. However, Roya changed her look from a natural
appearance to a very modern European look which is not acceptable in a
city like Yazd, where women are expected to be modest and not to attract
attention through their appearance. Yazd is an urban centre with strict
views and strong support for Islamic traditions and conventions, therefore
women are under more scrutiny than men in terms of their religious
practices. In contrast, in Tehran women wear more modern European
fashions, such as coats with jeans, and women wear scarves that do not
hide all their hair. When I travelled to Yazd for interviews I wore a loose-
fitting tunic and a proper hijab in order not to attract attention and to avoid
any problems caused by my appearance. So when I saw Roya for the first
time in our interview, I was very surprised by her appearance and her lack

---

[45] Roya, (2010). Personal interview. Yazd, at my cousin's house. 5 May 2010.

of fear of being arrested by the moral police. She is a tall woman with blond hair, who was wearing tight jeans and a top with a medium-length cardigan revealing her neck and chest. She had a very loose scarf which showed her hair at the back and front. Listening to her story, her life seems to have been transformed by participation on this spiritual path. As she indicated, *"I found God on this path and feel I am happier"*. She is no longer worried about what others may think of her because she believes in herself as a human being who belongs to the world, not just to that traditional community. This spiritual strength she gained from her involvement with *Inter-universal Mysticism* gave Roya the ability to deal not only with Islamic rules and hijab, but with how she wants to think about her individuality: it shifted her thinking about all aspects of her life not just religion. Separating religion from spirituality, Roya and women like her associated spirituality with finding true identity and peace. This illustrates the view of Tisdell (2003), that spirituality is a movement toward authenticity and that

> The notion of spirituality as moving toward a sense of greater authenticity or a more authentic identity … means having a sense that one is operating more from a sense of self that is defined by one's own self as opposed to being defined by other people's expectations.[46]

For Roya, "integrating new insights from different paradigms and new spiritual traditions was an important part of [her] spiritual development"[47] in *Inter-universal Mysticism*. Almost all of the 55 women talked about spirituality as related to this growing sense of true identity, which was strongly related to gaining belief in their higher self: a sense of being close to God and feeling his presence, which had not been happening to them before through their Islamic religion.

Ghazaleh and Roya's conceptualization of spirituality is as a reaction against the perceived rigidity and inconsistency of the official Islamic regime. In the discussion groups, women argued that they have seen many *mazhabi*/religious people who are pious in front of others but who, in private, are not committed to their religion. This issue of hypocrisy also came up in individual interviews. For instance, Maryam from Mashhad, 36 with a BA, married, and working part-time for her husband, said:

> *For these mazhabi people, religion is just hijab and praying. From morning to evening they go to jalaseh, from evening to night they go to the*

---

[46] Tisdell, 2003, p. 32.
[47] Tisdell, 2000, p. 331.

*shrine and then from night to morning they pray. But if you see their
private life, they break their daughter-in-law's heart and hurt her a lot
without fearing God. I wish they would agree to join these classes to
become open-minded.[48]*

In comparing *mazhabi* people with the followers of *erfan*, these women
think that spiritual people are more committed to their stated values,
beliefs, and identities. In these women's opinion, official Islam is defined
by formal rules about how to behave, whereas spirituality is about having
a personal relationship with God and achieving perfection. Such views
suggest that, for them, spirituality is not the same as religiosity and it is
possible for people to be spiritual even if they are not affiliated with
traditional religion.

One key idea notable in most studies of spirituality is some form of
search for "the meaning of life" and I found that 27 women were seeking
to make sense of their life in this way. For them, spirituality was
conceptualized as a fulfilling relationship with God that fosters a
purposeful life. The notion is clearly articulated by Zhaleh from Tehran,
43, a housewife with a high school diploma:

*I was looking for myself, I wanted to find myself and where is God, what
should I do? I was always thinking that I have a mission/duty, I should find
it...Just this reason that I can help others in this way and develop closer
relationships is very good.[49]*

Zhaleh's words suggest that spirituality is about questioning the purpose
of her life, in an attempt to improve it, and changing things around her.
Such a definition of spirituality is consistent with the understanding of
growth and development in spirituality. Asking existential questions
establishes self-definition or a meaningful identity, values and roles, as we
see in Zhaleh's story. Additionally, Zhaleh's notion of helping others
through her spirituality on this path is one of the important concerns in
some of the other women's understandings of spirituality.

As well as indicating the pursuit of meaning, belonging, and identity,
these women's stories reveal that being a good human and believing in
God and in some aspects of their religion are dominant descriptors of
spirituality. Although this could also be seen as a description of religiosity,
my interviewees nuanced this by suggesting they have more belief in God
than in religion. Some women's descriptions of spirituality in other

---

[48] Maryam, (2010). Personal interview. Mashhad, at Ghazaleh's house. 23 May
2010.
[49] Zhaleh, (2010). Personal interview. Tehran, at Nahid's house. 8 April 2010.

contexts suggest that spirituality is about being "our true self in God"[50]. According to Benner (2011) this kind of integrated, free and true being is the essential characteristic of anything deserving to be called spirituality. He suggests that spirituality is a fundamental part of being a human. He states: "because it is a way of living, it is not something that can ever be reduced to beliefs or practices"[51]. Spirituality, therefore, plays an indispensable role in the human developmental journey as the fulfilment of one's humanity happens through certain core spiritual ways of living. For instance, Mahin from Mashhad, 57, married, and retired, associated spirituality with humanity, stating that

> *Without spirituality we are apart from ensaniyat* (humanity). *Religion is different from spirituality. It means I may not be religious but I can be a perfect human and have belief in God.*[52]

Here, *ensaniyat*/humanity is a key theme to the meaning of spirituality for Mahin. Through her definition of *ensaniyat*, she argues that to be spiritual, one should see beyond the self and also be concerned with or compassionate about others. What Mahin suggests is that spirituality also allows one to identify with the rest of humanity rather than experience a feeling of isolation. In other words, there is a link between developing spirituality for oneself and simultaneously changing one's relations with others. Spirituality is thus not only about the search for a true or inner self, but also about caring for others, which is a distinctive tenet of *Inter-universal Mysticism*. This aspect is important because it connects the changes in women's relations with their families and with society.

Spirituality within Religion

For some women, practicing their own religion posed no contradiction with practicing spirituality on this path. The principles of *Inter-universal Mysticism* are not too distinct from Abrahamic religions; therefore spirituality on this path is not in competition with other forms of religiosity. The accounts of these women suggest that the spiritual development of women from different religious beliefs occurs through a process of rational and critical analysis of their experiences of religion while they remain open to new spiritual experiences. Spiritual development for these women, therefore, entails the "intentional identification and

---

[50] Benner, 2011, p. xii.
[51] Ibid.
[52] Mahin (2010). Personal interview. Mashhad, at Ghazaleh's house. 24 May 2010.

integration of their beliefs and values in the processes of identity formation, making meaning, and seeking purpose"[53]. In particular Shia Islam, as is clear, is an important factor in the shaping of almost all my interviewees' identities. Official Shia Islam offers a particular context in which these women have built a personal belief system maintained since their childhood.

There is a long tradition of women having shared religious and spiritual activities, such as visits to cemeteries and attending female gatherings of *rowzeh* and *sofreh*, which were as much about ritual and activity as about studying Islamic texts and discipline. In her study, The politics of women's rights in Iran (2009), Osanloo found that readings of the texts have empowering effects on women in a new set of circumstances in which women begin to "fly in the face of state-instituted practices and interpretations of Islam"[54]. In this way, she suggests that bringing the Qu'ran into dialogue with women's status in the Islamic republic "not only gave women agency, but also allowed women to assert themselves as credible social and political actors with knowledge of Islamic texts, practices, and traditions"[55]. In so doing, they declare a form of agency that is authorized. Similarly, I would argue that religious or spiritual meetings, such as the meetings of *Inter-universal Mysticism*, are one example of a dialogical situation in which ideas about rights are developing all over the country. They are a part of the new positions in which women become involved in different discussions, share experiences, and learn from one another, to find their way in the complex social, political, and religious context of Iran. For example Hamideh, one of the women in my individual interviews, said that as women learn more about religion and its aims in human life, particularly Islam as is stated in the Qu'ran, they would no longer follow those *ulama* who manipulate Islamic texts in order to rule their followers.

Before participating in *Inter-universal Mysticism*, these women had been or are still attending or running women's Qu'ranic meetings. They, therefore, have constructed their religious and spiritual meaning through symbols and rituals that are part of an Iranian Islamic background and cultural tradition. This is described vividly by Nastaran, a 41 year-old married legal advisor from Mashhad:

---

[53] King et al., 2011, p. 173.
[54] Osanloo, 2009, p. 95.
[55] Ibid.

We had different jalaseh[56] in our house for the imams or the Qu'ran but I never got answers for my questions like: why we are living? What will happen after death? The answers in religion were always short and ambiguous. My religious belief came from my family and limited to doing good to have a good next life. Love of our Imams and praying were inherited in all of us in the family and it was not an obligation. Ramadan month has always brought good feelings in our house and I always thought that there was something spiritual [happening]. But it was not enough for me and [it was] my thought that something was missing that urged me to look for it in spirituality. Spirituality to me is love of goodness, that is the most important and stable principle in life.[57]

Nastaran connects the practice of spirituality with the spiritual feelings she found in her traditional religious practices, for instance, fasting during the month of Ramadan. "During the month of Ramadan, more than at any other time, the goal is to gain spiritual excellence and control over the body"[58].Women like Nastaran are adding value to existing religious support for spirituality rather than rejecting that support. However, in joining *Inter-universal Mysticism*, Nastaran does not locate spirituality exclusively within her Islamic practices and does not believe that her religious tradition is the only source for spirituality, as she criticizes her religion for not providing her with full and clear answers. Similarly, Hamideh, a 36 year-old housewife from Yazd with a BA, argued that

our religion gave us fears of death and hell... They never tell us all the truth.[59]

Both Nastaran and Hamideh's criticism of their religion came from thinking about and questioning what they saw as problematic in existing traditional and religious practices. Nastaran found that she could not get full answers from her Shia Islamic religion and Hamideh thought that Shia Islamic leaders did not tell the truth and instead tried to scare their followers in order to increase their dependence on those leaders. These women draw on a belief that we are not only nourished by the traditions we grow up with, but that we have spiritual resources within ourselves, although we may need to learn how to explore and use these. In thinking about the narratives of these women, it is clear that there are many women

---

[56] *Jalaseh* is a women's religious gathering.
[57] Nastaran, (2010). Personal interview. Mashhad, at Ghazaleh's house. 23 May 2010.
[58] Torab, 2007, p. 27.
[59] Hamideh, (2010). Personal interview. Yazd, at her house. 03 May 2010.

who, like Nastaran and Hamideh, found spiritual meaning on spiritual paths other than their religion, at same time as continuing to practice the Islamic religious tradition in which they grew up. Nastaran and Hamideh both stated that spirituality strengthens their religious belief and they have gained insights into their religion which have increased the quality of their prayers. They said that they no longer pray because of a fear of hell or because it is an obligation, but that they pray for the love of God and enjoy doing so. Hamideh said

The God I knew before is very different from the God I know now.

Equally, another interviewee, Majidi, a 45 years old housewife from Mashhad, said that since she joined this movement she understands her Sunni lessons better.[60] These women have not moved away (either partly or completely) from their religion, and still think that it has a spiritual foundation for them. According to Tisdell, the "spiritual development of most of us as adults cannot be completely separated from how we were socialized religiously as children. In most cases, such childhood exposure was the foundation of spiritual development"[61]. This matter is well expressed by Sharifi, a 60 year-old housewife from Mashhad with a high school diploma, and Narges, a 40 year-old single hairdresser with a high school diploma from Mashhad. Sh. states:

We are born with spirituality, it is in our blood. We cannot be separated from it. In fact, when we open our eyes and grow up in an environment in which we see our mother is praying, unconsciously we get it.[62]

Narges concurs, saying:

I grew up with Erfan. I was interested in books such as Tadhkirat al-uliya[63], Qu'ran interpretation, etc. I was very enthusiastic in my prayers. I

---

[60] Majidi, (2010). Personal interview. Mashhad, at Mellat park which was a public park. 24 May 2010.
[61] Tisdell, 2003, p. 29.
[62] Sharifi, (2010). Personal interview. Mashhad, at Mellat public park. 24 May 2010.
[63] A 72-chapter book written by the Persian poet and mystic Attar (1142-1220). It is an invaluable source of information on the early Sufis, Muslim Saints and Mystics (See Britannica Online Encyclopaedia).

grew up in a religious family and Erfan was always in our family. It was not something that we chose or searched for.[64]

Such narratives confirm why many women's childhood religion is central to their adult spirituality. Nastaran's conceptualization of spirituality as *"love of goodness"* is drawn from her childhood religion: she mentioned that *"my religious belief was from my family and limited to doing good to have a good next life"*. This normative perspective is consistent with Islamic religious traditions in Iran; for example, we see evidence of this in the cultural and spiritual significance of Ramadan for Nastaran, who was brought up in a religious and spiritual atmosphere. This aspect of the cultural significance of spirituality may also be in part why another woman, Mina, a 59 year-old married retiree with a Master's degree from Mashhad, continued to attend Qu'ran classes and have *jalaseh*/women's religious meeting in her house. Although there were aspects of her religion (Shia Islam) she found problematic, it affirmed her cultural identity as Muslim.

Nastaran, Hamideh, Mina and the eight other women did not choose spirituality over religion because of the positive ways they have constructed meaning within those traditions, rituals, and symbols. They chose spirituality because there were some dichotomies as well as deficiencies between their personal beliefs and the official creed or ideology of their Islamic traditions. They found the official creed lacking in something (e.g. their aspirations and needs) which they have found by pursuing spirituality in *Inter-universal Mysticism*. In short, these women retained the religion of their childhood, either out of habit or because, for some of them, it does indeed nurture their spiritual growth and they are committed to their family and cultural traditions. They thus continue their religious adherence in profound and significant ways alongside spiritual development within *Inter-universal Mysticism*.

Spirituality and Religion as the Same Resource

Spirituality for 5 women in my study is tied neither to beliefs and practices rooted in established Islamic traditions, nor in personal experience, regardless of whether or not they practice their childhood religion or Islam. For them, religion and spirituality are both resources for humans to use to reach *kamal*. They believe in God, the non-material world, and life after death. Although in different ways, they think of both religion and

---

[64] Narges, (2010). Personal interview. Mashhad, at Ghazaleh's house. 23 May 2010.

spirituality as resources to guide people's conduct in their lives, and to help them experience divine existence and transcendence. What is interesting about the stories of these women is that while they consciously identified no difference between religion and spiritually, in their accounts there can be this confusion for the reader that they may go under one of the other categories discussed above. Even though they say they do not distinguish between spirituality and religion, they have multiple ideas about spirituality simultaneously that it might seem as though they do see them as different terms. The responses of the three interviewees I quote here indicate different ways in which these women make sense of spirituality without distinguishing it from religion.

When I asked Afsar, a 45 year-old married GP from Mashhad, about her definition of spirituality, she said:

> *Spirituality is what gives meaning to life or it is feeling* (experiencing) *life in a way that is meaningful. It may be very difficult to define spirituality, but for me it is like oxygen in that if they take it from you, you cannot breathe.*[65]

Her description picks up on one of the main ideas of spirituality as broadly related to meaning-making. Afsar's definition highlights this aspect but also hints at something more: she emphasizes spirituality as the breath of life, indicating that spirituality is always present in life even if it is unacknowledged. Having this perception, Afsar experiences both religion and spirituality as ways to make sense of life. Nevertheless, she was opposed to traditional aspects of religion and said:

> *I do not believe in mazhab* (religion) *in its traditional way. I think everything that becomes as a matter of routine, distances people from their full meaning… the mazhab we have is totally traditional. It is what we have got from our families. But when I started practicing spirituality, I found the real meaning of mazhab … and that both spirituality and mazhab intend to say the same thing.*

What is important for Afsar is that religion is "untouched": not manipulated through time into a tradition or an official institution of rules and doctrines. She goes further to state that anyone, even secularists, who feels inner peace and has that sense of meaning in his or her life, is spiritual. This suggests that having a meaningful life is at the centre of being spiritual, regardless of having faith in any particular religion. While, in her view, spirituality can have different definitions

---

[65] Afsar (2010). Personal interview. Mashhad, at her office. 24 May, 2010.

and interpretations, she said that the truth behind any religion is the same as the truth one searches for in spirituality.

Sara, a 32 year-old single university Physics lecturer from Tehran, had questions about the purpose of human creation and living life. Because of huge contradictions in all she had learned from her parents, she became interested in the mystical and spiritual path of *Inter-universal Mysticism* as a way to find the truth. Considering her family background, Sara's mother is a traditional and religious woman while her father is not at all religious. This huge difference between her parents left Sara conflicted, wondering how such a major difference could exist. Her non-religious father was, in her view, happier in his life compared to her mother whose life, Sara considered, was limited by religion. Sara chose neither way of living and was looking for something higher in human existence. Studying different religions and Islamic *erfan* for the last few years and then participating in *Inter-universal Mysticism* had taught her that:

> *Mazhab and erfan are one way and one resource, not the only and final way. The truth is inside one's own self.*[66]

Sara's view is that human beings have a spiritual dimension which connects them to a higher power (e.g. God) and through which one finds the truth behind living. Her main concern is communion with God or, rather, connecting the inner self with the life force to find the truth without choosing between religion and spirituality since both, in her view, are means to the same goal. In other words, for her, both religion and spirituality guide humans to the same destinations, but in different ways. So it is a matter of personal choice to prefer one way over the other.

Sogand, 43 year-old housewife with a BA from Mashhad, talked about spirituality as a resource in relation to her cultural identity. After discussing her Islamic cultural heritage and her upbringing in a less religious family, she explained that both religion and spirituality are, for her, resources for finding out who she is and how to define it despite the changing conditions of her life.

> *Something inside me attracts me to spirituality. My essence is spiritual, my real identity is being spiritual. I came to this path to elevate this*

---

[66] Sara, (2010). Personal interview. Tehran, at her house. 10 April 2010.

spirituality. This erfan is not apart from religious thoughts. Erfan makes religious thoughts alive.[67]

It can be easy to get a sense of identity by fulfilling others' expectations. Wearing strict Islamic hijab against her family's wishes, Sogand found courage to take a stand through spirituality, determining for herself what she believes and how to understand her identity. This sense of feeling was defined by her as a spiritual process that brings her into contact with her essence or deepest spirit. A key point here is that both spirituality and being religious are, for her, about moving toward this greater sense of one's deepest spirit. Sogand invoked aspects of spirituality to gain confidence in her wearing of hijab and practice of Shia Islam. These practices are in contrast to Roya who, as I mentioned earlier, found herself by relaxing her use of hijab. These different manifestations suggest that what is deemed spirituality seems to encourage women's finding of their true selves, and to allow them to manage a range of different relationships between spirituality and religion.

Commonalities among All Women's Understanding of Spirituality

A belief in life after death was common to all the 55 women's understanding of spirituality. None of the women in the discussion groups, individual interviews, or observations talked about death as the end of life and related it to spiritual life. The spiritual learning within *Inter-universal Mysticism* allows these women to understand more about life after death: it guides them to make a connection between how they should live now and how their life will be after death. As such, they conceptualized spirituality as a form of life direction. These women's responses suggest that God guides human beings and provides life instruction through transcendent forces (e.g. nature, inter-universal intelligence). For instance, Aram, a 29 year-old housewife with a diploma from Tehran, asserted that *"without spirituality, life is not complete ... without spirituality we humans will be lost"*[68]. Some women suggest that the absence of spirituality is associated with distress and restlessness. For example, Afrooz, a 34 year-old divorced university student working full-time as a teacher in Tehran, said "*I do not think those who do not believe in spirituality have deep peace inside*

---

[67] Sogand (2010). Personal interview. Mashhad, at Ghazaleh's house. 25 May 2010.

[68] Aram, (2010). Personal interview. Tehran, at Nahid's house. 8 April 2010.

themselves"[69]. Masoomeh, a 28 year-old single computer engineer from Tehran, also confirmed that *"I have never seen someone who does not believe in God and spirituality and [who] has a peaceful life"*[70]. She stated that this experience is not describable in words and can be felt only by the heart, which constructs meaning, and by what she honours as the feeling of peace in life. What she suggests is that there is a relationship between believing in God and spirituality. Spirituality is a close and personal connection with God through which one finds a meaningful life and experiences peace.

Furthermore, for these women the relationship with God was associated with the experience of power, autonomy, insight, inspiration and the transcendence of boundaries. They argued that their close relationship with God brings change to their lives. In other words, this intimate relationship permeates spirituality with its power to transform their lives. For example Zahra, a 38 year-old married housewife from Mashhad, said:

> *I believe that if I commit a sin tonight, I will not wake up for morning prayer by Azan call; and vice versa if I wake up, that day is a good day.*[71]

Whereas some women like Zahra thought that the lack of such a relationship with God is associated with negative experiences or negative life outcomes, other women such as Mahnaz, a 44 year-old housewife with a high school diploma from Yazd, lived with "a sense of assurance that even seemingly serendipitous events are connected as part of a larger plan"[72]. She said: *"now anything that happens, I say it is God's will so I would not get upset and ask why it happened, I trust his will"*[73].Their trust in this larger plan and in the compassion of God leaves these women with the certainty that all events happen for a greater good and/or as a part of destiny.

---

[69] Afrooz, (2010). Personal interview. Tehran, at Nahid's house. 15 April 2010.

[70] Masoomeh, (2010). Personal interview. Tehran, in my house. 27 May 2010.

[71] Zahra, (2010). Personal interview. Mashhad, at Ghazaleh's house. 23 May 2010.

[72] Mattis, 2000, p. 117.

[73] Mahnaz, (2010). Personal interview. Yazd, at the place I was staying while I was in Yazd/ my cousin's house. 3 May 2010.

Conclusion

Spirituality and religiosity influence almost every aspect of Iranian women's lives: understandings their relationship with God, the self and others; the meaning, direction and purpose of their life; and their responses to oppression and life difficulties. I argued that both spirituality and religion play central roles in structuring these Iranian women's interpersonal relationships, including their ideas about their femininity and motherhood, their way of living (e.g. whether to wear hijab or not), and their definition of official Islam and its social obligations towards women. Through my theoretical underpinnings, I argued that there is a trend to dichotomize religion and spirituality too much, whereas my study shows that although people do make a distinction, there is much that overlaps. For these women, *Inter-universal Mysticism* is an enriching and stimulating environment in which they can express a range of views about the relationship between religion and spirituality. This movement has thus given them conceptual agency and enabled them to have a sophisticated theoretical engagement on their own terms. Therefore, my analysis of the meaning of spirituality for my interviewees develops the work done on spirituality and religion in the west, and shows how growing up and living in a particular (Islamic) cultural tradition affects one's understanding of spirituality.

As a result of their participation in *Inter-universal Mysticism*, these women have developed their mental and spiritual capacities as well as their capacities to think about their conceptual understanding of their spirituality and their lives. I showed how they distinguished the differences or similarities between their religious views and spirituality and how they could apply those understandings in their lives. For these women, experiencing spirituality on this path has actually sharpened and opened up their conceptual agency and enabled them to discover something about life that they had not found outside of the movement. Although there are other ways in which women could experience spirituality in Iran (for example, the path of *erfan*), my respondents have chosen *Inter-universal Mysticism* as a very particular and effective way of experiencing spirituality. In addition, the *erfan* tradition is not particularly woman-friendly as it is quite an androcentric tradition. But *Inter-universal Mysticism*, because of its ideas (e.g. the relationship between love and reason), somehow enables these women to grasp ideas of religion and spirituality in a number of different ways: it doesn't prescribe which direction to choose, with some preferring to keep them together rather than separate them and others dividing them.

All these women, before being drawn to this spiritual path, were religious by belief and/or culture. Choosing to participate in *Inter-universal Mysticism* as an alternative spirituality is, for these women, an experience of going both inward and outward. Their spiritual journey is associated with self-awareness, true identity, inner strength, peace, and the clarification of core values and beliefs. Something about *Inter-universal Mysticism* enabled these women to manage or negotiate the relationships between their personal aspirations and needs, cultural and family influences, and official religious demands and pressures. All these women "strive to make sense of the world and to assert their place in it"[74]. The beliefs, worldviews, and understandings of the values of religious traditions and spiritualties provide an ideological context in which they "can generate a sense of meaning, order, and place in the world that is crucial to their definition of spirituality"[75]. In short, dimensions of spirituality for women inside *Inter-universal Mysticism* involve making personal meaning out of their life circumstances: coming to an understanding of their true self and of compassionate wisdom (the relationship between the realm of *eshq* and *aql*); helping others; and appreciating the importance of connections with God, others and the whole world.

---

[74] King et al., 2011, p. 173.
[75] Ibid.

CHAPTER FIVE

TRANSFORMING LIVES:
CHALLENGING EVERYDAY PATRIARCHY THROUGH INTER-UNIVERSAL MYSTICISM

One of the powerful insights I gleaned from my study was women's own surprise at how life had changed for them. These changes are mainly of two kinds: first, women reported some substantive alterations to their lives; and secondly, women feel able to cope with the lives they have by re-arranging their relations in a way that gives them more satisfaction. Thus, they recounted finding the courage to challenge patriarchal relations and constraints in their homes in situations which had kept them suppressed and unable to have autonomy since childhood. As a researcher, I found myself seeking ways to make sense not only of the changes the women told me about, but also of their amazement at the extent of the changes they achieved.

The key factor in the process of self-transformation on this spiritual path is the practice[1] of *Inter-universal Mysticism* (*ettisal*/connection) in which women are engaged and which determines their aspirations. In particular, I would like to draw your attention to the shift these women made from self-ignorance to self-determination as seen in their narratives of finding themselves on this path, and the conceptual relationship between the practice of *ettisal* and the construction of the self or the practice of women's empowerment in this movement. In this chapter, I argue that there is a relationship between these Iranian women's self-esteem, their identity as women, and their development of faith. I show that there is a connection between how these women think about themselves and the development of their faith through their commitment to *Inter-universal Mysticism*. They experience something inside themselves and realize their own potential which changes their self-image. The path leads them to learn about their capabilities to re-think and re-make their

---

[1] On the path, followers are asked to practice the connections daily or more than once a day if they wish to, in order to benefit from them.

lives on the basis of a new self-understanding and self-confidence. These women begin to see themselves as people who have agency and not as females who are limited in their autonomy in a patriarchal society like Iran.

Understanding Women's Empowerment

Empowerment can be considered as either a process or an outcome and some scholars, such as East (2000) and Staples (1990), have declared it to be both. However, most theorists (e.g. Gutierrez, 1995; Kaminski et. al., 2000; Nelson et al., 2001) have described empowerment mainly as a process, involving the personal transformation of the individual (Pandey, 1996; Zimmerman, 1995). Staples (1990) further proposes that "although the process of empowerment can result in the attainment of particular personal, social, and political goals, empowerment is inherently dynamic, dialectal, and on-going"[2]. He argues that "just as there is no final synthesis, there is no final state of empowerment. Rather the empowerment process strengthens the on-going capacity for successful action under changing circumstances"[3]. While the idea of empowerment as an outcome can be considered, process-oriented definitions have emerged as the more revealing approach to understanding women's empowerment in *Inter-universal Mysticism*. I consider women's empowerment as a process within this movement that enhances women's self-worth and self-determination, allowing them to make choices and gain control over key aspects of their lives.

Because of patriarchal structures and ideologies in Iran, many women have limited control over their lives and lack the self-confidence and opportunity to make choices and manage their lives as they wish. In this sense, for these Iranian women, empowerment involves a process of making change. I agree with Kabeer's notion of choice which "implies the possibility of alternatives, the ability to have chosen otherwise"[4]. She argues about the "move from a position of unquestioning acceptance of the social order to a critical perspective on it"[5]. The kind of power I am referring to, then, is the capacity to bring about change and this change can be in the self, in insights, in social structures, and in relationships with others. I carefully consider the conception of empowerment, as both

---

[2] Staples, 1990, p. 30; also cited in Carr, 2003, p. 11.
[3] Ibid, pp. 31-32.
[4] Kabeer, 1999, p. 437.
[5] Ibid, p. 441.

Gutierrez and Carr suggest, being "a process of increasing personal, interpersonal, or political power so that individuals, families, or communities can take action to improve their circumstances"[6]. Later we will see how the constant process of empowerment through the practice of *ettisal* enables women to make different choices or to know how to act in different situations. It enables some women to say "no" or to express their disagreement and give their own opinions, which they were unlikely to do before their participation in *Inter-universal Mysticism*. In this respect, I suggest that we think of agency as "the ability to define one's goals and act upon them"[7]. I understand agency as a process of decision-making, as well as negotiation, adoption and management. Kabeer suggests that:

> Agency is about more than observable action; it also encompasses the meaning, motivation and purpose which individuals bring to their activity, their sense of agency, or 'the power within'. While agency tends to be operationalized as 'decision-making' in the social science literature, it can take a number of other forms. It can take the form of bargaining and negotiation, deception and manipulation, subversion and resistance as well as more intangible, cognitive processes of reflection and analysis. It can be exercised by individuals as well as by collectivities.[8]

Women's empowerment and autonomy within *Inter-universal Mysticism* involves a capacity both for action and for resistance to, or confrontation with, patriarchal power relations. For the majority of these women, the agency they gain on this path is not a challenge to patriarchy: rather, they have used a number of strategies (e.g. the adoption of ways for conversation and the re-arrangement of their relationships) to deal with patriarchy in their homes. For example, they find ways to disagree with their husbands without damaging their relationship. Their agency in this sense means that they may continue to do what they always did but that they do it with a different state of mind and act based upon their own choices. *Inter-universal Mysticism* has increased these women's agency and ability to change, manage or control their lives in their own ways. Within their new consciousness and strengthened confidence, these women gained the courage to assert control in their lives and to participate in decision-making in new ways. They resist the dominant male order by reducing patriarchal power in their lives and creating opportunities for their own interests and agendas. Their agency can, thus, also be

---

[6] Gutierrez, 1990, p. 149.
[7] Kabeer, 1999, p. 438.
[8] Ibid.

understood as "the capacity to realize one's own interests against the weight of custom, tradition, transcendental will, or other obstacles"[9]. Through the agency they have gained in *Inter-universal Mysticism* these women challenge and transform the existing power relations first in their own homes and then, potentially, in society.

It is important to realise that there are aspects of Iranian patriarchal tradition and culture which are so taken for granted that they have become both normalized and internalised. As Isaacs argues, "one of the ways that oppression disadvantages individuals is by making their subordination invisible. It is seen as the natural order of things rather than as a situation of injustice, so it is not something that we notice"[10]. For example, some Iranian women undermine themselves by seeing it as normal to serve and obey their husbands and mothers-in-law, to take on pressures and problems without complaining, to sacrifice their needs to their families, and not to express their own ideas. They internalize their own lesser status and power without thinking about it. The majority of the women in my study, particularly women in the discussion groups, think that Iranian women are subordinate because, since their childhood, they have learned to be submissive and obedient. Expressions which emerged in the fourth discussion group, such as "*You are going to be a housewife so you should learn to be obedient to your husband*"; and "*You should do everything he wants in order to be satisfied by him and your mother-in-law*"[11] reveal this learned behaviour.

Despite some of our needs, interests and responsibilities which are clearly differentiated by gender in our daily life routines; "there are other needs and interests which do not have this self-evident nature because they derive from a "deeper" level of reality, one which is inscribed in the taken for-granted rules, norms and customs within which everyday life is conducted"[12]. Being a self-sacrificing mother is a key norm within Iranian patriarchal tradition and culture that has become naturalized for many women. Listening carefully to these women's stories, I interpret women's low self-confidence as "evidence of women's internalization of their own subordinate status: their tendency to put the needs of others in the family before their own"[13]. Indeed, patriarchy subordinates women in ways that encourages them to "be passive, dependent, maternal and nurturing,

---

[9] Mahmood, 2001, p. 206.
[10] Isaacs, 2002, p. 138.
[11] Fourth discussion/focus group conducted by myself on 25 May 2010 in Mashhad, at Mellat public park.
[12] Kabeer,1999, p. 441.
[13] Kabeer, 1999, p. 459.

concerned about others, compromising, unambitious, less competitive, disproportionately concerned about physical attractiveness to men. In essence, it encourages women to accept a subordinate place in society, and indeed, hardly to recognize it as subordinate"[14]. However, my interviews indicate that through participation in *Inter-universal Mysticism*, women no longer think that in order to be a good woman and mother they should be self-sacrificing. For example, Sharareh, a 49-year-old married woman who lives in Mashhad, said:

> *I believe Iranian women need these classes because they learn about their family, marital relationship, and their rights both in both home and society. There are many women who do not know about these things and still think that they should sacrifice themselves for others and have no right to even think about it.*[15]

The move from self-ignorance to self-awareness on this path allows women to find their own "self" and act upon it. However, women's autonomy on this path does not happen in isolation. There is a relationship between these women's courage in asserting themselves as individuals and their connection to their family and social life. Eisenstein's notion of choices, self and others is that:

> Individuality can imply autonomy and connection; one can choose to act individually while also recognizing obligations and responsibilities. This requires recognition of the self-determining woman and her choices while recognizing that these choices are not utterly free and unrestricted. This sense of self is interconnected with others, although the self is also independent.[16]

For these women, self-realization has happened within their relationships with others. In other words, their empowering process is relational, as it is not possible to have a sense of "self" which is not in part connected to others. In this regard, Isaacs proposes that "we think of the self-in-relation, not in terms of the obligations or responsibilities that being in relation generates, but rather in terms of the possibilities for action that being a self-in-relation creates"[17]. Here we understand these women's rethinking of "self" which consequently has affected their relationships with "others".

---

[14] Isaac, 2002, p. 131.
[15] Sharareh, (2010). Personal interview. Mashhad, at Mellat public park. 25 May 2010.
[16] Eisenstein, 2004, p. 192.
[17] Isaacs, 2002, p. 137.

In my interviews, women talked about how the experience of *Inter-universal Mysticism* deepened their personal integrity as individuals while enabling substantial bonding to take place with their family and friends. They understand themselves differently from their pre-path selves, but they also appreciate their relationships with others. Even though this was not what they expected, participating in this movement has enabled these women to make important shifts and changes in their relationships and, following changes they have made in their connections with others, to see the world and themselves differently.

The Practice of *Ettisal*

My study of *Inter-universal Mysticism* indicates that women's "discovery" of a sense of self evolves throughout the transformation process on this path. In my introduction to *Inter-universal Mysticism*, I mentioned that in order to understand the impact of this movement on women, it is necessary to explain the significant aims of this mysticism and how these work in practice. The process of people's self-realization on this path is significantly different from realizing oneself through self-transformation in other mystical traditions, e.g. Sufism. The search in most mystical and spiritual traditions is centred on the "interior life" and the person's relationship with God. It means seeking "perfection" and going beyond the requirements of ordinary life, for example using practices like *zikr*[18] or *muraqaba*[19] in Sufism. The Sufi's aim is "to reach a state through which they would be in direct relationship with God, unite with God, be annihilated in God, subsist in God, and then attest to the oneness of God"[20]. But in *Inter-universal Mysticism*, followers do not need to undertake this type of journey because this path argues against the interiorized and exclusive tradition of spirituality. It talks about spirituality in a way that is not exclusively about personal integrity and transcendence, but is about perfection and growth toward a whole human life, rather than just an interior life. It is the process of integrating every aspect of being and living. It is a very distinctive feature of *Inter-universal Mysticism* that spirituality on this path transforms relationships between others and the inner-self.

---

[18] *Zikr* means reminding oneself or mention. See glossary.
[19] The practice of *muraqaba* can be likened to the practices of meditation attested in many faith communities. See glossary.
[20] Angha, 1996, n.p.

The spiritual quest for completeness within the self is part of the larger goal on this mystical journey. This process follows a spiral rather than linear path and takes place within the context in which the realities and truth of life are interdependent. In *Inter-universal Mysticism*, a person who attends to both reality and truth is called *rend*[21]. A *rend* has moved beyond perceiving a dualistic split between the inner and the outer journey, the natural and the supernatural, matter and spirit, self and other, humanity and nature. This can be compared to similar thoughts in other religious and mystical traditions, for example, the Christian distinction between matter and spirit[22], or outer and inner meaning in the Iranian mystical tradition of *erfan*. In *Inter-universal Mysticism*, reality is not sacrificed to truth nor truth to reality. The *Rend* is a person who looks for truth in reality and vice versa: i.e. they can see both reality and truth. This concept is another way of looking at the ideas considered in my discussion of *aql* and *eshq*, where I argued that experiencing spirituality on this path means to be present in both modes at the same time. Therefore practices of seclusion, sheltering in a cave, asceticism, and the torture of the body, which are common on some mystical paths like Buddhism or Sufism, make no sense for *rend*.

The interdependence of lived realities, in the view of *Inter-universal Mysticism*, means that every life form is essentially related to every other. So the process of the self, becoming whole (*tan-e vahedeh* in Farsi means 'united body',[23] a phrase to which Mr. Taheri refers), does not entail isolation since the self is essentially connected to God, to others, and to the whole world. It has to do with the self, becoming aware of its interconnectedness and then living in ways that nurture the relationships between self, others, God, and the world: this is described by Mr. Taheri as being in *magham-e solh* which, in Farsi, means "peace position". The process involves finding peace with the self, then with God and the world, and finally with others, which is the most difficult part because of the

---

[21] Taheri, 2008.

[22] Thomas, 1971.

[23] The best description of this term in *Inter-universal Mysticism* is in a poem by Saadi, one of the major Persian poets (1213-1291). The poem reads:

Human beings are members of a whole,
In creation of one essence and soul.
If one member is afflicted with pain,
Other members uneasy will remain.
If you have no sympathy for human pain,
The name of human you cannot retain. (M. Aryanpoor translation)

existing differences between people.[24] In a broader sense, spirituality on this path centres on one's awareness and experience of relatedness and relationships. It is this relational component of lived experience which has enabled these women's lives to be transformed.

The growth process in *Inter-universal Mysticism* starts through gaining insight into the aim of human creation and existence as a "united body". The majority of my participants (49 out of 55 interviewees) described the spiritual practice of *ettisal*/connection as their first influential spiritual experience and, thus, as a significant life event. The role of the spiritual practice of *ettisal* in the making of these women's selves is crucial, even if they do not continue practising. 52 women indicated that even if they are absent from classes and movement activities such as spiritual healing, they still benefit from its positive effects in their lives. For them, this spiritual practice of *ettisal* in *Inter-universal Mysticism* develops inner wisdom for outer change.

I observed one of the introductory sessions of *Inter-universal Mysticism* conducted by Nahid at her house on 8 April 2010. The session was attended by 20 women and 5 men with the aim of helping them become familiar with this path and to decide whether they wanted to participate in its classes. The interesting thing for me was that when Nahid asked them to close their eyes and experience *ettisal,* everyone did it without any question. To their surprise, people reported that during this activity they felt cold or hot in parts of their body and became relaxed. Here, I need to mention that *ettisal* has both a physical and a psychological effect. Therefore, anyone experiencing *ettisal* is able to comment on both its physical and psychological effects.

In my individual interviews, Sayeh, a 41 year-old educated housewife from Mashhad, described her first experience:

My first experience of ettisal was before my participation in this movement. I had an exam and my friend asked me to try the ettisal to overcome my stress. It was indescribable. I got high self-confidence. This experience made me believe that there is a supernatural power that it is beyond our imagination and is helping us. Then I joined the movement.[25]

---

[24] This is taken from the teaching handbook used internally by practitioners and Masters for teaching. Mr. Taheri approved this translation from Farsi to English in 2006.
[25] Sayeh. (2010). Personal interview. Mashhad, at Mellat public park. 25 May 2010.

Sayeh's experience indicates how this practice affects many of the women I encountered in my interviews, focus groups and observations. The practice of *ettisal* strengthened women's self-esteem and enhanced their confidence and belief in their abilities and, in general, their belief in themselves as human beings.

One of the features of *Inter-universal Mysticism* is its indirect use of *ettisal*. This means that followers can practice *ettisal* on behalf of anyone who is not inside the path. Through this type of connection, one person can gain some of the advantages of *ettisal* as practiced by an *Inter-universal Mysticism* follower indirectly, without his or her knowledge. In other words, this type of *ettisal*[26] is intended for those who are not inside the path to connect to the inter-universal common sense network themselves. The women in my interviews talked about using this type of *ettisal* to construct better relationships with their family members, indicating how this practice has brought peace into their homes. For example, practising the indirect use of *ettisal* on her sister, Sayeh was very surprised by its result: she reconciled with her sister after a separation of many years. She said that as soon as she learned about this indirect use of *ettisal*, she practised it for her sister. She was at a social gathering when she saw her sister and was shocked when her sister came towards her and unexpectedly said hello. The majority of the women recounted similar experiences of the indirect influence of *ettisal* on their husbands, children, family members or friends. If a woman practices *ettisal* for someone else, she may actually then relate to that person differently, and that is one of the changes in women's lives brought about through *Inter-universal Mysticism*.

Summing up my understanding of empowerment processes through the practice of *ettisal*, I argue that what women learn in *Inter-universal Mysticism* is self-esteem and self-confidence, which enables them to discover who they are and who they want to become. This circular process of empowerment redefines what it means to be an autonomous woman: they understand themselves better, find a sense of their own worth and potential, and develop good relationships with others. As Meyers suggests, these "agentic skills bring women's voices into alignment with their individual identities and their lives"[27]. They therefore have more confidence which enables them to do things differently, either through changing their attitudes or, if it is a question of acceptance, gaining acceptance through their own choices rather than having such choices forced upon them.

---

[26] See Taheri, 2008, p. 101.

[27] Meyers, 2002, p. 1.

Women's Narratives of Self and Life Transformation

Participating in this movement has enriched women with their self-knowledge, revealed their emancipatory potential, and strengthened their ability not only to define themselves in their own terms, but also to act upon their identities as they understand them. The women's stories, in this section, reveal various aspects of these Iranian women's lives in relation to patriarchy, and show the changes they were able to make through the empowerment process in *Inter-universal Mysticism*.

The extensive influence of this movement is illustrated by Afrooz's story. Afrooz is a 34 year-old twice-divorced woman who lives alone in a small house with her landlord. She has experienced emotional and financial hardship throughout her life. Her parents divorced and remarried so she was forced into her first marriage by her father–to a criminal and drug addicted man with whom she has two children–when she was just 14. When her husband beat her harshly on the street, observers called the police and rescued her upon which she gained her first divorce. Because of the patriarchal tradition in Iran and Islamic laws regarding divorce, Afrooz had to give up custody of her children to her in-laws and suffered a mental breakdown shortly after, since she would not see her children for more than ten years. Her second husband, the love of her life as she put it, left her after two years of marriage because he no longer wanted to live with her. Afrooz heard about *Inter-universal Mysticism* at a desperate moment during her second divorce. The person she thought of as the oldest and most trustworthy and knowledgeable man in her family suggested that she participate in this movement when Afrooz asked for help.

Before joining *Inter-universal Mysticism*, Afrooz was a very angry and aggressive woman who used to take tranquilizer pills. She did not participate in or attend any social gatherings or celebrations and she used to get tongue tied whenever she met new people. But she has changed a lot on this path and her life has been significantly transformed. Afrooz was among those women who independently volunteered to participate in my study and at the time of our interview she was very calm and confident. She told me that

> *Maybe it is interesting for other women. Just being on this path for two years now I am a university student. I could not finish high school as I was forced into marriage. But this path made me powerful. Now I am a good provost and a teacher at an adult school and everyone respects me and likes me.*[28]

---

[28] Afrooz, (2010). Personal interview. Tehran, at Nahid's house. 15 April 2010.

Afrooz thinks that if she was not on this path, because of her two heart-breaking divorces and difficult life, she would have become very depressed. In *Inter-universal Mysticism* feeling the presence of God in *ettisal* and gaining the insight that humans are not left alone on this earth gives women like Afrooz the strength and power to face their problems and seek a better life. Afrooz said that since she participated in *Inter-universal Mysticism* not only has she become successful in her education (she finished her high school education and was a second-year university student at the time of our interview), but she has also been promoted in her job because of the changes to her aggressive attitude and an improvement in her performance. She was confident that now she is happy with her life, she can help other women in similar situations,[29] a relevant point for my later argument about the feminist potential of the *Inter-universal Mysticism* movement.

One of the most common issues among women was their inability to say "no" to others' demands. Women have accepted this position because of the fear of damaging important relationships. Participating in *Inter-universal Mysticism* has enabled these women to assert their power and say "no" in situations in which they are normally expected to behave submissively. For instance, Sharareh is a 49-year-old married woman who lives in Mashhad. She is a housewife with no university degree but who has developed a strong personality which led her to criticize the traditional roles of women in families. She found out about *Inter-universal Mysticism* from her sister-in-law who lives in Tabriz and talked about her participation in this movement. Sharareh, who changed from being an obedient wife to become a self-confident woman, says:

> *I have got complete self-confidence. Now I can speak for myself very easily. I was very conformist and would do everything for others, even if I would not like to do so. I would not say 'no' because I thought I should keep my family and husband happy and satisfied without paying attention to myself and what I want. But I am not like that anymore. Now I say 'no' very easily and nobody becomes angry. I have found peace of mind.*[30]

---

[29] Afrooz works in an adult school in one of the poor areas of Tehran. I mentioned in chapter one that girls who are married or who have been married cannot attend ordinary schools and thus special adult schools exist for them. The girls who Afrooz is working with have mostly experienced the same difficulties that she herself has gone through. So by teaching them about this movement and the practice of *ettisal*, Afrooz is now happy that she can help them.

[30] Sharareh, (2010). Personal interview. Mashhad, at Mellat public park. 25 May 2010.

This comment from Sharareh indicates how women continue to fight an inner struggle between their personal wishes and the expectations of others. She spoke about how participating in this movement and practicing *ettisal* led her to begin to believe in herself, to learn how to say "no" and live without needing to please others. Through this change she created conditions for her autonomy which, she was surprised to find, maintained her good relations with others and gave her peace of mind. Therefore, she no longer experiences a conflict between her desires and those of others.

Another perspective was offered by Nooshin, a 41-year-old married housewife who lives in Yazd. She came to *Inter-universal Mysticism* because of her daughter's illness, but never imagined that it might influence her own life. She told me she had never attended any classes because she had believed that she was a very strong, calm and positive woman, so that whenever she had a problem she had thought that she could handle it herself. But when she came into *Inter-universal Mysticism* she was surprised by the new things she found out about herself.

> *Although I used to think I did not have any problems, now I understand the extent to which I was depressed* (unhappy). *Now I say oh my God what a problem I had...[31]*

While she had thought she was self-sufficient before joining *Inter-universal Mysticism*, Nooshin found that she had been living with a hidden depression reinforced by the belief, which she now saw as mistaken, that a good woman should sacrifice her desires for the sake of others, should be strong and tolerate all burdens without complaint. This is a good example of women's internalization and unthinking replication of their own lesser status in a patriarchal culture. Nooshin used to be silent and very obedient during any arguments since she thought that she should be like that. She used to think and care about others and, as she put it, had never realised that she was a human being too. This endorses my general understanding of Iranian women who often do not see that they too have their own human rights. In patriarchal culture, the identity of many women is usually regulated by their male guardian who holds the power: this is generally first their father, then their husband. For example Zhaleh, a 43-year-old housewife from Tehran, thought that she did not have any right to think for herself. She said:

> *I thought that I did not have any authority. In our childhood, our fathers have authority over us. Then when we marry, our husband and his family*

---

[31] Nooshin, (2010). Personal interview. Yazd, at my cousin's house. 3 May 2010.

*have this authority. So I thought that we have no authority and identity for
ourselves as a human being...[32]*

Indeed, the traditional ethic of self-sacrifice demands women's denial of
their own needs for the sake of others, thus limiting their sense of their
own value. The ways in which patriarchy in Iran controls women's lives
psychologically makes them internalize what they understand to be their
own value. Iranian women first learn to ignore the self and ultimately to
deny their own inherent worth. This internalized self-ignorance caused
Sharareh, Nosshin, Zhaleh and 25 other women to talk about how they
remained silent, denying their own needs in order to please others, and
behaving in an obedient way accepting that, as women, they are of
secondary importance.

However, the availability of alternative ways of thinking in *Inter-
universal Mysticism* has enabled these women to recognize that in order to
be a good woman and mother they do not need to be oppressed and self-
sacrificing, as is understood in Iranian culture. Most of the changes are not
dramatic; some of the women's descriptions of their lives since joining the
path continue to feature self-sacrifice yet the self is perceived differently
by them and they find ways to manage their circumstances differently. As
I see it, these women's processes of empowerment and self-transformation
through the practice of *ettisal*, involves not only a deep understanding of
patriarchy, but also a willingness to discover their own personal power and
ability to effect change. Hence, the knowledge of their own inherent value
and self-affirmation lets them find their own unique "self" and the
capability to live by taking account of both their wishes and those of
others. This can be understood as an experience of awakening or
enlightenment.

The practice of *ettisal* has enabled these women to move from self-
ignorance to self-awareness and self-confidence and has defined a shift
from authority imposed on women from the outside, to authority derived
from within. I call this process empowerment: the turn to the self. It
encourages women to express their inner journey and outer struggles.
Nooshin, for instance, became aware of this deeper reality of her 'self' and
moved toward knowledge of her own inner authority and inherent value by
healing her 'self' through the spiritual practice of *ettisal*. She says:

*Before I was timid and worried that if I said something, it might make them
angry. But I am not like that anymore. This path has made my spirit*

---

[32] Zhaleh, (2010). Personal interview. Tehran, at Nahid's house. 8 April 2010.

stronger and I am much more energetic. Now *if my husband says something, I respond to him and won't be quiet and let him say whatever he wants* (she laughs). *Although I say my words in a good way I do say them and everyone is surprised that I have become like this.*

According to *Inter-universal Mysticism* and its collective practice of *ettisal*, an awakening to the potential for autonomy does not take place solely within the individual. It strengthens people's ability to be individual without making them isolated and enables them to rebalance their relationships with other people. Women inside this path experience direct union with God, others and the whole world. The concept of the "united body" in *Inter-universal Mysticism* gives confidence to women to be individual and have good relations with family and friends. Rather than losing their own self in interpersonal relationships they come to an authoritative and confident but relational sense of self. Nooshin's words– "*although I say my words in a good way I do say them*"–indicates that while she has gained the confidence to express herself, she looks for ways to maintain good relations and this shows how she deals with others to manage her family situation.

Another interviewee, Sayeh, a 41-year-old married housewife with a BA in nursing from Mashhad, said she had serious family problems at the time that she learned about *Inter-universal Mysticism*. Her husband had left her and her children and her relationship with her family was about to be destroyed because of a major misunderstanding. She repeatedly tried, unsuccessfully, to save her relationship with her husband until her friend who was inside *Inter-universal Mysticism* asked for Sayeh's consent to help her with *ettisal*: this is an example of the indirect use of *ettisal*. Sayeh was not inside the path and her friend practiced *ettisal* on her behalf to help her. Sayeh thinks that without the help of divine consciousness on this path she could not have changed and saved her marital life.

My husband returned home. All problems were solved. It was like something is working behind curtains and solving problems one by one. It was amazing, unbelievable.[33]

After joining *Inter-universal Mysticism* herself, Sayeh said that throughout the 11 months that she had been inside the movement (she was at level 7 of the path at the time of our interview) many good things had happened to her. She was able to influence her husband and change his patriarchal

---

[33] Sayeh. (2010). Personal interview. Mashhad, at Mellat public park. 25 May 2010.

attitude towards her. She said *"now he is a very calm and loveable husband"*.

Now I want to turn to a contrasting conception of agency that I encountered in my interviews, "a contrast that sheds light on how we might think of agency not only as the capacity for progressive change but also, importantly, as the capacity to endure, suffer, and persist"[34]. Some professional women dealt with pressure in their lives by practicing *ettisal* in *Inter-universal Mysticism*, which increased their tolerance. These women perceived it as a positive influence. For instance, Misha, a 30-year-old single full-time engineer from Tehran, has practiced *ettisal* since she heard about it from one of her close friends. She has never attended *Inter-universal Mysticism* classes because she thinks that the experience of this mystical journey through the practice of indirect use of *ettisal* alone is sufficient for her and that she does not need its lessons. She found that the experience of practicing *ettisal* via her friend inside the path really helps her whenever she has a problem or feels angry, anxious or sad. It helps to calm her down and make her more patient. She said:

> *I am not taken as seriously as men in my work place in any position and this problem really bothers me. The spiritual practice on this path helps me to tolerate and accept the situation. Although it does not change it, at least it helps me to be less annoyed.*[35]

In another case, Azam, a 36-year-old married psychologist from Yazd, thinks that the most important influence of this path in her life was the increase in her stamina and endurance. Azam lives with her husband, who is psychologically sick, and her daughter. She learned about *faradarmani*/spiritual healing in *Inter-universal Mysticism* from a friend when she had lupus, a serious health problem. First, she enquired about this spiritual healing and then decided to join the path. After two months in this movement, her health improved. Azam was also looking for relief from other burdens and pressures in her life. In my interview with her she said that although she was not yet very satisfied with her expectations of the movement, she was happy that her health was better and her life was less stressful, so she can accept things the way they are. In her words:

> *I have not got the capability that I want to have because I am still in level three. But I saw women from higher levels that have more satisfaction and have achieved more powers. In my private life, I have got more power to*

---

[34] Mahmood, 2001, p. 217.

[35] Misha, (2010). Personal interview. Tehran, in her house. 7 April 2010.

accept things for the way they are. I learned to be less sensitive and have
fewer expectations. In the work place too, I have less stress and deal with
problems easier.[36]

Likewise, Maryam learned to cope with her life through joining *Inter-*
universal Mysticism. Maryam is a 36 year-old educated married woman
from Hamadan, who has lived in Mashhad since her marriage. She works
part-time as an accountant for her husband. She was lively and excited
during our interview. She said that she had been forced very early to marry
someone who had a very different cultural and religious background from
her. She said that if she could go back she would not have married early
nor married someone from Mashhad, which is a centre of strict religious
observance, being a major pilgrimage site. Her husband and his family are
dogmatic Muslims and continually criticize her hijab and religious
practices. Since she moved to Mashhad, Maryam has had to wear strict
hijab, adapt to new rules and accept her new family. For example, she told
me she is not allowed to read books in front of her husband or to be out of
the house when her husband is due to return home.

> *I am very patient; I tolerated huge pressures. Before* (participating this
> movement) *I used to cry at night. I did not let anyone to find out how much*
> *I suffer. But now it is much easier for me to tolerate. I feel much better and*
> *feel less pressure.*[37]

Maryam was at an early stage of the path–level 2–when I interviewed her.
She was very excited and said she likes to attend multiple sessions in a
week and hoped to pass all the levels very soon. She said she would
become very sad if the government were to ban these classes. She thinks
that after only 3 months inside the path her capabilities are growing daily
and she is more determined than before. She said she performs her duties
better and has improved relations with others. Most importantly for
Maryam, she can now help her daughter, who strongly disagrees with both
her father and brother's strict religious beliefs and is under great pressure
from them to wear Islamic hijab. Maryam said her teenage daughter used
to cry and ask her for help, because she (her daughter) likes to look like
modern, fashionable girls since in her view they are more beautiful than
those who wear Islamic hijab. Although Maryam could not resist her

---

[36] Azam, (2010). Personal interview. Yazd, in a waiting room at a public hospital.
1 April 2010.
[37] Maryam, (2010). Personal interview. Mashhad, at Ghazaleh's house. 23 April
2010.[38] Maryam, (2010). Personal interview. Mashhad, at Mellat public park. 25
May 2010.

dogmatic husband and his family, she has tried to help her daughter by providing her with colourful cloths and scarves in different styles to look nice even with her Islamic hijab. Maryam said that she also practises indirect use of *ettisal* for her daughter and talks about everything she learns in the class with her in order to help her to cope better with her situation and find ways to live the life she desires.

What the narratives of women like Misha, Azam, Maryam and the 12 other women reveal is that the practice of *Inter-universal Mysticism* does not necessarily enable one to change reality. It does, however, enable them to accept or tolerate situations, both within the family and in wider society, which in the past have not been tolerable. The influence of connections in Misha's problem solving, or Azam's healing of her disease through *faradarmani,* are experiences on this path which enable women to become stronger and wiser in their everyday lives. Furthermore, via such connections women actually feel power through wholeness. The ability to effect change comes from the process in which women begin to experience unity with others. For example, Azam said

> I do not have problems with my husband anymore because I understand him as an ill person'. Similarly, Maryam said: 'I accept my husband and his family's attitudes towards me more easily as I understand they are restricted to their dogmas and do not have correct insights.

As Azam and Maryam started to perceive their interrelatedness to their husbands and others and the concept of the 'united body', it became easier for them to be more tolerant of difficulties in their lives. In short, what we have here is a notion of agency defined in terms of individual acceptance of a social structure. Just as the women's self-esteem structured the possibilities for action, as it did for Sharareh and 26 other women, so too did it increase the endurance of Misha, Azam, Maryam and 12 other women. However, these changes might not be tolerated by their patriarchal society.

Criticisms of the *Inter-universal Mysticism* Movement

In order to give a rounded picture of the benefits as well as the difficulties experienced by the women participating in *Inter-universal Mysticism*, I will now examine different kinds of critical responses to women and to the movement. It will be helpful to first explain some of the criticism that women dealt with personally, then to consider how women themselves criticised some aspects of *Inter-universal Mysticism*, and finally to explore how the movement itself has recently come under criticism.

Some husbands and families could not tolerate changes in women and complained that these women were not the same people because they were no longer obedient. When I asked Maryam, a 39-year-old married architecture engineer from Mashhad, about the reactions of others to the changes she has made in herself she replied:

> *Everyone criticizes me now and says I am not the person I used to be and they do not like the new me just because I am not obedient anymore and speak of myself. But I am very happy because gradually I am feeling: I am my 'self'.*[38]

Similarly, in my interview with Hamideh, a 36-year-old housewife with a BA from Yazd, she mentioned that:

> *I used to be very obedient: everything that my mother-in-law forced me to do, I would accept. But I changed; now I give my opinion and politely disagree with her. She is angry with me and wonders why I have changed.*[39]

Such quotes vividly indicate the patriarchal relations these women deal with at home or, rather, the patriarchal culture in which many Iranian women are living and in which they are expected to be submissive. However, I would mention that such negative and critical reactions to the confidence women have gained in *Inter-universal Mysticism* could later change; we have seen, for example in Sayeh's story, how some of these women can affect their families through the indirect use of *ettisal* and change their husbands' attitudes towards them.

Despite the fact that these women experienced criticism for the changes they made in themselves, they had their own criticisms of the movement. In my interviews, women had different views on the structure of *Inter-universal Mysticism*. For example, while some women think that an enrolment fee for the classes is necessary, others think of it as a kind of obstruction to joining the movement for those who cannot afford it. On the other hand, some complained about the high number of participants in a class which hinders them from participating in discussions or asking questions. Interestingly Maryam, who is a doctor and homoeopathist, criticized the disparity of educational level in her class. She said:

---

[38] Maryam, (2010). Personal interview. Mashhad, at Mellat public park. 25 May 2010.
[39] Hamideh, (2010). Personal interview. Yazd, at her house. 03 May 2010.

There are highly educated people in the class sitting next to some with less education; and this difference in educational level causes problems. Because some women start to talk about their experiences, family problems, their relations with their husbands, etc. which makes class like a story telling and those who are not interested become bored.[40]

In addition, those women with higher education criticized the ability of Masters and commonly said that many Masters, particularly those with only high school diplomas, could not deliver the lessons of *Inter-universal Mysticism* in the way Taheri does. They criticized Taheri's training of students to become Masters and argued that simply by passing a few levels on this path, someone who is not highly educated or who does not have enough knowledge in similar fields cannot be qualified to teach *Inter-universal Mysticism*. For example, Roya, a married 31-year-old with a BA working full-time from Yazd, and Sogand, a 43-year-old housewife with a BA from Mashhad, both said that

Masters with no or less education mostly deliver lessons from their own points of view, not Taheri's view, and this causes problems (Roya).[41]

We need experts in this field who have done research in order to be Masters not just anyone who passes 6 levels on this path (Sogand).[42]

While for some women with less education and a lower social status becoming a Master is considered a kind of empowerment in terms of being able to teach in front of others and earn money, as was the case for two Masters I interviewed, for other women, especially those with higher education or a higher social status, the possibility that anyone can qualify to become a Master seems to be an inefficiency of *Inter-universal Mysticism*'s system.

In addition to such criticism by women and their families, more recently anyone involved in the movement has faced both official and unofficial criticism from the regime. My primary textual materials show that critics of *Inter-universal Mysticism* in Iran call this movement one of

---

[40] Maryam, (2010). Personal interview. Yazd, at Hamideh's house which was a safe place to conduct the interview. 3 May 2010.[41] Roya, (2010). Personal interview. Yazd, at my cousin's house. 5 May 2010.

[41] Roya, (2010). Personal interview. Yazd, at my cousin's house. 5 May 2010.

[42] Sogand (2010). Personal interview. Mashhad, at Ghazaleh's house. 25 May 2010.[43] There are different articles written against this movement published on websites and in newspapers, all of which I gathered during my fieldwork in Iran. These are listed in my primary material reference list.

the deviant sects which does not benefit from official Islamic doctrine.[43]
By contrast, Taheri, the founder of this movement, argues that this path is
a new approach to the thousand year-old teachings of *erfan* and Iranian
Islamic mysticism and is based on religious beliefs. Apart from critics'
uncertainties about the principles and teachings of this mysticism, their
main concerns are the high number of women on this path, mixed gender
classes and meetings of men and women in which women do not wear
proper Islamic hijab. The blogs of opponents of this movement published
pictures of women without hijab with men at parties or mixed social
gatherings–which are opposed by the regime's ideology and policy–falsely
claiming that these were *Inter-universal Mysticism* classes. Using their
authoritarian Islamic ideology, such opponents criticize women in *Inter-
universal Mysticism* and deny that mysticism can be practiced by women
who wear makeup and who do not have proper Islamic hijab. For example
on *Bonyan Marsoos* (2010), one of the blogs whose function is criticism of
deviant religions and sects, they ask,

> How it is possible for someone to reach God while she or he is
> participating in mixed classes, in which young women attend without hijab
> and sit next to boys? How can they purify their souls while there exists
> female coquetry and intellectual pretension? Isn't it the strict order of
> Islamic religion that we should avoid participating in places where Islamic
> values are not respected? Don't our distinguished Shiite jurisprudents
> prohibit the relationships between strange men and women?.[44]

Critics think that the high numbers of women participating in such
activities is damaging to families. For example, on 14 March 14 2010 *Raja*
news wrote:

> We witnessed some families, whose members had good and warm
> relationships, torn apart because of the *Inter-universal Mysticism*
> movement. This movement, by resorting to mysticism and metaphysic
> sciences, attempted to deceive and then abuse its followers.

Inter-universal Mysticism is accused of opening a way for women to act
freely, a criticism which was heightened after President Ahmadinejad, in
October 2006, "called on Iranian women to return to the family home and

---

[43] There are different articles written against this movement published on websites
and in newspapers, all of which I gathered during my fieldwork in Iran. These are
listed in my primary material reference list.
[44] Translated by myself.

devote their energies to their primary responsibility of raising children"[45]. Such critics think that women do not make proper use of the freedom they find in this movement. In fact, it is a long established argument that women begin to believe that they have freedom and will consequently lack moral concern and restraint so that they become self-willed and cause family conflict and moral corruption.

However, my discussion with women inside *Inter-universal Mysticism* suggests that the opportunity and freedom the women have found in this movement have enabled them "to both formulate and enact self-determined goals and interests"[46]. 15 women described *Inter-universal Mysticism* as a form of support: in fourteen cases women managed to improve their marital relations and in one case that of Afrooz mentioned above, strength was gained to live as a divorcee. Aram, a married housewife of 29 with a high school diploma, said that because of certain problems her relationship with her husband had become cold and they had decided to li
ve apart for a few months before deciding on their future. At the same time, she joined *Inter-universal Mysticism* which helped her lot. She said:

> *Fortunately, participating in these classes and practicing ettisal helped me very much and we reconciled very soon, after being apart for one and a half months.*[47]

In contrast to what official critics argue, Aram's experience and those of 14 other women show that not only has participation in *Inter-universal Mysticism* benefited these women's marital lives, but has also improved it. Even where divorce is some women's best solution, involvement with this path helped them to have a better life as a divorcee.

Regardless of these criticisms, both from opponents of this movement and from its followers, the stories of these women show how women's lives have been substantially transformed since they chose to participate in *Inter-universal Mysticism*. Although two women, who were at a very early stage of the path, said that they had not seen any changes either in themselves or in their lives, analysis of the remaining 53 narratives show that women's freedom and self-determination happens in this movement as a result of their experience of exploring, finding and affirming their own self, or strengthening their knowledge of their inherent value through searching for an authentic spirituality on this path. In other words, while

---

[45] Barlow and Akbarzadeh, 2008, p. 22.

[46] Mahmood, 2001, p. 207.

[47] Aram, (2010). Personal interview. Tehran, at Nahid's house. 08 April 2010.

these criticisms are important, the weight of evidence from the interviews, the focus groups and observations provides substantive proof of how their lives have transformed since they joined this movement. Women's stories in interviews emphasise various practical, personal and emotional ways in which they have benefited from participation in *Inter-universal Mysticism*.

Conclusion

There is specific gender component to the question of choice in contemporary Iranian society: it is not just about people not having a choice, but it is something about being a woman. There are particular difficulties associated with being a woman in Iran. In other words, there are ways in which choices are more difficult for Iranian women than for Iranian men. I am not saying that Iranian men do not encounter difficulties–indeed this movement also offers men the opportunity to be more in charge of their lives and more able to choose–however, there are particular aspects of the movement which are important for women because of the particularities of Iranian women's lives in a patriarchal society. In this chapter, I demonstrated how women's participation in this movement has transformed their lives. I argued that joining *Inter-universal Mysticism* has affected these women in different ways and, for some of them, has changed their everyday lives. What women learn inside the movement gives them new tools, sources and insights which they can use to change their lives or, if they are living the same life, to find strategies for greater happiness. *Inter-universal Mysticism* encourages them to transform self-doubt, feelings of worthlessness, and a lack of confidence into the courage to be autonomous and look within for insight that heals themselves and their difficult lives.

CHAPTER SIX

THE RELATIONSHIP BETWEEN FEMINISM AND WOMEN'S ACHIEVEMENTS IN INTER-UNIVERSAL MYSTICISM

All but one of the women participants did not want to be called a feminist, yet although these women distanced themselves from the concept of feminism, I will suggest that there are aspects of feminist thought which are illuminating for understanding their experiences. While this poses a challenge for me, I argue that their rejection of the term feminist is related to both social and cultural influences currently dominant in Iran which encourage negative views about being a feminist, and to the specific influence of *Inter-universal Mysticism*, a movement which is gender neutral as it evokes spirituality beyond gender. Feminism is a rich intellectual cultural tradition within which there are many tools that I could draw on in order to shed light on what these women said about themselves, even as they themselves would not be happy with that term.

I have shown how women's participation in the *Inter-universal Mysticism* movement has begun to change their life in various ways, whether enabling them to behave differently, or helping them to find strategies for coping with existing relationships in their family or at work. This "empowerment" of women's lives raises interesting questions about how such personal changes might or might not be understood in a feminist way. When I asked my participants if they suggested this path to other women (without even mentioning the word "feminism" in my question) their responses were: "*Yes, but I do not have a feminist view about it*"; "*there is no difference, I recommend Inter-universal Mysticism to both men and women*"; "*I am not a feminist, I suggested it to women more just because I am more comfortable with women than men*". However, despite these responses I wanted to consider whether feminist thought is relevant for understanding these women's lives. One of the main reasons I undertook this study is because a large percentage of the followers of *Inter-universal Mysticism* are women, so much so that many of the meetings I attended felt like a "women's group". Although *Inter-universal*

Mysticism does not deal directly with women's family and social problems and its purpose is to help all humans reach perfection through spirituality, these women's stories reveal its role in women's real lives. In other words, the issues I talked about in the previous chapter regarding these women's agency and self-determinations are ones which have engaged much feminist thought and research, and so it makes sense to investigate the relevance of such understandings to women's experience of *Inter-universal Mysticism*, as well as to assess where this study may extend or challenge existing feminist perspectives.

Here, then, we find an interesting contradiction; on the one hand, these women push away from the term feminism, but on the other, the substance of what they are saying about themselves and their lives echoes feminist scholarly thought about feminist context or feminist implications. In this chapter I examine this interesting contradiction. Women's achievements on this path, such as realizing themselves to be powerful, being able to challenge things in their own way, and their sense of seeking *kamal*/fulfilment, can be all read as aspects of feminism. Asking, why these women reject feminism? How being on the path changes their conception of gender in both their daily and spiritual lives? What kinds of notions of feminism, particularly spiritual feminism, might be useful for understanding women's achievements in *Inter-universal Mysticism*? These issues are considered in the following three sections.

Social and Cultural Influences

There are cultural reasons why these women are not particularly attracted to the idea of feminism. Early twenty-first-century Iranian women are not very interested in using the term feminism because cultural norms are quite anti-feminist. There is also a lack of knowledge about the diversity of feminisms in the world today. Except for a few women's groups and activists, the majority of people in Iran–like many people around the world–do not have a positive opinion of feminism as they have assumed that feminism is about hating men and exists mainly for educated and privileged women. Here I should note that there are men and women in Iran who believe in feminism, but that it is not common for them to use the word "feminist", instead substituting the label followers of "women's rights movement in Iran". In this regard, in her interview with parazit on 13 March 2011, Shadi Sadr, an Iranian feminist and women's rights activist, said that the feminist movement in Iran does not have a long history. Although there have been women's rights movements in Iran for nearly 100 years, feminism is a new movement for both its fans and opponents. The negative connotations of feminism have been reinforced by the dominant group who benefit from the gender rules of the Islamic government and the present structuring of power in Iran. This misrepresentation of feminism has occurred for the same reasons that Iranian women's lives have been manipulated within official Islamic patriarchal culture, particularly after the Islamic revolution in 1979. It is noticeable that both government and religious authorities consider education to be the foremost means to reproduce and expand their version of Islamic culture and to shape Muslim believers. They have enforced reform of the philosophy, objectives, policies and assessment of education at both basic and higher levels in accordance with Islamic principles, through which they have made a sharp distinction between their Islamic views and the secular views of the west. They define themselves as pious and morally superior Muslims and represent western people as heartless, tyrannical and unjust.

In terms of women's issues, the regime sometimes defends its position by arguing that while they do not think of women as unequal, they do think of women as different, and I would argue that this is the tradition of male Muslim thinking which goes back mostly to the 1960s and early 1970s. For example, Ayatollah Morteza Mutahari, a famous Iranian cleric and politician, argued against the equality of rights between men and women in the west in his book, *Woman and her rights in Islam,* and viewed the women's rights movements as the deterioration and corruption of the family. He stated:

> They forgot that equality and liberty related to the relations between human beings, as human beings only. No doubt, woman, as a human being, is born free like any other human being and in that capacity she has equal rights. But woman is a human being with certain peculiarities, as man is a human being with certain other peculiarities. The traits of their characters are different and their mentality is distinct. This difference is not the result of any geographical, historical or social factors, but lies in the very making of them. Nature has purposely made them different and any action taken against the intention of nature would produce a disastrous result.[1]

More generally there have been difficulties for politically minded Iranians when dealing with gender politics and feminism.[2] For example, in her article "Troubled relationships: women, nationalism and the left movement in Iran", Moghissi (2004) argues that nationalists and leftists in Iran were

---

[1] Mutahari, 1974, p. 5.
[2] See for example Afary,1989; and Paidar,1995.

concerned that feminism is un-Iranian. Therefore, there is a long established and widely spread resistance to the implications of gender politics and feminist movements which has been more forceful since the Islamic revolution. In the religious authorities' view, an intellectual term like feminism, which deals in particular with gender matters, is inappropriate because it originates from the west and is therefore a threat to official Islamic values and gender ideology. In this way, the education system and the dominant Islamic ideology, plus the legacy of Iranian culture over many decades, have created a very negative presentation of feminism. My own experience can here offer an example which illustrates this point well.

During my fieldwork in Iran, I visited the women's studies centre at Tehran University, as I had been invited to share my knowledge with their students. The teachers told me that I was not allowed to talk about feminism in class because it is a negative western term, and therefore not deemed applicable to Iran. Surprisingly, I found that the research subjects in women's studies were limited to women in Islam and women in the family: gender, sexuality and violence against women were banned subjects. When I asked students why this was so, they responded that it is because of their political connotations. One of the girls jokingly commented: "*here even if you drink water, it is political*". This quote shows to what extent the official Islamic government is seen to have an effect on people's lives and can control their interests. Interestingly, on 22 May 2012 news reports claimed that the Community Council to promote development and the Humanities Council of Cultural Revolution headed by Gholam Ali Haddad Adel had changed the title of "women's studies" courses at universities in the country to "women's rights in Islam" in order to be in agreement with the Islamic order. One of the lecturers there gave me books and articles by academics, all of which criticized feminism. For example in an article on feminism and family, Maryam Farahmand, an expert on women's issues in the humanities and cultural studies, wrote:

> Although the principles and foundations of this movement are built on the struggle against patriarchy and discrimination against women, the misconstruction and radicalization of the movement has led the situation and status of women to be more complex. Although we cannot ignore the considerable changes in women's situations, women have paid a heavy price for these changes, which is noteworthy. Through the failure of the family structure, marriage, and the freedom to prescribe the limitless bounds of sexual stereotypes of women under the excuse of fighting against women's oppression, all radical, liberal and lesbian feminisms in all three waves of this movement not only damaged women's dignity and personality, but also severely undermined the position of women in the

roles of mother and wife and reduced them to a sexual attraction. In addition, with too much emphasis on employment issues and women's social and political participation, feminism draws women into another valley in which they have to be assertive and to demonstrate masculine identity. Feeling of insecurity, lack of focus in terms of family, personality instability due to frequent contradictions of feminist identity, depression, loneliness, sexually transmitted diseases in terms of relationships and abortion are the full implications of feminist waves.[3]

I would argue that this attack is directed specifically towards feminists in the west, rather than feminism elsewhere. Some critics of feminism think that only westerners are feminists, which is not the case. Here, I need to acknowledge that even those who advocate women's rights in Iran often don't like the term feminism, and argue that it is a white, middle-class movement. Attacks on feminism as a western phenomenon are part of a broader chauvinist trend in Iranian culture, both official and non-official, which is anti-westernism. Western feminists are blamed for the breakdown of the family and some think that the way in which western feminists consider women's issues and family needs are wrong. For example, based on their Islamic view of the difference between men and women, officials criticize western feminists for considering men and women as similar, regardless of what they see as their natural differences. However, criticism of feminism in the west by people like the women I met at the Tehran women's studies centre does not mean that they accept patriarchy. They reject the idea that women should be isolated at home to raise children and serve the family, arguing that the roles of the family should not be forgotten and that the status of women as mothers and wives should not be reduced through their full-time participation in public and in the community. They think that women need a balanced position and that through a systematic approach–which they see as Islamic–all aspects of women's physical and psychological concerns are considered and their individual and family demands are addressed. In this respect, there are different forms of feminism in Iran.

There are two main groups of feminists in Iran: Islamic feminists, who argue that "women's problems result from misguided male interpretations of Islam's holy texts, as opposed to the principles"[4] underlying Islam; and secular feminists, who base their arguments on appeals to a non-religious principle of human rights. In their article on "Prospects for feminism in the Islamic Republic of Iran", Barlow and Akbarzadeh argue that: "building a

---

[3] Farahmand, 2007, pp. 2-6, translated by myself.
[4] Barlow and Akbarzadeh, 2008, p. 25.

state to uphold and promote Islam is part and parcel of religious-oriented feminism as it considers the attainment of Muslim women's rights and dignity to be entirely possible in the context of a consummate Islamic state"[5]. On the other hand, secular feminists view the role of Islam in politics as central to the problems that Iranian women face. In their view, addressing women's issues "is seen to depend to a very large extent on the separation of the state and its legal codes from Islam"[6]. Despite putting up a long and hard battle, neither group of feminists has fulfilled their goals, meaning that "they could not produce substantive and lasting changes to the status of women in Iranian society"[7].

Thus, one of the reasons my respondents rejected feminism is that they think feminists cannot make changes in women's real, practical lives. Women in my fourth discussion group gave the example of divorce in Iran and how it is difficult for a woman to continue her life as a divorcee. They argued that although feminists' efforts to change laws are noteworthy, they cannot change people's attitudes, such as how they regard divorcees or how a mother can live without her children. They also commented that feminists have not dealt with child custody issues or those of temporary marriages. They argued that it is in *Inter-universal Mysticism* that women gain the power to renew their lives and feel happy, as was the case for Afrooz. For these women, it is the humanism of the path which gives them confidence and, as I now argue, influences their views on feminism.

Inter-universal Mysticism's Influence

I contend that these women's perceptions of feminism are not only affected by the negative messages of society and culture, but also by the thinking of *Inter-universal Mysticism*. This mystical path holds human equality to be ideal and values all human beings. These women consider that feminism prioritizes women over men or is even hostile to men, which goes against the notion of the value of all human beings: the aspiration of the movement is to transcend gender. Followers are committed to a concept of humanity that is gender neutral, which raises a paradox. On the one hand, my respondents do feel enabled to handle their female situation differently, more effectively and more happily, but at the same time they experience themselves as having something beyond gender.

---

[5] Ibid, p. 26.
[6] Barlow and Akbarzadeh, 2008, p. 32.
[7] Ibid, p. 26; see also Ahmed-Ghosh, 2008.

My interviews with these women indicate that before joining this movement many of them had what I would term feminist thoughts, even if they did not see it that way. For instance, Zhaleh, a 43-year-old housewife from Tehran, told me that she used to fight for equality and say that men and women are equal, even though her husband used to tell her to forget about these thoughts. She assumed she should agitate and do something, but she did not achieve these aims. In this movement, she said, her insights transformed and she changed her attitudes towards men since she learned that all human beings are equal and that gender does not matter.[8] In fact, *Inter-universal Mysticism* talks about the world of unity in which humans come to understand the concept of the unified body of the world of existence, the world whose component parts are all considered the manifestations of God. In this condition, humans find themselves interacting and unified with all the constituents of the world of existence. This message leads its followers beyond the boundary of human thought and reflection to promote what is considered the highest level of intellect and insight and make them aware of the fact that human beings are part of the same body. Thus, followers not only expand their insight and reflection beyond tribal, national, racial and even international limits, but also direct their thoughts, perceptions and insights to the world of existence.[9] Majidi, a 45-year-old housewife from Mashhad, indicated how she changed from being a feminist to thinking beyond gender.

> *Since I was at high school, I used to have feminist thoughts and think that women should be feminists: sexual difference really mattered to me. I had this feeling towards my husband. But now I think I had a lot of oppositions all of which are solved on this path. Now I think there is no difference: gender does not matter, we all are human beings in one body. I used to make myself apart from my husband but now I could easily forgive him.[10]*

The path provides a ways of re-conceptualizing the self and its relationship to the other (and to the universe). It offers a view of reality as a continuous expression and manifestation of a single source and reflects the unity behind the multiplicity of our divine natures. This realization of interconnectedness between living beings and with the universe is what led women like Zhaleh and Majidi to distance themselves from feminism. However, there are notions of feminism which might help to make sense

---

[8] Zhaleh, (2010). Personal interview. Tehran, at Nahid's house. 8 April 2010.
[9] Taheri, 2008.
[10] Majidi, (2010). Personal interview. Mashhad, at Mellat public park. 24 May 2010.

of these women's experiences, even if they consider that feminism is
irrelevant.

The Applicable Notions of Feminism

Why do I use the word "feminism" when these women object to its
separatist associations? I do so because, like Cooke, I believe that
feminism is much more than a driving ideology which organizes political
movements. Beyond all its bold attitudes, I think that by considering
women's lives through a feminist point of view, feminists understand the
role of gender in society and the way it is organized. That is why I can
make the case that even people who reject the term need to take this kind
of feminist thought seriously because it asks questions of the workings of
culture, society and politics. Through feminism, research such as this
study is facilitated by analytical tools through which the unjust situations
of women can be assessed and the gendered dynamics of society, culture,
and politics explored. Cooke argues that "feminism provides a cross-
cultural prism through which to identify moments of awareness that
something is wrong in the expectations for women's treatment or
behaviour, of rejection of such expectations, and of activism to affect
some kind of change"[11]. Feminism, as a rich school of varied thought,
analyses women's lives and looks for something better. Eisenstein argues
that

> There will be a variety of ways that women's equality, freedom, and justice
> are expressed and defended; as long as self-determination–which
> encompasses individual choices and access (equality) to them exists as part
> of this process. So, feminisms belong to anyone who is committed to
> women's ability to choose their destiny; to be the agent of their own life
> choices as long as they do not colonize another. As such, no one simply
> owns feminism's particular meaning.[12]

In my view, feminism is about what different women have in common and
how women go about conducting their lives. Because of patriarchy,
women experience oppression, disadvantage and inequality in their
choices and actions. "All feminists–theorists and activists alike–regard the
questions of why women suffer these wrongs, and how they can be righted
as crucial"[13]. In diverse and evolving movements, "feminists understand

---

[11] Cooke, 2000, p. 92.
[12] Eisenstein, 2004, p. 186.
[13] Meyers, 2002, p. 2.

gender inequality and interpret women's experience in relation to patriarchy, men and other women"[14]. I use these perspectives on feminism as an intellectual framework for analysing how these Iranian women's lives have changed inside *Inter-universal Mysticism*.

The main subject matter here, however, is the unity women on this path are looking for: unity among men and women, not just women. These women do not see themselves as self-determined individuals who search for independence from unjust male control, but as deeply connected to each other, to their husbands and their families, and ultimately to God. Despite the fact that one can be connected but also be unequal or powerless, women in my study criticize the ideal of self-directed independence in feminism as they understand it. They think that the language of feminism does not describe their understanding of self as connected or in relation with others as well as the nature of their engagement with the powers they gain through *Inter-universal Mysticism*. However, I would argue that feminism is not necessarily about women's individualization. Eisenstein's work on feminism, for instance, points to connections and relationships rather than individualization and separations. She argues "it is a feminist articulation of individuality which recognizes the autonomy of the woman without imagining her as solely alone, nor negating her identity as one and the same with her family or community"[15]. Her work and my study of feminism confirm the notion of self in relation to others.

To argue against an individualistic interpretation of feminism, it is worth comparing two notions of individualism by Sampson (1988): "self-contained individualism and ensembled individualism". Self-contained individualism reflects a psychology of the person or self that is exclusionary. For example, Spence defines individualism as "the belief that each of us is an entity separate from every other and from the group"[16]. Sampson notes that this belief:

> [L]eads to a sense of self with a sharp boundary that stops at one's skin and clearly demarks self from non-self. The psychology of ensembled individualism, by contrast, is based on a more inclusive conception of the person or self: the circle would include others within the region defined as self.[17]

---

[14] Ibid.
[15] Eisenstein, 2004, p. 206.
[16] Spence, 1985, p. 1288, cited in Sampson, 1988, p. 16.
[17] Sampson, 1988, p. 16.

There are many feminists, for instance Islamic and black feminists, who imagine a social notion of the individual that is connected to family or community. Their feminism is "the recognition of the communal, familial and interconnected concepts of the self"[18]. All these types of feminism bear relation to the self-determining women in *Inter-universal Mysticism* who see themselves "free but not alone; obligated yet independent; equal and also unique"[19].

One of the strands in feminism is a particular concern for gender equality and this converges with *Inter-universal Mysticism*'s spiritual concern with human justice. I argue that there are areas of common ground between *Inter-universal Mysticism,* these women, and contemplative feminist spirituality. Feminist spirituality originates in the process of feminist consciousness-raising. At the heart of this new consciousness is the conviction that all beings are interconnected: each affects the other in the movement toward future life[20]. These feminists recognize that being individualistic is problematic and alternatively interpret the self not as independent and unconnected, but as essentially in relation to others[21]. However, one common argument among feminists is that it is women's close alignment with "caring" roles and behaviour that keeps them subordinate. Meyers argues that "many feminists have wondered whether this understanding of the self and care-based agency may be encouraging continued participation of women in their own subordination"[22]. In both the discussion groups and individual interviews, women argued that it is not only men who are responsible for their bad behaviour, but that women themselves contribute to their subordination as they go along with it.

> *I used to think women are victims of our male dominant tradition. But now I find that women have been oppressed by themselves due to a lack of belief in themselves and self-confidence. All that caused them to be submissive.*[23]

To make a change, they argued that they need to change themselves and that it is also important for them to struggle with male power. They think that the changes in their families and husbands will happen when they start

---

[18] Ibid, p. 193.
[19] Eisenstein, 2004, p. 214.
[20] Zappone, 1995.
[21] Isaacs, 2003.
[22] Meyers, 2000, p. 377.
[23] First discussion/focus group conducted by myself on 17 April 2010 with Masters of the path in Tehran, at Nahid's house.

to make changes in themselves. Aram, a 29-year-old housewife with a diploma from Tehran, clearly explained

> *Inter-universal mysticism is excellent. The least it can do is that you will find yourself. I think it is very good for women more than others. Because women think they have been born to serve others. But here they learn about unity and that it is they who give direction to their lives. Our women do not believe in themselves and this is why we have patriarchal practices. Women always worry about divorce and being alone. Because of their dependencies, social taboos and these fears, unconsciously they open a way to patriarchy. But here on this path they find out about their values, goals and abilities. This path helps them to find their essence and raises their insights which give them power and strength.[24]*

In this vivid quote we can see what I consider to be the growth process on this path. Finding the self and its essence followed by heightened insights can be interpreted as the empowerment process and gaining agency and strength to manage things differently. Notions of agency and autonomy are vital to feminist attempts to understand women's subordination and oppression, and so I understand these women's ability to be effective agents and active participants against their subordination as a kind of feminist agency. It is also important to note the perception of gender by Aram when she says "*I think it is very good for women more than others*". Here, Aram articulates the interesting paradox of the gender non-specificity of the path and how she thinks of gender by making a distinction between women and others (men).

Analysis of my interviewees' stories revealed that all these women had some sort of feminist thought before joining *Inter-universal Mysticism*, either consciously or unconsciously, which has been influenced by the insights they have gained in this movement. I contend that these women are conflicted between their previous feminist views and the beyond-gender insights of this path. For example, women at higher levels of the path considered that as women gain self-confidence and self-esteem on this path, they will no longer allow themselves to be recognised as worthless and that this is very good for "women". This is interesting for if, as these women say, gender does not matter, why are women here more important than men? These women, who are not interested in feminism, to some extent want an un-gendered or beyond-gender view of spirituality on this path, yet nonetheless know that the world in which they live is shaped by male dominance. I have chosen some of the women's narratives which

---

[24] Aram, (2010). Personal interview. Tehran, at Nahid's house. 8 April 2010.

illustrate the feminist implications and inconsistencies in their words (I have bolded the expressions which, in my view can be read as feminist):

> ***This is very good for our girls*** *however it is good for both girls and boys.* ***But first for women*** *as the role of women to influence men is more than that of men on women. But there is no difference: every human being could have influence on the world. There is no gender for Inter-universal Mysticism, but it depends who has the more effective word.*[25]

Or

> *Yes,* ***I want women to grow****. Of course there is no difference between men and women, but because* ***women have more problems in our society*** *and they also do not believe in themselves, I can say they need this path more. But I do not say this through a feminist view of the matter that just women not men [need the path]. No, it is not like that. The important matter is that we achieve change.*[26]

Or

> *I wish we could reach a stage in our lives where there is no difference between men and women. Women accept this more easily than men, whose pride does not allow them. If there was not such political situation around this movement* ***we women could change this view among men.***[27]

Reading these comments shows that these women understand themselves to be separate or distinct in some ways from men, even while they say that there is no difference between men and women. What, then, does gender mean to them?

The dominant Iranian culture views men and women as different, while the thoughts of *Inter-universal Mysticism* go beyond gender. Thus, there are two approaches: one is that women think about their gender in relation to acceptance or rejection of the conventions and traditions of patriarchy in their culture, the other is that they see themselves either as women or as un-gendered human beings. I argue that ideas of gender differ from context to context; hence, *Inter-universal Mysticism* provides an opportunity for these women "to rethink the constructions of womanhood and then remake

---

[25] Fourth discussion/focus group conducted by myself on 25 May 2010 in Mashhad, at Mellat public park.
[26] Aram, (2010). Personal interview. Tehran, at Nahid's house. 8 April 2010.
[27] Second discussion/focus group conducted by myself on 12 May 2010 with women at an early stage of the path in Tehran, at Nahid's house.

them"[28]. So, Aram's point about women is that women need to think more and remake their definition of being a woman. In my discussion group consisting of Masters of *Inter-universal Mysticism,* women agreed that a lack of self-confidence and self-knowledge caused them to be oppressed. Therefore, although this path is not gender specific and aspires to transcend gender, it does not reject gender and, furthermore, teaches people how to live in this world and reach perfection or fulfilment, which means that "gender" matters. These rather open ended views of gender and feminism help to understand the way in which these women could learn how to live with their difficulties and opens up questions of their agency and self-esteem.

Although these women do not openly identify with feminism, their goals and ideas have feminist implications. In three of my discussion groups, women commonly said that they thought they had contributed to *mardsalari* (patriarchy) in society as they treat their daughters and sons differently. They let their sons do whatever they want while their daughters are expected to be obedient and to stay at home. Recognizing this and changing traditional ways of raising their children in order to eliminate patriarchy from their homes is, to me, "feminism". In this context, these women become activists who negotiate for social and political change. Whether it is in their homes or in public, as O'Reilly argues, "anti-sexist childrearing, from this perspective mother work, is redefined as a social and political act through which social change is made possible"[29]. These women also argue that Iranian women contribute to their own oppression, thereby showing their awareness of the traditional beliefs that legitimize male domination, such as the traditional preference for sons. They discussed how they are brought up to be submissive and obedient to their fathers, brothers and later their husbands' wishes and their critique of this pattern is also what I consider a feminist view.

In another discussion group, women who were at the first level of the path talked about the different positions of women as both wives and mothers and argued that if each of them is able to influence men in their families, they can influence society more widely. This is in tune with the thinking of *Inter-universal Mysticism*, which suggests that human beings will survive in unity not isolation. To grow and reach perfection, each person is responsible for helping others to grow as well. All 55 women I interviewed also talked about the indirect influence of *Inter-universal Mysticism* on parents, siblings, husbands, children and friends. This is

---

[28] Scheiwiller, 2009, p. 214.
[29] O'Reilly, 2010, n.p.

quite remarkable when considered from a feminist perspective, because the indirect effect of this mysticism on members of the family, particularly fathers and husbands, is one of the most important factors in challenging patriarchal relations at home. These women talked about how their involvement in *Inter-universal Mysticism* has changed their husbands' attitudes and increased their respect and love, as mentioned in Sayeh's story in the previous chapter. Their attempts to alter their husbands' behaviour through indirect use of *ettisal* and to fight against patriarchal practices from within their homes are actions that, I argue, have feminist implications. One of the women at the first level of the path gave the following example:

> *Today I called my friend to ask why she did not come to our class. She said her husband does not allow her [to attend] anymore; because of the political situation and official condemnations of such movements, her husband told her he would not let her participate in such movements which are like a sect. So I think that as this woman could not influence her own husband how could she change a patriarchal society? We women ourselves should start from our homes; even training our sons or our children is very important. There is no expectation of this change happening very fast, but Inter-universal Mysticism has made it fast through its connections.*[30]

She is plainly talking about changing patriarchal practices through changing gender power relations at home–treating husbands differently, and the importance of training sons–which all are relevant to feminist thought, even if these women do not see it that way or do not want to use the term feminist. Significantly, these women, who were at the beginning stage of the path and had not had much experience of the effects of the movement, were talking about gender, which indicates how the lessons of *Inter-universal Mysticism* can later affect a feminist way of thinking.

Most of the women inside this movement invited men in their family or network of friends to consider a similar journey. They think that the shared experience of the path between women and men is one of the essential components of a free and peaceful culture. In my interview with Nahid, a Master on this path whose students are mostly women, I asked if the increasing number of women in this movement was important for her. She explicitly responded that she does not have feminist point of view and said that men and women should grow together. In her opinion, a self-determined woman cannot be successful unless a man accompanies her.

---

[30] Second discussion/focus group conducted by myself on 12 May 2010 with women at an early stage of the path in Tehran, at Nahid's house.

We have seen empowered women in our families, workplaces and society, but men have poisoned their way. So in my view, men and women should rise to the same level. If we see that women's groups have problems and are not successful, it is because they only think about women and not men. While here, both men and women, both highly educated and less educated groups will reach the same level of insight on this path as they become a united body.[31]

Likewise Hamideh, a 36-year-old married housewife with a BA degree from Yazd, said she likes women to participate in this movement but, for her, gender is not generally important. She thinks that if men join women on this path it will be much easier for women to progress. She said there is a big difference between talking with a man who grows on this path and one who does not understand any of it. In her words, '*in truth, if men join the movement, it is a help for women'.[32]*

These women, and even men in solidarity with women inside this path, argue that if they really are one part of the whole, the healing of others is necessary for the health of self. The pursuit of mutual relationships is an indispensable step toward reaching perfection, as understood on this path. All of my respondents share the view expressed by Zappone that the "main force for Cultural Revolution emerges when women's personal power is nurtured to effect political change. But this is not just any kind of power"[33]. Like spiritual feminists these women are, in my view, talking about "potency for effecting change that only comes when one acknowledges that we are each part of a vast organism that is in trauma"[34]. I would argue that although feminism can focus on how patriarchy affects women's lives, feminist movements, likewise, involve men just as deeply as they do women, albeit in dramatically different ways. In other words, "to the extent that feminism is about patriarchy as a whole and how we all participate in it, then change requires that both men and women understand it, since each brings distinct points of view to the work"[35]. Despite the fact that only women themselves can speak about their own "experience of oppression, men have a lot to contribute to understanding patriarchy as a whole, and particularly male privilege and men's participation in it"[36]. Therefore, I do not see any disparity between

---

[31] Nahid, (2010). Personal interview. Tehran, at her house. 8 May 2010.

[32] Hamideh, (2010). Personal interview. Yazd, at her house. 3 May 2010.

[33] Zappone, 1995, p. 41.

[34] Ibid.

[35] Johnson, 2005, p. 101.

[36] Ibid.

feminism and these women's desire to have men beside them when making changes in their lives.

The aim of women's life transformation in *Inter-universal Mysticism* is dependent on "collective solidarity in the public arena as well as women's autonomy in the private space"[37]. Involvement in *Inter-universal Mysticism* gives women the capacity to rethink, remake and reimagine the world and therefore to live in the world differently on the basis of their self-confidence and self-understanding. This, I am arguing, is the relationship between feminism–feminist spirituality–and women in this movement. Feminists in spirituality similarly seek personal integration of mind, body, emotions, and spirit while remaining in relation with others. In her book, *The hope for wholeness: a spirituality for feminists*, the spiritual feminist Zappone argues,

> [S]piritualities of women's power critique the suppression of female power both in the psyches of women and in the construction of the social order. Within this context women examine the psychological and sociological effects of patriarchy on the inner life and examine outer struggles of women to become themselves and take responsibility for creating a new order.[38]

She further argues that spiritual feminists:

> [D]elve to the deepest parts of themselves – alone, with others, with nature – to break apart the patriarchal conditioning that they are powerless, unimaginative, and unable to heal themselves or the rest of life. They reach inside the self to find a new source of energy beyond patriarchy.[39]

Even though feminists are commonly interested in raising awareness and in the elimination of patriarchy, several strands of feminism, including spiritual feminisms, are concerned with humanity and aim for equality in life. Such feminist aims are similar to the main target of women in this movement, which is to live in a world of unity and be a 'united body'. Hence, I suggest that the connection between these spiritual women and feminism is their shared impetus towards a new world and a new way of being in the world.

Furthermore, in my fourth discussion group in Mashhad women argued that it is good if feminist groups cooperate with women inside this movement.

---

[37] Kabeer, 1999, p. 49.
[38] Zappone, 1995, p. 18.
[39] Ibid, p. 41.

The least this movement can do for women is that women get their self-confidence or increase it, because they see themselves in connection with something supernatural. With this mentality, they move, they talk, they behave, etc. It gives them power in their actions. If feminist groups act under this mysticism, they will be more effective and can gain people's trust in themselves. If these groups were successful, they would do something, or at least could convince women. We have women who follow such groups but they do not believe they can be successful: but here women move themselves.[40]

They suggested that as women choose to participate in this movement, their knowledge effectively expands, their insights change and they begin to reflect on their lives. They begin to identify why they are living and thus become critically aware of their relationship to others and to the whole world. This re-constructs their identity and offers new possibilities for their agency, which is a crucial point in making changes in their lives. The practice of *ettisal* on this path fosters the creative, intuitive, healing and relational activities of these women. But these women think that feminist organizations and Islamic and secular feminists in Iran have more access to social and political organizations, even though women's agency and empowerment exists inside the path. Therefore they think that if feminists and women inside *Inter-universal Mysticism* movement cooperate they will achieve more. They said that the cooperation of women's organizations and this movement in particular can have an important role to play in creating the conditions for change.

Conclusion

In this chapter I examined the paradox that exists among women in relation to feminism: on the one hand these women refused the term feminism–either for cultural or spiritual reasons–but on the other hand, we have seen that the term has some value for understanding what has happened to them. Speaking for myself, as the researcher, I have found these concepts useful because I am myself a woman who is involved in the *Inter-universal Mysticism* movement, who has experienced the same conflict between what I have learned on the path and my understandings of feminism, and I have changed from being passionate about women's issues (before joining the movement)–in particular the elimination of violence against women–to thinking beyond gender (after gaining new

---

[40] Fourth discussion/focus group conducted by myself on 25 May 2010 in Mashhad, at Mellat public park.

insights on the path) and then to reconciling both through conducting academic research about women inside this movement from a feminist perspective.

I approached women's narratives through a feminist lens, which was helpful in understanding their stories. I suggested how the women's changes in *Inter-universal Mysticism* could be read from the perspective of a scholar in feminism. On the one hand, these women do not find the labels of feminist or feminism helpful; on the other they do have a clear sense of a changed perspective on their gender subjectivity. *Inter-universal Mysticism* for them is about raising self-awareness that allows them to gain confidence and to understand themselves as gendered human beings. Therefore, they are less submissive wives and mothers as they have gained the confidence to renegotiate those roles which are gendered. Like Cooper, who studied Plotinus and feminism, I contend that although the lessons in *Inter-universal Mysticism* "might be seen otherworldly and far from the concern of feminists, there are principles and intuition that may be valuable for feminists particularly for feminists' reconstructive works in religion and spirituality"[41]. I argued that the women inside this movement and feminists, particularly spiritual feminists, both share the deep experience of personal integrity and interrelatedness of life's realities which motivates inspiration and action to transform the world.

Finally, my analysis from a feminist perspective shows that there is a feminist potential in *Inter-universal Mysticism* which provides positive ways of re-conceptualizing the self that identifies "who these women are and how they are constructing new identities and negotiating a new presence"[42] in their family and society. As a result of this process of bringing my feminist perspective to the women's own words and analysis, I feel I am in a position to make some original propositions about the potential relationship between Iranian women, spirituality and feminism or female self-realisation and self-fulfilment. This is perhaps one of the most unexpected and original thoughts to have emerged from this study.

---

[41] Cooper, 2007, p. 73.
[42] Cooke, 2000, p. 91.

CHAPTER SEVEN

CONCLUSION AND RECOMMENDATIONS

Give up searching and you will find
Suspend your mind and all will bind
The deeper you dive the surface hides
The surface you seek the depth confides
The core and shell are all but one
So rest your soles, for here you're found
In His presence, safe and sound (Mowlana)[1]

It was a big and beautiful park, busy with people exercising on a warm, sunny morning in May 2010. We entered the women only section of the park where women could practice different sports and exercise in a relaxed environment. In a corner of the playground under the shadow of a big tree I saw a group of nearly 20 women, ranging in age from early 20s to late 60s, wearing different kinds of hijab, sitting next to each other on a cloth on the ground and chatting. On my final day of doing field work in Iran these women welcomed me warmly. I was very surprised, as I did not expect that number of women to be there voluntarily taking time to share their experiences with me. They told me it had been three years since five of them had started studying *Inter-universal Mysticism* with a Master in their homes and now they are a group of nearly 100 women. They were smiling and looked happy and healthy. Among them was an old lady wearing a black chador with a walking stick sitting on a bench near us. She said she could not walk well but she had come to this meeting as she would do anything in support of this movement.

I end as I began, with a story drawn from my experience of women on the path. The stories of these Iranian women whose participation in *Inter-universal Mysticism*, in increasing numbers over the past few years has been active in developing a movement, offered: insight into the resultant changes in their lives and reflected the importance of understanding that women's choice of spirituality on this path has shifted their consciousness and visibly altered their ways of functioning in the world which, in turn,

---

[1] Mowlana is one of the great mystical poet of Iran: see chapter three for further information. Translated by myself.

could profoundly affect the way women view themselves and others, the transformation that I like to call "the birth of celestial light" in these women's hearts.

My study has emphasized the importance of understanding how women use faith and spirituality for personal and social support and as sustaining resources to deal with gender based discriminations. I maintained that this is part of a tradition in which Iranian women have often turned to various religious and spiritual practices for support, believing that such rituals help them to connect with the higher being and with their inner strength so they can endure the hardships of daily life. The development of spiritual paths like *Inter-universal Mysticism* after the Islamic revolution, as I mentioned before, provides insights into a society that is complex and disillusioned with unfulfilled religious revolutionary goals. Women's choice of this movement is one of the ways in which women, as both social and political actors, express their critical dissatisfaction with the regime and challenge patriarchal and gendered relations in Iran in both the public and the private spheres. Having identified important reasons for women joining this movement, I have been able to argue that for women, *Inter-universal Mysticism*, with its flexible and broad framework, provides a range of support for helping them maintain their efforts to manage difficult situations and adversities in their lives (chapter three).

I argued that spirituality for these women is connected to their belief in God, feeling his presence and the transcendent dimension of life (chapter four). Examining women's perceptions of the two constructs of religion and spirituality, I opened up the discussion to suggest that while these women's perception of spirituality is rooted in Iranian Islamic cultural and religious traditions, it forms a distinctive and important self-described identity for all the women I interviewed. Among many available ways of "being spiritual", these women have been attracted to *Inter-universal Mysticism* because it presents an experience of spirituality in a modern way rather than the traditional way that they know about, uses rational discourse, and also allows them to be spiritual (and if they wish, religious) but to distance themselves from the dominant orthodoxy of present-day Iranian Shi'ism. I also showed that the spirituality these women experience in *Inter-universal Mysticism* is relational, which means not only that they have a sense of a relationship with their own selves, gaining self-awareness and self-confidence, but that they also feel a connection with God, the whole world, and with other people. Through their participation in this movement, spirituality for them centres on the awareness and experience of this relatedness or relationship. Having conducted such an analysis of women's spiritual experiences, I am able to argue that this particular exploration of spirituality and the relational component of lived experience–which is appreciated, discussed, and enjoyed by women inside *Inter-universal Mysticism*–upholds their agency and has enabled their lives to be transformed.

I further explored ideas of agency alongside women's understandings of self-realisation and life transformation (chapter five). From the personal stories of the narrators, it can be seen how they questioned inherited patriarchal traditions and negotiated a balance between their own wishes and what others expect from them. I have argued that this is a (re)construction of identity and belonging that requires women to question who they are and who they want to be. This movement acts as an accessible space in which not only can women's life and health problems be alleviated, but in which they can also negotiate conflicts between officially prescribed religious practices and their own religious beliefs and aspirations. These women's stories suggest that observers should recognize the role of this movement in encouraging and facilitating women's self-empowerment and life transformation. These women gave many examples of how "being spiritual" helps them to move through and beyond difficult life situations. Of course it should be acknowledged that such changes can also come about in other ways, but for these particular women "deep structural changes of thought, feeling, and actions spring from"[2] the realm of spirituality in *Inter-universal Mysticism*. Involvement in spirituality is appreciated by them as a way of approaching life in terms of how the spiritual and the material can interact. Thus, the narratives of these Iranian women in *Inter-universal Mysticism* not only offer some hitherto unexplored approaches to the topic of spirituality that is framed in the language of religious feeling or practice, but they also reveal life transforming insights and the capacity for women to make use of them. My conclusions may be similar to those of research on spiritual movements in Europe or America, but they are new within the field of feminist research on Iran. Specifically, my study contributes to knowledge of how the spiritual and the material interacts to transform both women's self and life.

It has been my aim to look at women's spiritual experiences in *Inter-universal Mysticism* using a feminist lens that is "capable of articulating the intersection of personal and social transformation"[3]. I argued that the themes discussed by women in groups and individually have important

---

[2] Chin, 2006, p. 28.
[3] Ibid, p. 41.

feminist implications, in particular for spiritual feminism and for the notion of self-in-relation agency (chapter seven). The experiences of women on this path enhance women's agency and autonomy which emerge from participation on this path, and thus, I argue, are an important site for feminist understanding. This analysis constitutes new knowledge within the field of feminism and is part of a growing movement to include religion and spirituality within intersectional feminist understandings. The women participants in this study have found forms of emancipation within this movement through self-determination, agency, and the construction of new ways of being, acting and identifying which break free from the constricting norms of official Islam and its patriarchal rules. Therefore, in my view, not only do they act as examples for other women in similar situations, but they use their choice of this path to empower themselves as individuals and, by working with and for other women through practicing *ettisal*, they generate new and empowering views and modes of living. My study has presented and explored different possibilities for women in *Inter-universal Mysticism*, possibilities that could also be useful for other women outside of this movement in order to enhance their own search for self-development and life improvement.

The findings of this study have implications for feminist practices and research in Iran. Although more research is needed about the spiritual experience of various groups of women in Iran and its influence in their lives, I have highlighted the role of spirituality as a culturally relevant factor in coping with life difficulties for Iranian women in *Inter-universal Mysticism*. The women's ideas and experiences, combined with both their own conceptualisations and my analysis, build an understanding that there is space in women's experience on this path for Iranian feminism, and space in feminist theory and activism for spirituality. In conducting this research, then, I can argue for the emancipatory and feminist potential of this movement for women. Through my feminist reading of these women's narratives, I suggest that feminist researchers in Iran could develop both their theory and their practice by considering the changes that this movement can make in women's lives. I also consider that those who are interested in women's emancipation and in campaigning for women's rights in Iran might wish to consider that feminism is relevant to women's progress on this path. They could learn from the insights and experiences of the women who have been involved in the *Inter-universal Mysticism* movement. The ideas and experiences of the women who participated in this study may contribute to the understanding of, and engagement with, spirituality in Iranian women's lives.

Although it is beyond the scope and purpose of this study to discuss the full range of feminisms in Iran, I want to argue that the inclusion of spirituality within Iranian feminism is something different from attaching it to a religious agenda for feminist activities, the current practice of Islamic feminists. Rather, I propose that there is real value in exploring spirituality for its powerful effect on women's agency and ability to make changes in their lives. At this point, I distinguish spirituality from religion. I am not talking about spirituality in religion in the way that Islamic feminists do, in terms of being engaged with the structures of Shia Islam in Iran; my point is that there is a practical, emancipatory potential in spirituality for Iranian women in this movement that can be considered from both a secular and Islamic viewpoint within Iranian feminism. Feminism, from this perspective, is therefore viewed as usefully integrating both Islamic and secular views of women's choice and agency. In this respect, I propose that rather than thinking about feminism in Iran as a binary of Islamic and secular, there is another perspective in spirituality. The educated spiritual women in this study showed that through their involvement in *Inter-universal Mysticism*, their lives are changed in a way that might not be significant for them as individuals, but can be important for society in general. Islamic and secular feminists would do well to reflect on these women's experiences. In other words, my study recommends that feminists in Iran (both secular and Islamic) may need first to identify the effectiveness of spirituality in everyday life and then to conceptualize and link spirituality to women's self-empowerment, raising questions such as: how do engagements in spiritual movements change an Iranian woman's insight and view of the world?; What new forms of knowledge and ways of knowing emerge as a result of spiritual growth and change?; How does spirituality shape the (re)construction of self?; And how can spirituality lead to new and positive understandings and experiences of being a woman in Iran?

I suggest that instead of simply identifying binary oppositions between types of feminism in Iran as either secular or pious Islamic, we should think of something different: a way in which we can see a future for female agency and female self-assertion through mobilizing the kinds of resources that women in my study have found in their individual lives in some more collective way. These women's changes in self and life can be used to support discussions about spirituality and feminism and provide a base for future research on Iranian women. I would argue that the construction of such empowering factors and their contribution to women's real life experiences could help to effect change for women in Iran. It is hoped that this study will generate more interest and dialogue among different groups of feminists and women's activists in Iran in exploring women's self-empowerment through spirituality. The challenging task going forward is to focus on the empowering aspects of spirituality rather than the official Shia Islamic religion to provide elements of vision and hope in women's struggles for change in Iran. I end with a popular quotation from Taheri:

> *Men have started the path of erfan and women will accomplish it. Who did the job is who finishes it and those are women* (2005).[4]

---

[4] This quote was stated by Taheri in our classroom in 2005.

APPENDIX I

BIOGRAPHICAL SKETCHES OF THE INTERVIEWEES

The purpose of these brief biographies is to serve as an introduction to the women who participated in this research. The names given here are actual names although in cases where respondents did not tell me their first name, I used their family name. I left out certain details in order to protect their privacy.

Tehran

Afrooz, aged 34 and divorced (twice) with two children. She was in her second year at university and was working as a teacher at an adult school. She had had very difficult marriages and a hard life situation before she participated in *Inter-universal Mysticism*. She was at level 7 and used to talk about what she was learning on this path to some of her students in order to help them cope with their own difficult lives.

Afsaneh, aged 38 and single. She had a BA and was working full time. She was at level 4 and was very interested in developing *Inter-universal Mysticism* further by translating its lessons into English. She was one of the translating committee members.

Aram, aged 29 and married. She left university after two years of study and was a housewife. Having a difficult relationship with her husband, she participated in *Inter-universal Mysticism*. She was at level 5 and was happy about the changes she had made in her life.

Banafsheh, aged 25 and single. She had a post-high school[1] diploma and lived with her parents. Suffering badly from bone cancer and feeling

---

[1] A post-high school diploma is a qualification between a high school diploma and a university degree. After finishing high school, students can study for two more

hopeless about her medical treatment, she found out about the spiritual healing in *Inter-universal Mysticism*. She was at level 1 and was surprised by the improvement she had noticed in her cancer even in that short period of time.

Fereshteh, aged 37 and married. She had a difficult relationship with her husband, so much so that she ended up in a mental hospital until her sister suggested that she practice spiritual healing in *Inter-universal Mysticism*. As soon as she felt better she left her husband and participated in the movement. She was at level 5 when I interviewed her and was surprised by the extent of the changes she had had in her life. Later her husband joined her on the path.

Farnaz, aged 28 and married. She had a BA and was working full time as a computer engineer. She became interested in *Inter-universal Mysticism* as it offered modern teaching of spirituality with scientific examples. She passed level 1 and did not continue for two reasons: first because she was not happy with the Master she had; and secondly, her life circumstances did not allow her the time to look for another Master to continue with the path.

Jalili, aged 33 and single. She had a PhD in civil engineering and was working full time. She was at a very early stage on this path, level 1, and was interested in following it to the end.

Jalili, aged 48 and married with children. She had a high school diploma and was a housewife. Being at just the first level on this path, she could feel its influences in her difficult life and wanted to experience it further.

Lara, aged 30 and married with a child. She had a high school diploma and was a housewife. She was heavily pregnant when her husband became bankrupt, which caused her to lose her house to creditors and live with her parents. Being severely depressed, she gave birth to her daughter and could not take care of her as she had expected. Through a friend's suggestion, she chose to participate in *Inter-universal Mysticism* and was at level 1 when I interviewed her.

---

years at particular universities and gain a post-high school diploma. If they wish to continue and get a university degree, they need to study for two further years after gaining their post-high school diploma.

Manijheh, aged 47 and divorced. She had a BA and was working full time. She passed all levels up to level 8 and became a Master but never tried teaching.

Masoomeh, aged 28 and single. She had a BA and was working full time as a computer engineer. Not being satisfied with her life, she participated in *Inter-universal Mysticism* and was at level 5 when I interviewed her.

Misha, aged 30 and single. She had a BA and was working full time as an agricultural engineer. She never joined *Inter-universal Mysticism* but benefited from its indirect spiritual experience through a friend. Interestingly, she suggested this movement to others while not thinking that it was worth her spending time on its classes herself: she believed that simply practising its indirect *ettisal* was sufficient for her.

Nahid, aged 43 and married with three children. She had a high school diploma and was a house wife before participating in *Inter-universal Mysticism*. Passing level 8 on this path, she became one of the most active and popular Masters in Tehran and Yazd. She converted one of the rooms in her house into a classroom and was teaching up to nearly 20 students at each level. Due to requests from some women in Yazd, she rented a place there and used to travel to Yazd once a week for teaching. I chose my interviewees mostly from among her students in both Tehran and Yazd.

Pasyar, aged 38 and married with two children. She had a BA and was a nurse at a hospital. She found out about *Inter-universal Mysticism* from one of the patients at the hospital who was healed by spiritual healing on this path. Witnessing such healing, she became interested in learning more about it and potentially practising it on other patients. She was at level 1 when I interviewed her.

Paygani, aged 42 and married with two children. She had a high school diploma and was a housewife. She was interested in energy therapy and wanted to learn about spiritual healing in *Inter-universal Mysticism*. She was at an early stage of the path: level 1.

Pooravaz, aged 43 and married with two children. She had \ high school diploma and was a housewife. She was at level 1 and had no idea about the effect of *Inter-universal Mysticism* in her life, but her curiosity kept her on the path. She believed that it was worth spending time on its classes as there were many new things to learn.

Reyhaneh, aged 31 and married with a child. She had a BA and was a housewife. She passed level 8 and became a Master but because she moved to the UK she did not get a chance to teach. However, she would help anyone who asked with *Inter-universal Mysticism*'s lessons or healing.

Sara, aged 32 and single. She had a master's degree in Physics and was a university lecturer. She was at the final stage of the path, having passed level 8, and became a Master in 2006. She was active in teaching *Inter-universal Mysticism* to small groups of friends.

Shahla, aged 47 and a widow with children. She had a high school diploma and used to be a dress maker before learning about *Inter-universal Mysticism*. She passed all 8 levels on the path and became an active Master in Karaj (a city near Tehran).

Zahra, aged 52 and single (a divorcee). She was a housewife with a university master's degree. She passed the final stage of the path, level 8, in 2006 and became a Master but was not active in teaching *Inter-universal Mysticism*.

Zhaleh, aged 43 and married with two children. She had a high school diploma and was a housewife. Being interested in spirituality since the age of 15, she had tried many spiritual paths and had not felt fulfilled until she joined *Inter-universal Mysticism* on a recommendation from a friend. She was at level 5 on the path and was very enthusiastic about telling others of her experiences.

Yazd

Azam, aged 36 and married with two children. She had a BA and was working full time in a laboratory. She was suffering from lupus and was desperate for healing. When she found out about the spiritual healing in *Inter-universal Mysticism* she researched it before deciding to participate. She was practicing *faradarmani* along with her medical treatments and experienced some improvement in her condition. She was at level 3 and felt that her expectations were not satisfied as much as those of other women at higher levels, so she was determined to follow the path further.

Mahnaz, aged 44 and married with two children. She had a high school diploma and was a housewife. She was at level 4 and was very happy to talk about her experience on this path and the changes she had noticed in her life.

Hamideh, aged 39 and married with two children. She had a BA and was a housewife. She had many religious questions which had previously gone unanswered and which were responded to clearly throughout the 7 levels that she had progressed through on the path. She kindly offered the use of her house for me to conduct some of my interviews.

Maryam, aged 32 and married with two children. She was a homeopath and had her own clinic. She was the main advertiser of *Inter-universal Mysticism* in Yazd as she used to recommend its spiritual healing along with her remedies to all her patients. She was at level 7 and believed that it met all her spiritual needs which could not be satisfied through her religious studies.

Maryam, aged 28 and married with children. She was studying at university and was very interested in supernatural and paranormal powers. Being at level 7 of the path, she was happier than before and believed that the love between her and her husband was increased because she is no longer dependent on him.

Maryam, aged 24 and newly married. She had a BA and was a housewife. She participated in *Inter-universal Mysticism* with her husband and they were both at level 3. Her husband helped extensively to develop this movement in Yazd by offering safe places for its classes and, interestingly, attended her interview with me. They kindly invited me for dinner after my interview and showed me one of the most beautiful and oldest bazaars in Yazd.

Nooshin, aged 41 and married with two children. She had a high school diploma and was a housewife. She joined *Inter-universal Mysticism* to help her daughter, who was sick and severely depressed because of her divorce and could not participate on the path herself. She was in Mashhad to pray for her daughter when someone in the lounge of her hotel accidentally told her about the spiritual healing in *Inter-universal Mysticism*. As soon as she returned Yazd she looked for its Master. She was at level 2 and was surprised by the changes she had noticed in her own self. She said she came onto this path just to help her daughter and had not expected such improvement in her own life.

Roya, aged 31 and married with a child. She had a BA and was working full time in a travel agency. She had a difficult relationship with her husband and was thinking about divorce when she learned about *Inter-universal Mysticism*. On her mother's suggestion, she asked one of the Masters in Tehran (Nahid) to travel to Yazd and teach there. Her mother offered her house for the classes and this was how the movement started in Yazd. Roya was at level 8 and wanted to become an active Master. She also allowed her 9 year-old daughter to attend classes and pass the first level on the path as she thought it would help her in future.

Mashhad

Afsar, aged 45 and married with children. She was working full time as a medical doctor and was the manager of a health centre. Interested in spirituality, she was a Master in Reiki and had a few students. When she found out about *Inter-universal Mysticism* she became curious and wanted to learn more about it so joined the path. She was at level 1 and said she had not found any disparity between the insights on this path and those in Reiki.

Malihe, aged 70 and married with children. She had a high school diploma and was a housewife. She had a grandmother who could heal people through her hands. Desiring to follow her grandmother's way and become a healer, she unsuccessfully tried different spiritual paths until she learned about *Inter-universal Mysticism*. First, she asked her son to join the movement to find out how it worked, and then she herself joined. She was at level 2 and was happy with the insights she had gained on the path and its spiritual healing.

Faezeh, aged 35 and married with children. She had a high school diploma and was a housewife. She joined Inter-universal Mysticism because of her husband's illness. She was at level 3 of the path and was critical of the amount of enrolment fees for the classes.

Ghazaleh, aged 39 and married with two children. She had a high school diploma and was working full time selling homemade cakes and cookies. She offered part of her house to one of the Masters (who was her relative) to teach *Inter-universal Mysticism*. She did not believe in religion and spirituality and chose to join this movement to save her married life with an alcohol addicted husband. She was at level 3 and could see its effects on herself and her daughters, but not yet on her husband.

Shirin, aged 63 and married with two children. She had a high school diploma and was retired. She had a difficult relationship with her daughter who lived at home who, as she said, was a trouble-maker. After passing 8 levels on this path, she was surprised by the changes she saw in her daughter through using its indirect *ettisal*.

Arezoo, aged 50 and married with children. She had a BA and was one the Masters in Mashhad. She had started teaching *Inter-universal Mysticism* with just five students, who were all women, in her house and had more than 100 students when I was introduced to her through one of the women I interviewed. As soon as she found out about my interviews she voluntarily contacted me and suggested that I recruit some of my interviewees from among her students. Through her I conducted two focus groups and a few more individual interviews.

Maryam, aged 50 and married with children. She had a BA and was working full time. She was at level 3 at the time of my interview with her and was determined to continue on the path.

Majidi, aged 45 and married with children. She had a high school diploma and was a housewife. She was at level 5 when I interviewed her.

Mahin, aged 57 and married with children. She had a high school diploma and was retired. She was at level 3 and believed that Iranian women should participate in this movement to eliminate patriarchal culture in Iranian society.

Marjan, aged 28 and single. She had a university master's degree and was looking for a job. She was at level 2 and was looking for more new insights that *Inter-universal Mysticism* could offer.

Maryam, aged 39 and married with two children. She had a BA and was working as an architect. Having unsuccessfully tried different ways to increase her self-confidence, she found this path very helpful. She was at level 2 and believed that Iranian women need to experience the spirituality in *Inter-universal Mysticism.*

Masoomeh, aged 32 and single. She had a BA and was working full time. She was at level 3 when I interviewed her.

Maryam, aged 37 and married with children. She had a high school diploma and was working part-time. She was at level 7 when I interviewed her.

Mina, aged 59 and married with children. She had a university master's degree and was a retired teacher. She was at level 2 and wanted to use this movement to experience spirituality.

Narges, aged 40 and single. She had a post-high school diploma and was working full time as a hair dresser. She had believed in spirituality for years before joining *Inter-universal Mysticism* and said she was famous among her customers for her spiritual support. She was at level 3 of the path.

Nastaran, aged 41 and married with children. She had a BA and was working full time as a legal advisor. She was at a very early stage of the path, level 1, and said she had to spend a few months convincing her husband that she would benefit from participating in this movement.

Roksana, aged 27 and single. She was studying for a master's degree at university. Having parents from two different religious beliefs (a Muslim father and a Christian mother) she was looking for spirituality. She found *Inter-universal Mysticism* to be thought-provoking and an environment in which she felt no conflict between her mixed religious beliefs and could experience spirituality. She was at level 2 and wanted to get more from the path.

Sayeh, aged 41 and married with two children. She had a BA in nursing and was a housewife. She experienced the indirect effects of *Inter-universal Mysticism* on her life through a friend, before joining the path. Her married life was going to be destroyed when she chose to try the help of *ettisal* and was highly surprised by the results. She was at level 7 and said that it also affected her husband, changing him to a more caring husband.

Sharifi, aged 60 and married with children. She had a high school diploma and was a housewife. She passed 8 levels on the path and informed one of the other Masters in Mashhad, whom I did not know, about my research and gave her my contact details.

Maryam, aged 36 and married with two children. She had a BA and was working part-time as an accountant for her husband. She had a very difficult relationship with her husband and mother-in-law because of their dogmatic religious views. She learned about *Inter-universal Mysticism* from one of her friends and used to attend its classes without informing her husband, who would not allow her to be present. She was managing her time in order to return home before her husband. She was very enthusiastic in talking about her life and the support she received from this path. She was at level 2 and was worried about the official closure of the classes and wanted to pass all the levels as quickly as possible.

Sharareh, aged 49 and married with children. She had a high school diploma and was a housewife. She was critical of the patriarchal culture in which she (and many other women) grew up and believed that this movement could change this culture by giving women confidence and agency. She was at level 5.

Sogand, 43 and married with children. She had a BA and was a housewife. She grew up in a secular family and chose to become a pious Muslim and wear hijab against the wishes of her family. She was at level 5 and believed that *Inter-universal Mysticism* complemented her spiritual feelings and experiences.

Takaloo, aged 43 and married with children. She had a high school diploma and was a housewife. She was at level 7 when I interviewed her and was happy with her choice to participate in this movement despite of her daughters' disagreement.

Tayebeh, aged 35 and married with children. She had a high school diploma and was a housewife. She had difficult relationships with her in-laws and was surprised by the changes she felt in her life just at the first level of the path.

Fatemeh, aged 68 and married with children. She had just five years of primary school education and was a housewife. She had had a difficult life, with financial pressure and health problems. She was at a very early stage of the path, level 1, and was very enthusiastic about it. She had serious knee problems and used to use a walking stick. She came to my interview walking comfortably upright without a stick and said she owed the improvement in her health to the movement and would do anything? to support it.

Zahra, aged 38 and married with two children. She had a high school diploma and was a housewife. She was at level 2 and was not yet sure how much her participation in this movement could help her. Practising her religion, Islam, and believing in spirituality, she thought that the lessons of *Inter-universal Mysticism* sounded familiar to her.

GLOSSARY

aql: wisdom, intellectual knowledge

akhund: colloquial Persian term for a Muslim religious specialist (mullah)

aref (plural: *urafa*): someone with expertise in *erfan*, a mystic

basiji: literally 'mobilized person', nowadays the name for the resistance force created under the Islamic republic

bazar: traditional centre for business, trade, and artisan production in an Iranian urban settlement

bazari: bazar trader or businessman

chador: literally means a tent. In Iran it is the term used to describe the full-length loose cloak-like cover worn by women, which covers the body from head to toe. At official gatherings women usually wear a black chador, while on unofficial occasions women might choose to wear a colorful chador

cheshm hamcheshmi: herd mentality

darvish: itinerant self-proclaimed religious specialist, often with Sufi affiliations

din: religion in general

dowreh: social gathering of a group who usually share particular culture or political interests or affiliations

erfan: mystical thought and practice

ettisal: literally means connection. It refers to spiritual practice in *Inter-universal Mysticism.*

ensaniyat: humanity (from *ensan* = human being)

eshq: love

Farsi: the official and predominant language in Iran

faqih (plural: *fuqaha*): an expert in Islamic Law, jurist

faradarmani: spiritual healing in Inter-universal Mysticism

gharbzadegi: literally 'west-struckness / west-intoxication'; it came into wide use from the 1960s following its appearance as the title of an influential dissident text by the radical writer Jalal Al-e Ahmad to label Iranians seen as excessively/inappropriately influenced by western culture

haqiqah: ultimate truth

heyat: pious gatherings

hijab (*hejab*): describes [1] the principle of modest/concealing dress said by some Muslims to be incumbent upon pious Muslim women; [2] an article of women's closing which covers her head and protects her from the eyes of male strangers

jalaseh: a gathering, meeting

jashn-e Ebadat or Taklif: 'Celebration of Worship. A special ceremony invented by the Islamic regime, specifically for girls when they reach the age of 9 to prepare them for puberty and to mark their transition into adulthood in Shia Islam. Central to the ceremony is the performance of the daily prayers by the novice, who must also display competence in answering questions posed by adults on her religious duties

kamal: perfection, completeness, fulfilment. It refers to the human's spiritual growth toward perfection

komiteh: grouping of local enforces and moral police established after the 1979 revolution

khoshnami: good reputation, honor.

khoshnam: a person who has a good reputation.

madraseh: school

magham-e solh: peace position. It is one of the main principles of *Inter-universal Mysticism*. The process involves finding peace with the 'self', then with God and the world, and finally with others

mahr: bride-price agreed between the families of the bride and groom and written into the marriage contract. It is supposed to be paid by the husband to the wife on demand after the consummation of the marriage. But the normal practice is for it to be paid on divorce

majles (*majlis*): the Iranian national assembly or parliament

majles-e do'a daramani: healing ritual

majles-e khebregan: assembly of religious experts

manaviyat: spirituality

maraji-'i taqlids: the supreme religio-legal authority, or the source/model to be emulated

mardsalari: patriarchy

mazhab [noun]: literally means a creed or sect. nowadays *mazhabi* [adjective] is applied to a self-consciously religious (Muslim) person or group

muraqaba: the practice of *muraqaba* can be likened to the practices of meditation attested in many faith communities. The *muraqabah* (watching) fills the Sufi with either fear or joy according to the aspect of God revealed to him (see Britannica Online Encyclopaedia)

namaz jome: Friday prayer in Islam

polygamy: form of marriage in which a person has more than one spouse at the same time

rahbar: religious leader (literally a guide)

rowzeh: mourning rituals and recitations commemorating the martyrdom and virtues of the founding leaders of the Shi'a tradition (see below), especially Ali, Husein and Zahra.

Shi'ism [noun], *Shi'a* or *Shi'i* [adjective]: the version of Islam whose founders supported Ali, the Prophet Muhammad's nephew and son-in-law. Shi'i believers consider that after the Prophet's death the leadership of the Muslim community should have gone to Ali and his descendants and were therefore called the supporters (Shi'ah) of Ali. Shi'ism has several branches, and the majority of Iranian Muslims are followers of the 'Twelver' branch of the Shi'a tradition

sigheh: temporary marriage, fixed-term marriage. A form of marriage mainly confined to the in Shia branch of Islam. It is based on a contract, which is bound by a time-limit of between one hour and ninety-nine years

sofreh: ritual feasts with a religious purpose, mainly organised by and for women

tan-e vahedeh: united body. It is the most important principle of *Inter-universal Mysticism*, through which one understands that human beings are members of the whole, in creation of one essence and soul, therefore cannot be indifferent toward each other

tariqah [plural: *turuq*]: way, path

ulama (Olama) [plural, singular: *alim*]: professionally trained Muslim religious specialists

velayat-e faqih: a Shi'a religio-political concept (literally 'the guardianship of the jurist/*faqih*) supporting the supervisory authority of religious specialists in matters of governance; in the Islamic Republic of Iran it designates the constitutional and political authority of a chosen senior member of the '*ulama*' and the Council of Experts

zikr: literally 'reminding/recollection' or 'mention' (of a person or topic). It is used to describe the prayers, recitations, or other rituals practiced by Muslim mystics (Sufis) for the purpose of glorifying God, and used as a means to achieve spiritual perfection through closeness to God

REFERENCES

Primary Material

Personal Notes taken in *Inter-universal My*sticism classes, 2004, 2005 and 2006.

Teaching handbook used internally by practitioners and Masters of *Inter-universal Mysticism* for teaching, 2005 and 2006. Also available online at http://amoozeshemajazi.wordpress.com [Accessed 31 January 2013].

Internally recorded interviews of Taheri in his office. During my field work in 2010, I could collect copies of these interviews from some of the Masters who had access to them before the closure of *Inter-universal Mysticism* institution by the government.

Taheri's interview regarding the criticisms against his movement. April 2010. [Online]. Available at http://archive.org/details/interuniversal [Accessed 31 January 2013].

Taheri, M.A. (2009). Ramadan prevents the way of Satan. *Farhang ashti*, 6, p. 7.

—. (2010). The role of insights in life. *Hemayat*, 15, p. 13.

—. (2010). Movement and stability in the context of conflict. *Sobh eghtesad*, 13, p. 8.

—. (2009). Inter-universal Mysticism articles. *Farhang amoozesh*, 14 (4).

Books and Articles against *Inter-universal Mysticism*

Avini, M. (2011). Evolution or development. *Keyhan*, 11 April 2011. [Online]. Available at http://www.kayhan.ir/900122/6.htm#other601 [Accessed 31 January 2013].

Aiin (2011). *Criticism and evaluation of deviant sects and religions.* [Onine]. Available at http://aiin.blogfa.com/cat-11.aspx [Accessed 31 January 2013].

Adyannews (2010). *Inter-universal Mysticism and disrespect of Shia Islamic Imams.* [Online]. No longer available.

Bonyan Marsoos. (2010). *Claim of Inter-universal Mysticism.* [Online]. Available at http://bonyanemarsoos.blogfa.com/post-117.aspx [Accessed 26 May 2012].

Fars News Agency (2010). *Inter-universal Mysticism: a trap for university students and graduates.* [Online]. Available at http://www.farsnews.net/newstext.php?nn=8902040466 [Accessed 31 January 2013].

Gerdab (2010). *Inter-universal Mysticism: an Iranian mysticism or Cosmic mysticism?* [Online]. Available at http://www.gerdab.ir/fa/pages/?cid=1862 [Accessed 31 January 2013].

Ghasemi, M. R. (2011). Connection to Inter-universal intelligence. *Fars news agency*, 11 April 2011. [Online]. Available at http://khabarfarsi.com/ext/469974 [Accessed 31 January 2013].

Iran Track (2009). *What is Inter-universal Mysticism?* [online]. Available at http://forum.irantrack.com/thread58488.html [Accessed 31 January 2013].

Jamejam online (2010). *Criticism of Inter-universal Mysticism's principles.* [Online]. Available at http://www.jamejamonline.ir/newstext.aspx?newsnum=100876081883 [Accessed 31 January 2013].

—. (2010). *Inter-universal Mysticism's inconsistency with Qu'ran.* [Online]. Available at http://www.jamejamonline.ir/newstext.aspx?newsnum=100874711080 [Accessed 31 January 2013].

Javanemrooz (2010). *Arrest of the head of a deviant sect by anonymous solders of Imam Zaman.* [Online]. Available at http://javanemrooz.com/news/page-3128.aspx [Accessed 31 January 2013].

Keyhan, (2010). Criticism of Inter-universal Mysticism's principles and theories. 18 October 2010, p. 6. Also available online at http://www.kayhan.ir/890726/6.htm [Accessed 31 January 2013].

Mansoureh (2010). *Mirage of Inter-universal Mysticism.* [Online]. Available at http://www.damehalghe.blogfa.com [Accessed 31 January 2013].

Mashreghnews (2011). *Deviant Inter-universal Mysticism cult: from rise to down.* [Online]. Available at http://www.mashreghnews.ir/fa/news/61346 [Accessed 31 January 2013].

Mohakemeh (2010). *Inter-universal Mysticism, conspiracy against Shia Islamic Imams.* [Online]. Available at http://www.mohakeme.com/news-1135.html [Accessed 31 January 2013].

Mohammad (2010). *The Inter-universal Mysticism's networks are not Muslims.* [Online]. Available at http://www.askdin.com/showthread.php?t=5799 [Accessed 31 January 2013].

Moosavi, H. (2010). *Criticism of Inter-universal Mysticism.* [Online]. Najva blog, no longer available.

Naserirad, A. (2011). *Spell of circle: review and criticism of Inter-universal Mysticism.* Tehran: Sayan.

Rajanews (2009). *Deviant cult activity in the country and exploitation of its followers.* [Online]. Availbe at http://www.rajanews.com/detail.asp?id=46413 [Accessed 31 January 2013].

Shia online (2010). *Inter-universal Mysticism: vows to God are kind of bribery.* [Online]. No longer available.

Tabnak (2011). *Arrest of the head of Inter-universal Mysticism.* [Online]. No longer available.

Zamani, M. (2010). *Inter-universal Mysticism, imprisonment cult in circle.* [Online]. Available at http://www.javanonline.ir/vdci5qapqt1av52.cbct.html [Accessed 31 January 2013].

—. (2010). *Downfall of Inter-universal Mysticism is continuing: return of a woman to religiosity.* [Online]. Available at http://mohammad-zamani.blogfa.com/post-123.aspx [Accessed 31 January 2013].

BIBLIOGRAPHY

Adelkhah, F. (1999). *Being modern in Iran.* Translated by Jonathan Derrick, London: Hurst & Company.

Afary, J. (1989). On the origin of feminism in the early 20th-century Iran. *Women's history,* 1 (2), 65-87.

—. (2009). *Sexual politics in modern Iran.* Cambridge: Cambridge University Press.

Afkhami, M. & Friedl, E. (1994). *In the eye of the storm: women in post-revolutionary Iran.* London: L.B.Tauris & Co Ltd.

Aftab. (2010). *Annually one percent of Iranian population rich poverty line because of health expenses.* [Online]. Available at http://www.aftabnews.ir/vdcaaan6w49nwi1.k5k4.html [Accessed 9 November 2012]. Translated by myself.

Akhavi, Sh. (1980). *Religion and politics in contemporary Iran: clergy-state relations in the Pahlavi period.* Albany: State University of New York Press.

Ahmed-Ghosh, H. (2008). Dilemmas of Islamic and secular feminists and feminisms. *International Women's Studies,* 9 (3), 99-116.

Alavi, N. (2005). *We are Iran.* London: Portobello Books Ltd.

Amanat, A. (2009). *Apocalyptic Islam and Iranian Shi'ism.* London: I.B.Tauris & Co Ltd.

Ammerman, N.T. (2007). *Everyday religion: observing modern religious lives.* Oxford: Oxford University Press.

Angha, S.A.N. (1996). *Origin of Sufism.* [Online]. Available at http://mto.org/school/index.php?id=9 [Accessed 22 May 2012].

—. (2012). *Unity of religion.* [Online]. Available at http://mto.org/AOS/en/unity_religion.htm [Accessed 25 January 2013].

Arjmand, R. (2004). Education and empowerment of the religious elite in Iran. In H. Daun & G. Walford, eds. *Educational strategies among Muslims in the context of globalization: some national case studies (Muslim minorities, V. 3),* Library of Congress Cataloging-in-Publication data, Netherlands: Brill, pp. 63-81.

Asemi, F. (2012). *Ten-day trial of 189 dervishes without lawyer.* [Online]. Available at http://www.radiofarda.com/content/f4_iran_trial_dervish_gonabadi_no_lawyer/24573896.html [Accessed 22 May 2012].

Aune, K. Sharma, S. and Vincett, G. (2008). *Women and religion in the west: challenging secularization.* Aldershot: Ashgate Publishing Company.

Baker, D. C. (2003). Studies of the inner life: the impact of spirituality on quality of life. *Quality of life research*, 12 (1), 51-57.

Banks-Wallace, J. and Parks, L. (2004). It's all sacred: African American women's perspectives on spirituality. *Issues in mental health nursing*, 25 (1), 25-45.

Barlow, R. & Akbarzadeh. Sh. (2008). Prospects for feminism in the Islamic Republic of Iran. *Human rights quarterly*, 30 (1), 21-40.

Barry, C.M. Nelson, L. Davarya, S. and Urry, SH. (2010). Religiosity and spirituality during the transition to adulthood. *International journal of behavioral development*, 34, 311-324.

Bauer, J. (1985). Sexuality and the moral construction of women in an Islamic society. *Anthropological quarterly* 58 (3), 120-29.

Begolo, Z. (2008). Veiled politics. *History today magazine*, 58 (9), 42-44. Also Available online at http://www.historytoday.com/zephie-begolo/veiled-politics [Accessed 10 October 2012].

Benner, D. G. (1989). Toward a psychology of spirituality: Implications for personality and psychotherapy. *Journal of psychology and Christianity*, 5, 19-30.

—. (2011). *Soulful spirituality: becoming fully alive and deeply human.* Brentwood: Brazos Press.

Benson, P. L., Roehlkepartain, E. C., & Rude, S. P. (2003). Spiritual development in childhood and adolescence: Toward a field of inquiry. *Applied developmental science*, 7, 204-212.

Birbili, M. (2000). Translating from one language to another. *Social research update*, 31, 1–7. Also Available online at http://sru.soc.surrey.ac.uk/SRU31.html [Accessed 25 December 2012].

Black, H. (1999). Poverty and prayer: spiritual narratives of elderly African-American women. *Review of religious research*, 40 (4), 359-374.

Brannick, T and Coghlan, D. (2007). In defence of being "native": the case for insider academic research. *Organizational research methods.* 10 (1), 59-74.

Brown, C.F. (2005). Old religion, new spirituality, and health care. In A. Meier, T.J. O'Connor, and P. VanKatwyk. *Spirituality and health: multidisciplinary explorations.* Canada: Wilfrid Laurier University Press, pp. 191- 211.

Brayton, J. (1997). *What makes feminist research feminist? the structure of feminist research within the social sciences.* [Online]. Available at http://www.unb.ca/par-l/win/feminmethod.htm [Accessed 13 August 2012].

Britannica - *The Online Encyclopedia*. Available at http://www.britannica.com/.

Bruinessen, M.V. and Howell, J.D. (2007). *Sufism and the 'modern' in Islam*. London: I.B.Tauris,

Burke, J. (2012). *Free Mohammad-Ali Taheri*. [Online]. Available at http://www.gopetition.com/petitions/free-mohammad-ali-taheri-sentenced-to-five-years-and-7.html [Accessed 25 January 2013].

Burkhardt, M. (1994). *Becoming and connecting: elements of spirituality for women*. Charleston: Williams & Wilkins.

Burgess, R. (1984). *In the field: an introduction to field research*. London: Allen and Unwin.

Butler, J. (1990). *Gender trouble: feminism and the subversion of identity*. New York: Routledge.

Carr, E. S. (2003). Rethinking empowerment theory using a feminist lens: the importance of process. *Affilia*, 18 (1), 8-20.

Casagrande, J. B. (1954). The ends of translation. *IJAL*, 20 (4), 335- 340.

Chen, Y.Y. Subramanian, S.V. Acevedo-Garcia, D. and Kawachi, I. (2005). Women's status and depressive symptoms: A multilevel analysis. *Social science & medicine,* 60 (1), 49-60.

Chin, S.S. (2006). I am a human being, and I belong to the world: narrating the intersection of spirituality and social identity. *Journal of transformative education*, 4 (1), 27-42.

Coholic, D. (2003). Incorporating spirituality in feminist social work perspectives. Sage journals online, *Affilia*, 18 (1), 49-67.

Connell, R. (1987). *Gender and power*. Stanford: Stanford University Press.

Cook, R. (1994). *Human rights of women, national and international perspectives*. Philadelphia: University of Pennsylvania Press.

Cooke, M. (2000). Multiple critique: Islamic feminist rhetorical strategies. *Nepantla: Views from South*, 1 (1), 91-110.

Cooper, E. Jane. (2007). Escapism or engagement? plotinus and feminism. *Journal of feminist studies in religion,* 23 (1), 73-93.

Dehkhoda, (1955). *Persian dictionary Loghat-nameh*. [Online]. Available at http://www.loghatnaameh.org [Accessed 28 November 2012].

Delgado, CH. 2005. A discussion of the concept of spirituality. *Nursing science quarterly*, 18 (2), 157-162.

Denscombe, M. (1998). *The good research guide*, Buckingham: Open University Press.

Devault, M.L. 1990. Talking and listening from women's standpoint: feminist strategies for interviewing and analysis. *Social problems*, 37 (1), 96-116.

East, J. (2000). Empowerment through welfare-rights organizing: A feminist perspective. *Affilia*, 15, 311-328.

Eisenstein, Z. (2004). *Against empire: feminisms, racism, and the West*. London: Zed press.

Elkins, D. N., Hedstrom, L. J., Hughes, L.L., Leaf, J. A., and Saunders, C. (1988). Towards a humanistic phenomenological spirituality: definition, description and measurement. *Journal of humanistic psychology*, 28, 5-18.

Elton, L. and Mahdi, A. (2006). *Culture and customs of Iran*. Library of congress cataloguing-in-publication data, Westport: Greenwood Press.

Erricker, C. and Erricker, J. (2001). *Contemporary spiritualities: social and religious contexts*. London: Continuum International Publishing.

Esfandiari, H. (1997). *Reconstructed lives: women & Iran's Islamic revolution*. Washington: The Woodrow Wilson Centre Press.

Farahmand, M. (2007). Introduction. In S. Sadeghi-Fasaei, M. Farahmand, A. Bakhtiyari, Balali, E. M.A. Mohamadi, and M. Torahi, (Eds.). *Feminism and family*, Tehran: Ravabet Omoomi Shoraye Farhangi-Ejtemaei Zanan, pp. 2-6.

Fischer, M.M. J. (1980). *Iran from religious dispute to revolution*. Cambridge: Harvard University Press.

Fonow, M. and Cook, J. (1991). *Beyond methodology/feminist scholarship as lived research*. Bloomington: Indiana Press.

Friedl, E. (1989). *Women of Deh Koh: lives in an Iranian village*. London, New York: Penguin.

Ghavamshahidi, Z. (1995). The linkage between Iranian patriarch and the informal economy in maintaining women's subordinate roles in home-based carpet production. *Women's studies international forum*, 18 (2), 135-151.

Gilbert, M. C. (2000). Spirituality in social work groups: Practitioners speak out. *Social Work With Groups*, 22, 67-84.

Giordan, G. (2009). Spirituality: from a religious concept to a sociological theory. In K. Flanagan, and P.C. Jupp, (Eds.). *A sociology of spirituality*. Surrey: Ashgate, pp. 161 – 181.

Guest, M. (2009). In search of spiritual capital: the spiritual as a cultural resource. In K. Flanagan, and P.C. Jupp, (Eds.). *A sociology of spirituality*. Surrey: Ashgate, pp. 181 – 201.

Gutierrez, L. (1995). Understanding the empowerment process: Does consciousness make a difference?. *Social work research*, 19, 229-237.

Halkes, C. (1988). Feminism and spirituality. *Spirituality today*, 40 (3), 220-236.

Hashemi, F. (1982). Discrimination and imposition of the veil. In A. Tabari and N. Yeganeh, *In the shadow of Islam: the women's movement in Iran,* London: Zed Books, pp. 193-207.

Hassouneh-Phillips, D. (2003). Strength and vulnerability: spirituality in abused American Muslim women's lives. *Mental health nursing*, 24 (6-7), 681-694.

Hegland, M.E. (1986). Political roles of Iranian village women. *Middle East report 138*, 14-19.

Heelas, P. (2002). The spiritual revolution: from 'religion' to 'spirituality'. In L. Woodhead, P. Fletcher, H. Kawanami, and D. Smith (Eds). *Religions in the modern world*. London: Routledge, pp. 357-377.

—. (2009). The holistic milieu and spirituality: reflections on Voas and Bruce. In K. Flanagan, and P.C. Jupp, (Eds.). *A sociology of spirituality*. Surrey: Ashgate, pp. 63 - 81.

—. (2009). *Spiritualities of life: new age romanticism and consumptive capitalism*. Hoboken: Wiley Publisher.

Heelas, P., Woodhead, L., Seel, B., Szerszynski, B., and K. Tursting (2005). *The spiritual revolution. why is religion giving way to spirituality?* Oxford: Blackwell Publishing.

Heroy, M. (2009). *Sexual and reproductive health and rights situation report: Iran*. [Online]. Available at http://www.genderacrossborders.com/2009/11/09/srhr_sit_report_iran [Accessed 9 November 2012].

Hesse-Biber, Sh. N. (2007). *Handbook of feminist research: theory and praxis*. London: Sage.

Hesse-Biber, Sh. N. and Leavy, P. L. (2007). *Feminist research practice: a primer*. London: Sage.

Hill, P.C., Pragament, K.I., Hood, R.W., JR., Mccullough, M.E., Swyers, J.P., Larson, D.B. and Zinnbauer, B.J. (2001). Conceptualizing religion and spirituality: points of commonality, points of departure. *Journal for the Theory of Social Behaviour*, 30 (1), 51-77.

Hojat, M. and Mehryar, A.H. (circa 2002). *Iran-divorce-family and women*. [Online]. Available at http://family.jrank.org/pages/957/Iran-Divorce.html [Accessed 2 November 2012].

Holmes, P. R. (2009). Spirituality: some disciplinary perspectives. In K. Flanagan, K. and P.C. Jupp, (Eds.). *A sociology of spirituality*. Surrey: Ashgate. pp. 23 - 43.

Honarbin-Holliday, M. (2009). *Becoming visible in Iran: women in contemporary Iranian society*. London: Tauris Academic Studies.

Hooglund, E. (2002). *Twenty years of Islamic revolution political and social transition in Iran since 1979*. New York: Syracuse University Press.

Houtman, D. and Aupers, S. (2008). The spiritual revolution and the new age gender puzzle: the sacralization of the self in late modernity (1980– 2000). In K. Aune, S. Sharma, and G. Vincett, (Eds.). *Women and religion in the west: challenging secularization*. Aldershot: Ashgate, pp. 99 – 119.

Index Mundi. (2013). *Iran Demographics Profile 2013*. [Online]. Available at http://www.indexmundi.com/iran/demographics_profile.html [Accessed on 4 March 2013].

Iranianuk. (2012). *Women's studies title changed to women's rights in Islam*. [Online]. Available at http://www.iranianuk.com/page.php5?id=20120523145300018 [Accessed 23 May 2012].

Isaacs, T. (2003). Feminism and agency. *Canadian journal of philosophy supplementary, 28*, 129-154.

Isgandarova, N. (2005). Islamic spiritual care in a health care setting. In A. Meier, T.J. O'Connor, and P. VanKatwyk, (Eds.). *Spirituality and health: multidisciplinary explorations*. Canada: Wilfrid Laurier University Press, pp. 85 – 105.

Jahanbegloo, R. (2004). *Iran between tradition and modernity*. Washington: Lexington Press.

Javaheri, F. (2006). Prayer healing: an experiential description of Iranian prayer healing. *Journal of religion and health, 45* (2), 171-182.

Johnson, A.G. (2005). *Gender knot: unravelling our patriarchal legacy* (Revised and Updated Edition). Philadelphia: Temple University Press.

Johnson, R. (2004). *The practice of cultural studies*. London: Sage.

Jones, K. (1996). Trust as an affective attitude. *Ethics, 107* (1), 4-25.

Johnson, L.T. (2008). *Mystical tradition: Judaism, Christianity, and Islam*. [Online]. Available at http://www.thegreatcourses.com/tgc/courses/course_detail.aspx?cid=6 130 [Accessed 28 November 2012].

Kaar, M. (1996). Women and personal status law in Iran: an interview with Mehrangiz Kaar. *Middle East report, 198*, 36-38.

Kabeer, N. (1999). The conditions and consequences of choice: reflections on the measurement of women's empowerment. *Development and change, 30*, 435-464.

Kale, S.H. (2004). Spirituality, religion, and globalization. *Journal of macromarketing, 24* (2), 92-107.

Kamalkhani, Z. (1998). *Women's Islam: religious practice among women in today's Iran.* London and New York: Kegan Paul International.

Katouzian, H. and Shahidi, H. (2008). *Iran in the 21st century: politics, economics & conflict.* Canada: Routledge.

Keddie, N. (1986). Sexuality and Shi'i social protest in Iran. In Cole, J.R.I. & Keddie, N. *Shi'ism and social protest.* New York: Yale University.

—. (1998). *Islam and feminisms: an Iranian case-study.* New York: St. Martin's Press.

—. (2001). Women in Iran since 1979. *Social research,* 67 (2), special issue: Iran: Since the Revolution, 405-438.

—. (2007). *Women in the Middle East: past and present.* Perinceton: Princeton University Press.

Keddie, N. and Hooglund, E. (1982). *The Iranian revolution and the Islamic Republic.* Washington, D.C.: Middle East Institute.

Keddie, N. and Richard, Y. (2006). *Modern Iran: roots and results of revolution.* London: Yale University Press.

Khosrokhavar, F. (2002). Post-revolutionary Iran and the new social movements. In E. Hooglund, *Twenty years of Islamic revolution political and social transition in Iran since 1979.* New York: Syracuse University Press, pp. 3-19.

Kian-Thiebat, A. (2007). From motherhood to equal rights advocates: the weakening of patriarchal order. In H. Katouzian and H. Shahidi. *Iran in the 21st century: politics, economics and conflicts.* London and New York: Routledge, pp. 86-107.

King, U. (1993). *Women and spirituality, voices of protest and promise.* Pennsylvania: State University Press.

—. (2002). *Spirituality and society in the new millennium.* Brighton: Sussex Academic Press.

King, U. and Beattie, T. (2005). *Gender, religion and diversity: cross-cultural perspectives.* London: Continuum International Publishing.

King, P. E. Carr, D. and Boitor, C. (2011). Religion, spirituality, positive youth development, and thriving. *Advances in child development and behavior,* 41, 161 -195.

Kitzinger, J. (1995). Qualitative research: introducing focus groups. *BMJ,* 311, p. 299. [Online]. Available at http://www.bmj.com/content/311/7000/299 [Accessed 31 October 2012].

Koenig, H. G., McCullough, M. E., and Larson, D. B. (2001). *Handbook of religion and health.* New York: Oxford University Press.

Kousha, M. (2000). *Voices from Iran: the changing lives of Iranian women.* New York: Syracuse University Press.

Kousha, M. and Mohseni, N. (1997). Predictors of life satisfaction among urban Iranian women: an exploratory analysis. *Social indicators research*, 40 (3), 329-357.

Kusha, H. R. (2002). *The sacred law of Islam: A case study of women's treatment in the Islamic Republic of Iran's criminal justice system*. The University of Michigan: Ashgate.

Loeffler, R. (1988). *Islam in practice: religious beliefs in a Persian village*. Albany: State University of New York Press.

MacKenzie, C. and Stoljar, N. (2000). *Relational autonomy: feminist perspectives on autonomy, agency, and the social self*. New York: Oxford University Press.

Mahdi, A.A. (2003). Iranian Women: between Islamisation and globalization. In A. Mohammadi. *Iran encountering globalization: problems and prospects*. London and New York: Routledge, pp. 47-73.

Mahmood, S. (2001). Feminist theory, embodiment, and the docile agent: some reflections on the Egyptian Islamic revival. *Cultural anthropology*, 16(2), 202–236.

Marler, P. L. (2008). Religious Change in the West: Watch the Women. In K. Aune, S. Sharma, and G. Vincett, (Eds.). (2008). *Women and religion in the west: challenging secularization*. Aldershot: Ashgate, pp. 23 – 57.

Mattis, J.S. (2000). African American women's definitions of spirituality and religiosity. *Journal of black psychology*, 26 (1), 101-122.

Maynard, M. and Purvis, J. (1994). *Researching women's lives from a feminist perspective*. London: Taylor & Francis.

McGinn, B. (2002). *The foundations of mysticism: origins to the fifth century*. New York: The Crossroad Publishing Company.

Mehran, G. (1989). Education in post-revolutionary Persia 1979-95. In E. Yar Shater, *Encyclopedia Iranica*. Costa Mesa: Mazda Publishers.

—. (1990). Ideology and education in Islamic Republic of Iran. *Compare*, 20 (1), 53-65.

Meier, A. O'Connor, T. J. and VanKatwyk, P. (2005). *Spirituality and health: multidisciplinary explorations*. Canada: Wilfrid Laurier University Press.

Meyers, D. (2000). Agency. In A. Jaggar, and I. Young, (Eds.). *A companion to feminist philosophy*. Oxford: Blackwell, pp. 372-382.

—. (2002). Gender in the mirror: cultural imagery and women's agency. *Oxford scholarship online*. [Online]. Available at http://www.oxfordscholarship.com/view/10.1093/0195140419.001.000 1/acprof-9780195140415 [Accessed 22 May 2012].

Milani, F. (1992). *Veils and the words: the emerging voices of Iranian women writers*. New York: Syracuse University Press.

Mir-Hosseini, Z. (1993). *Marriage on trial: a study of Islamic family law, Iran and Morocco compared*. London & New York: I.B Tauris & Co Ltd.

—. (1996). Stretching the limits: a feminist reading of the Sharia in post-Khomeini Iran. In M. Yamani. *Feminism and Islam: legal and literary perspectives*. The University of Virginia: Ithaca Press, pp. 285-321.

—. (2000) *Islam and gender: the religious debate in contemporary Iran*, London & New York: I.B.Tauris Publishers.

Moghadam, V. M. (2002). Islamic feminism and its discontents: toward a resolution of the debate. *Women in culture and society*, 27 (4), 1135-1171.

—. (2003). *Modernizing women: gender and social change in the Middle East*. London: Lynne Reinner publishers.

—. (2004). Women in the Islamic Republic of Iran: legal status, social positions, and collective action. This article is in connection with her participation in the conference entitled *Iran after 25 years of revolution: a retrospective and a look ahead*, which was held at the Woodrow Wilson international center for scholars on November 16-17. [Online]. Available at http://www.wilsoncenter.org/sites/default/files/ValentineMoghadamFinal.pdf [Accessed 2 November 2012].

Moghissi, H. (1996). *Populism and feminism in Iran: women's struggle in a male- defined revolutionary movement*. New York: St. Martin's Press.

—. (2004). Troubled relationships: women, nationalism and the left movement in Iran. In S. Cronin. *Reformers and revolutionaries in modern Iran: new perspectives on the Iranian left*. London & New York: Routledge, pp. 209-229.

Mottahadeh, R. (2000). *The mantle of the prophet: religion and politics in Iran*. Oxford: Oneworld publication.

Mutahari, M. (1974). *Woman and her rights in Islam*. Translated by M.A. Ansari. Published by the Islamic Seminary Publications. [Online]. Available at http://www.iranchamber.com/personalities/mmotahari/works/woman_rights_islam.pdf [Accessed 11 January 2013].

—. (1987). *On the Islamic hijab*. Tehran: Islamic Propagation Organization.

Najmabadi, A. (1994). Power, morality, and the new Muslim womanhood. In M. Weiner, and A. Banuazizi, (Eds.). *The politics of social transformation in Afghanestan, Iran, and Pakistan*, Syracuse & N.Y.: Syracuse University Press, pp. 366-390.

Nasr, H. (1972). *Sufi essays*. New York: State University of New York Press.

Nelson, J.M. (2009). *Psychology, religion, and spirituality*. New York: Springer.

Nelson, G., Lord, J., and Ochocka, J. (2001). Empowerment and mental health in community: Narratives of psychiatric consumer/survivors. *Journal of community and applied social psychology*, 11, 125-142.

O'Reilly, A. (2010). *Twenty-First-Century Motherhood: Experience, Identity, Policy, Agency*. New York: Columbia University Press.

—. (2010). *Outlaw(ing) motherhood: a theory and politic of maternal empowerment for the twenty-first century*. [Online]. Available at http://www.faqs.org/periodicals/201001/2224850751.html#ixzz1RkD3 i3xa [Accessed 26 May 2012].

Osanloo, A. (2009). *The politics of women's rights in Iran*. New Jersey & Oxford shire: Princeton University Press.

Ostow, M. (2006). *Spirit, mind, and brain: a psychoanalytic examination of spirituality and religion*. New York: Columbia University Press.

Paidar, P. (1995). *Women and the political process in twentieth-century in Iran*. Cambridge: Cambridge University Press.

Pargament, K. (1997). *The psychology of religion and coping*. New York: Guilford Press.

Pargament, K. and Mahoney, A. (2002). Spirituality: Discovering and conserving the sacred. In C. R. Snyder and S. J. Lopez, (Eds.). *Handbook of positive psychology*. Oxford: Oxford University Press, pp. 646-659.

Price, M. (2006). Patriarchy and parental control in Iran. *Society on Podium*. [Online]. Available at http://www.iranchamber.com/society/articles/patriarchy_parental_cont rol.php [Accessed 31 January 2013].

Poya, M. (1999). *Women, work and Islamism: ideology and resistance in Iran*. London & New York: Zed Books.

Ramazanoglu C. and Holland J. (2002). *Feminist methodology: challenges and choices*. London: Sage.

Reinharz, Sh. (1983). Feminist research methodology groups: origins, forms, functions. In G. Bowles and R. Duelli-Klein, (Eds.). *Theories of women's studies*, Boston: Routledge and Kegan Paul, pp. 162-191.

—. (1992). *Feminist methods in social research*. Oxford: Oxford University Press.

Richards, A. Wrubel, J. Grant, J and Folkman, S. (2003). Subjective experiences of prayer among women who care for children with HIV. *Journal of religion and health*, 42 (3), 201-219.

Roof, W.C. (1999). *Spiritual marketplace: baby boomers and the remarking of American religion.* New Jersey: Princeton University Press.

Roof, J. (2007). Authority and representation in feminist research. In S. N. Hesse-Biber, *Handbook of feminist research: theory and praxis,* London: Sage, pp. 425-443.

Rostami Povey, E. (2001). Feminist contestations of institutional domains in Iran. *Feminist review*, 69, 44-72.

Saberi, R. (2006). *Growing popularity of Sufism in Iran.* [Online]. Available at http://news.bbc.co.uk/1/hi/4907406.stm [Accessed 28 November 2012].

Sadeghi Fasaiy, S. Farahmand, M. Bakhtiyari, A. Balali, A. Mohammadi, M. and Torabi, M. (2007). *Collective articles: feminism and family.* Tehran: Women's social and cultural council.

Sadeghi, F. (2010). Bypassing Islamism and feminism: women's resistance and rebellion in post-revolutionary Iran. *Remmm journal.* [Online]. Available at http://remmm.revues.org/6936 [Accessed 31 January 2013].

Safavi, S.G. (2010). *The practice of mysticism ('irfan-i 'amali) in Islam.* [Online]. Available at http://iranianstudies.org/articles/the-practice-of-mysticism-%E2%80%98irfan-i-%E2%80%98amali-in-islam [Accessed 28 November 2012].

Safi, O. (2000). Bargaining with Baraka: Persian Sufism, mysticism, and pre-modern politics. *The Muslim world*, 90 (3-4), 259–288.

Salehi, M.M. (1988). *Insurgency through culture and religion: the Islamic revolution of Iran.* New York: Praeger Publishers.

Samipersia, (2007). *Hafez.* [Online]. Available at http://blogpersia.blogspot.co.uk/2007/04/hafez.html [Accessed 25 January 2013].

Sampson, E. (1988). The debate on individualism: Indigenous psychologies of the individual and their role in personal and societal functioning. *American psychologist*, 43(1), 15-22.

Schirazi, A. (1997). *The constitution of Iran: politics and the state in the Islamic Republic.* London & New York: I.B Tauris Publishers.

Schimmel, A. (1975). *Mystical dimensions of Islam.* Chapel Hill: The University of North California Press.

Scheiwiller, S. (2009). On Iranian women. *Women: a cultural review*, 20 (2), 214-217.

Sedghi, H. (2007). *Women and politics in Iran*. Cambridge: Cambridge University Press.

Senter, K.E. and Caldwell, K. (2002). Spirituality and the maintenance of change: a phenomenological study of women who leave abusive relationships. *Contemporary family therapy*, 24 (4), 543-564.

Shahidian, H. (2002). *Women in Iran: emerging voices in the women's movement*. London: Greenwood Press.

—. (2005). Women, gender, and revolutionary movements: Iran and Afghanistan. *Encyclopaedia of women in Islamic countries*, pp. 417-419.

Shirazi, F. (2001). *The veil unveiled: the Hijab in modern culture*. Gainesville: University Press of Florida.

Staples, L. H. (1990). Powerful ideas about empowerment. *Administration in Social Work*, 14, 29-42.

Tabari, A. and Yeganeh, N. (1982). *In the shadow of Islam: the women's movement in Iran*. London: Zed Books.

Taheri, M.A. (2008). *Human from another outlook*. Translated by: Fatemeh Rezaie Pour, Tehran: Bijan Press.

—. (2010). Az nezareh ta nazar, special attachment to *Gozaresh monthly journal*. Tehran.

Tashakkori, A. and Thompson, V. D. (1988). Culture change and attitude change: An assessment of post-revolutionary marriage and attitudes in Iran. *Population research and policy review*, 7, 3-27.

Taylor, CH. (2007). *A secular age*. United States of America: Harvard University Press.

The green voice freedom. (2010). *Two million under poverty line*. [Online]. Available at http://en.irangreenvoice.com/article/2010/feb/21/1253 [Accessed 9 November 2012].

The New Encyclopedia Britannica, (1989), vol. 19. Chicago.

—. (1989), vol. 22. Chicago.

Thomas, G. F. (1971). *The vitality of the Christian tradition*. London: Harper & brothers.

Tisdell, E. (2000). Spirituality and emancipatory adult education in women adult educators for social change. *Adult education quarterly*, 50, 308-336.

—. (2003). *Exploring spirituality and culture in adult and higher education*. San Francisco: Jossey-Bass.

Tohidi, N. (1995). Modernity, Islamization, and women in Iran. In V. M. Moghadam, *Gender and national identity: women and politics in Muslim societies*, London: Zed Books, pp. 110-148.

—. (2002). The global-local intersection of feminism in Muslim societies: the cases of Iran and Azerbaijan. *Social research*. [Online]. Available at http://www.nayerehtohidi.com/wp-content/uploads/docs/tohidi-article-global-local-intersection-feminism-Muslim-societies.pdf [Accessed 31 January 2013]

Torab, A. (1996). Piety as gendered agency: a study of Jalaseh ritual discourse in an urban neighbourhood in Iran. *The royal anthropological institute*, 2 (2), 235-252.

—. (2002). The politicization of women's religious circles in post-revolutionary Iran. In S. Ansari, S. and V. Martin, (Eds.) *Women, religion and culture in Iran* (2002). Surrey: Curzon Press, pp. 143–168.

—. (2006). *Performing Islam: gender and ritual in Iran.* Boston: Brill.

Trend. (2013). *Divorce rate reaches alarming level in Iran.* [Online]. Available at http://en.trend.az/iran/2147065.html [Accessed 25 May 2013].

Trimingham, J.S. (1998). *The Sufi orders in Islam.* Oxford: Oxford University Press.

Usman, J. (2002). The evolution of Iranian Islamism from the revolution through the contemporary reformers. *Vanderbilt journal of transnational law*, 35 (55), 1679-1731.

Vries, H. (2007). *Religion: beyond a concept.* London: Fordham University Press.

Walter, T. and Davie, G. (1998). The religiosity of women in the modern West. *The British journal of sociology*, 49 (4), 640-660.

Watt. SH. (2004). Come to the river: using spirituality to cope, resist, and develop identity. Special Issue: *Meeting the needs of African American women*, 104, 29-40.

White, G. (2006). *Talking about spirituality in health care practice: a resource for the multi-professional health care team.* London: Jessica Kingsley Publishers.

Wiseman, J. P. (1979). *Stations of the lost: The treatment of skid row alcoholics.* Chicago: The University of Chicago Press.

Woodhead, L. (2009). Why so many women in holistic spirituality? A puzzle revisited. In G. White. *Talking about spirituality in health care practice: a resource for the multi-professional health care team.* London: Jessica Kingsley Publishers, pp. 115-127.

Wouter, J. (1999). New age spiritualities as secular religion: a historian's perspective. *Social compass,* 46 (2), 145-160.

Yeganeh, N. (1986). Sexuality and shi'i social protest in Iran, co-authored with Parvin Paidar. In N.R. Keddie, (2007). *Women in the Middle*

East: past and present, Princeton: Princeton University Press, pp. 297-325.

Yick, A.G. (2008). A metasynthesis of qualitative findings on the role of spirituality and religiosity among culturally diverse domestic violence survivors. *Qualitative health research*, 18(9), 1289-1306.

Yong, W. (2010). *Iran's divorce rate stirs fears of society in crisis.* [Online]. Available at http://www.nytimes.com/2010/12/07/world/middleeast/07divorce.html ?_r=2 [Accessed 9 November 2012].

Zali, A. (2010). Health problems. *Khabaronline.* [Online]. Available at http://www.khabaronline.ir/news-55591.aspx [Accessed 9 November 2012].

Zappone, K. (1995). *The hope for wholeness: a spirituality for feminists.* Mystic: Twenty-Third Publications.

Zavella P. (1993). Feminist insider dilemmas: constructing ethnic identity with "Chicana" informants. *Frontiers: a journal of women studies*, 13 (3), 53-76.

Zimmerman, M. (1995). Psychological empowerment: Issues and illustrations. *American journal of community psychology*, 23, 581-598.

Zinnbauer, B. J., K. I. Pargament, B. Cole, M. S. Rye, E. M. Butter, T. G. Belavich, K. M. Hipp, A. B. Scott, and J. L. Kadar. (1997). Religion and spirituality: Unfuzzying the fuzzy. *Journal for the scientific study of religion,* 36 (4), 549-64.